IN SEARCH OF
ETHICS

*Conversations with Men
and Women of Character*

Other Books of Interest:

DC Press

If It Weren't for You, We Could Get Along:
How to Stop Blaming and Start Living

The Motivating Team Leader

52 Ways to Live Success

How to Compete in the War for Talent

Becoming Real: Journey to Authenticity

Unleashing Excellence:
The Complete Guide to Ultimate Customer Service

Raising Children One Day at a Time:
A Daily Survival Guide for Committed Parents

Who's Right? (Whose Right?):
Seeking Answers and Dignity in the
Debate Over the Right to Die

IN SEARCH OF
ETHICS

Conversations with Men and Women of Character

Second Edition

By Len Marrella

PRESS

A Division of the Diogenes Consortium

SANFORD • FLORIDA

Published by DC Press
2445 River Tree Circle
Sanford, FL 32771
http://www.focusonethics.com

This book was set in Adobe Caslon
Cover Design and Composition by Jonathan Pennell

Library of Congress Catalog Number: 2004103882
        Marrella. Len,
In Search of Ethics, Second Edition
        ISBN: 1-932021-11-6

First DC Press Edition
10 9 8 7 6 5 4 3 2 1
Printed in the United States of America

DEDICATION

To the most important women in my life.

To Caroline, my mother, who laid the keel and worked hard to establish the values in my life.

To Tammy, Lani and Robin, my daughters, who reinforced and tested those values.

To Dee, my wife, who has made it all worthwhile.

TABLE OF CONTENTS

ACKNOWLEDGEMENTS

U PON REFLECTING ON THE JOURNEY traveled to put this book together, I have come to realize that, without the assistance of the following friends there would have been no book.

My sincere thanks go to Rush Kidder of the Institute of Global Ethics for his inspiration and leadership*. I am equally indebted to Michael Josephsen for his training on ethics in the workplace and for the fine book he edited, *The Power of Character*. And Gus Lee, who made two excellent and inspirational keynote presentations at the National Conference on Ethics at West Point. I was truly inspired by these three gentlemen.

It would be remiss of me to fail to acknowledge the lifetime impact on me of living up to the standard of the Honor Code at the United States Military Academy at West Point. I am ever thankful for the opportunity to fulfill my boyhood dream of going to West Point and to serve in the U.S. Army for twenty-two years.

The heart of this book is a reflection of the character of the moral exemplars I chose. I am indebted to each of them.

---

*I have been sufficiently impressed with Dr. Kidder that I have emulated his research methodology as found in his book *Shared Values in the Western World*.

Alice James typed and helped organize the original manuscript. Susan Esposito typed the final draft, while Nancy Brumbach and my daughter, Tammy Toso ensured that all of the interviews were scheduled and accomplished.

Sister Marian, from the Precious Blood Convent, and Colonel Pat Toffler, a trusted colleague and friend, provided preliminary reviews and edits. Les Horvitz and Danelle MacCafferty of New York, and Claudia Strauss conducted professional edits and comments.

A special note of thanks to Edie Wixon, for her "soul searching" review, analysis and edit. Her comments were at once thought provoking and inspiring.

Dennis McClellan for taking on the task of getting this book published and for his encouragement along the way.

Last, and most importantly, I want to thank my wife and life partner, Dee, for her continuous inspiration and encouragement.

Len Marrella
Wyomissing, Pennsylvania

PUBLISHER'S COMMENT

W HEN THE FIRST EDITION of *In Search of Ethics* came out, I wrote that it couldn't be coming at a better time. Relatively speaking, I might have been correct. However, since all things are relative at any given time, it appears the second edition couldn't be coming out at a better time as well. I wonder what that really says about our society.

At the time the first edition was released, our country had just emerged from sex scandals in the White House. A suicide squad had attacked the U.S.S. Cole, killing and injuring sailors...but we were not at war (as I wrote then, "in the purest sense"). However, in a few short months we surely were. Since the turn of the century new words and phrases have joined the common lexicon — often with shocking and sometimes confused meanings: 9/11, Osama bin Laden, Enron, weapons of mass destruction, Al-Qaeda, wardrobe malfunction, Jayson Blair, Paris Hilton, BALCO, homicide bomber, Scott Peterson, performance enhancing drugs, Jason Giambi, WorldCom, and Armstrong Williams. Older, well-known names, words and phrases found themselves being used in new and different ways – with new and different connotations: Martha Stewart, oil for food, Arthur Andersen, anthrax, lip synching, Halliburton, consensual sex, Kobe Bryant, liberal bias, CBS, Dan Rather, cloning, spam, and Tyco. We saw educators and coaches with fraudulent degrees and collegiate sports stars suspended for violations of NCAA rules including excessive partying, driving violations, grade fixing, illegal drug possession, even rape. While one can find bastions of civility, the movement that degrades girls and women (at home, at school, in the media) seems to be alive and well and showing no signs of letting up and time soon.

One contemporary author contends that the many forms of cheating to gain success in our society can be blamed on the dog-eat-dog economic climate that has persisted over the past twenty years. The concept of equal opportunity is quite literally threatened by what he called the "Winning Class" — that group with sufficient financial resources and clout to cheat without consequences, while an "Anxious Class" co-exists along side — a huge group of Americans who actually believe that by choosing not to cheat they might loose out on their only chance at success in this winner-take-all culture. Therefore…to cheat or not to cheat…that is the question.

In many ways the post 9/11 world was different than the days just before. But at the same time, it was evident that even the most shocking of events will not change how some men and women live their lives, conduct their businesses, and educate their young. For some it was ethics as usual. We may have faced a new enemy with a multitude of evil ways to harm us, yet it wasn't enough to shake many of us to the core of our character foundations. Even in the early days that followed the devastation in New York City, cheating and scheming wasn't put on hold. And since then, we've been witness to an array of discouraging examples of people placing self above family, faith, business, and country. This continues to be a very challenging time.

Making choices and carrying through on those decisions is what free will is all about. From the earliest moments of a child's life, we have an opportunity to teach by example (not merely by words) so that a child can grow into a sensitive, sensible, mature, and responsible adult. Parenting remains the most important source for teaching character, and yet, the critical institution of family remains under constant attack and erosion. It takes a strong knowledge of self to be a strong and effective parent. Coupled with a strong awareness of morality, a parent has the potential to create within a child character and a strong personal ethic. Society surely offers a wide range of ways for our youth (not to mention our adults) to opt out of making character-based decisions and actions. There has been an obvious change in society during the past fifty years — a relatively short time when compared to human history. The influences on our children from sources outside the family are innumerable. The question facing individual families is whether or not they are capable of instilling their own positive values, ethics, and character over the strong forces that impact our children each and every day. If the effort isn't made at home, the schools, religious centers, and other positive foundations have a lesser chance of effecting positive change. If the family fails, and the schools fail, if churches, synagogues and mosques fail, and if society in general falls on its face, why should we be shocked when the next generation outdoes us with their lack of ethics and character?

Most of us are given a boost when exposed to successful, resourceful, ethical people. In fact, we like to rub elbows with the highly productive members of society who have succeeded where others haven't. Many of us would like to know a Bill Gates, an Eleanor Holmes Norton, a Tommy Franks, an Oprah Winfrey, a Donald Trump, a Laura Bush, a Bernadine Healy, or a Michael Dell. Exposure to such successful people could have all manner of positive impact. At the same time, most of us are exposed on a regular basis to people who, in their own ways, are highly successful and capable of great motivation and influence. Each and every day we rub elbows with people of keen intellect and high ethical standards who point us in a direction toward higher achievement and higher moral planes. Some of those people are our parents, our teachers, our bosses, our peers, our employees, and sometimes ourselves.

The first edition of *In Search of Ethics* was highly praised and widely received by diverse audiences. Executives from corporate settings and the government, leaders from education and religion, parents and coaches have embraced the stories found on these pages. We've heard from students ranging from junior high schools through MBA programs. And we've received phone calls and letters from military personnel in all branches — from bases here at home to overseas locations to the hallowed halls of West Point. Since stories of character always inspire and encourage, we went in search of additional people to add to this new edition. It is my hope that this book continues to inspire and provide a foundation upon which we might continue to illustrate the importance of character, ethics, honor, humility, integrity, and moral fiber in everyday life.

Dennis N. McClellan
Publisher

FOREWORD

I N THE YEARS THAT HAVE PASSED since I wrote the foreword to the first edition of this book, many significant unethical events have occurred in the world. I need not elaborate at this time on the indiscretions of *some* government officials, *some* corporate executives, *some* members of the clergy, *some* educators, and unfortunately *some* high school and collegiate students. I emphasize some because not all is bleak — there are many parents, teachers, religious and business leaders making strong efforts at conducting themselves in a manner consistent with the moral values that make this a great nation.

I'll emphasize again what I stressed in my comments in the first edition. This book — especially this new edition — is a marvelous compendium and a valuable reference tool. Now Len Marrella has added new examples and a completely new chapter he calls "Show Me the Way." This is an important addition for it is instructional and actually teaches readers how we as individuals can develop exemplary character.

Probably the best endorsement for the book is the fact that for the past three years the United States Military Academy at West Point has sent a copy of *In Search of Ethics* to the homes of every new cadet for reading prior to their arrival at West Point. The Academy strives to be the premiere institution in the world in developing leaders of character and for these last years has begun the process with this book. Other schools (high school through college) and businesses are following

West Point's lead in using *In Search of Ethics* to train people of all ages and experiences.

It is my view that *In Search of Ethics* is a very effective tool for parents, teachers, clergy of all faiths, and business leaders. It should be a major contributing force in dealing with the challenge of developing leaders of character.

—Dana G. Mead
Retired Chairman & CEO Tenneco and
Chairman of the MIT Corporation
Greenwich, Connecticut

PREFACE

THE TEXT OF THE FIRST EDITION of this book was written in the late summer of 2000 and published in early 2001. Since then we have experienced a terrorist attack on America (September 11) as well as a number of serious scandals in corporate America. Moreover, we have witnessed serious allegations of misconduct by senior politicians and by members of the clergy. An ongoing survey conducted in our schools reveals that serious cheating continues to be a major concern. If there was any doubt about the importance of ethics and character to our national civility and survival, the events of the last several years should surely erase that doubt.

We will not survive the 21st century with the ethics of the 20th century. I first heard these words uttered by Dr. Rush Kidder, the President of the Institute for Global Ethics. This admonition is ominous and, I believe, quite true.

In modern society, one doesn't need a quotation from a famous ethicist to recognize that the pressure to succeed often tempts us to behave immorally or unethically. In a world of increasing expectations, rapid communication, global economics, and superb technology, our success and failures are magnified and leveraged. We are approaching a world where the unethical actions of others can do us considerable harm.

My purpose for this book is simple and practical. In search of ethics means just that. My intent was to search for and exemplify those people and institutions who have achieved success and who did so without lying, cheating, and stealing their way to the top. Was I looking for role models? You bet I was! Did I find them? You bet I did! I looked for leaders from various walks of life, and I examined the role that ethics, values and, ultimately, character played in their lives and in their successes.

There are people who will tell you that character doesn't count — that ethics and values are naïve and outdated notions. They will tell you that competence and drive are the primary prerequisites of success. Others will insist that vision, communication, and courage are the primary components of successful leaders. There are business executives who measure their success primarily by the bottom line. *Show me the bottom line — show me the money* is their rallying cry. They need not and must not be emulated — that is the message of this work.

This book is about leadership and ethics. Despite all the technical and economic progress that we have made in the past fifty years, I submit that many leaders aren't leading with character. Therefore, at the same time that we are facing national financial surpluses we are also facing moral deficits, ethical deficits, and an erosion of our traditional American values. Is it possible that there is a connection between the moral meltdown and the leadership vacuum?

It is my thesis that ***ethics is essential to effective leadership.*** In order to get commitment from those you lead, you must be trustworthy. You earn trust by being ethical. This means acting in accordance with good positive values, the values your followers share and respect. I will go so far as to say that character is the absolute cornerstone for successful leadership. There are other attributes of a good leader, but without character the leader's ultimate impact will be negative and harmful to most.

Today much is being written and taught about servant leadership and moral courage. True servant leadership not only facilitates a connection of the shared values and shared visions of leaders and followers, it also facilitates the connection of their spirits, their passions, and their souls. Moral courage provides the discipline and tenacity to tackle the difficult moral issues and to make the right choices. The most important ingredient common to both servant leadership and to moral courage is character — character based on the core ethical values that have been the foundation for all successful and vital civilizations.

So, at a time when the media is reporting and publicizing the corruption, the indulgence, the deceit, and the immorality of many of our politicians, our business leaders, and our sports heroes, I hope the uncompromised integrity and success of the exemplars in this book will be inspiring to you as they have been to me. By reading their stories we may be inspired to take the higher road, to choose the harder right versus the easier wrong, and to never be content with a half truth when the whole can be achieved.

INTRODUCTION

THE CORE OF THE BOOK is the powerful message derived from the interviews with the role models or the moral exemplars as I choose. This core is framed by initial chapters that review the ethical values shared by peoples the world over and present the results of surveys that show a deterioration (in this country) both in espousing these values as well as in conducting oneself in accordance with them; and by final chapters that explore how leaders can lead with character and discuss how values can become integral to the workplace. I conclude by offering some recommendations on how to get from where we are to where we want to be.

It is my goal to show through example that living by our values is more than the right thing to do. It is paramount to our success as individuals and a society. These exemplars I have chosen have done just that. Their successes, and their destinations, have been impressive.but it is their path to success that is inspiring.

Are they perfect? Of course not. None of my exemplars is perfect, and each would be the first to say so. Like the rest of us, they are human. Temptations, disappointments and discouragements have strewn their paths. But these are people and institutions that strive to do the right things for the right reasons and have been recognized for their high degree of consistency in doing so. They have solid values and they work hard at living their values. On the few occasions when they have fallen short, they've regrouped, picked themselves up, reconnected with their values, and recommitted themselves. Perhaps William James may have said it better:

> *"An act has no ethical value unless it be chosen out of several all equally possible"*

these people have chosen well.

SECTION I
THE MORAL
ENVIRONMENT

CHAPTER ONE

THE MORAL MELTDOWN

The shortest and surest way to live with honor in the world is to be in reality what we would appear to be. All human virtues increase and strengthen themselves by the practice and experience of them.

— *Socrates*

WHAT SOCRATES SAID is as true today as it was 2500 years ago. If you want to know the true character of an individual, watch his or her feet and not his or her mouth. Emerson may have said it better when he stated "What you're doing speaks so loudly that I can't hear what you're saying." Character can be measured by what you do or how you act when no one is looking. I believe that there is latent goodness in all of us, but it is our actions that indicate how we deal with the temptations and expectations we face. It is our actions that reflect our character.

Most of us know what is right and what is wrong. Many of us know how to differentiate between good and bad. But there appears to be a continuing erosion of our conduct. While we may want to do what is right, or appear as if we are upstanding moral people, more and more of us seem to be "sliding down the slippery slope" to routine unethical behavior.

Here is a sampling of some current thinking and some expressions that are prevalent:

"Don't give me that goody goody garbage—everybody cheats."

"What's the big deal? I see my parents doing it."

"So what if I take a few things? I am not stealing from a friend, I'm stealing from a big corporation and they can afford it."

"How dare that teacher punish my child. My son is a good kid."

"I can get anything I want from my parents. They feel guilty about leaving me while they work."

"What's the use? How can I make a difference? I don't vote. All politicians are crooks anyway.

"Whatever. Anything goes."

"I'm a bit discouraged. My boss is having an affair with one of my co-workers and she got a raise and promotion even though she is less qualified and less productive."

*"What has happened to the word **honor**? Our politicians seem to be people without honor and we are all diminished by having them in government."*

"Where have all the role models gone? I'm having trouble finding them."

These remarks are topics of conversations today. A skeptic might react to them by saying, "So what? Such expressions are nothing new and they don't prove a widespread deterioration in our values or our ethics." Unfortunately, statistical evidence demonstrates the pervasiveness not only of this kind of thinking but also this kind of behavior.

Disturbingly high percentages of high school students responding to a **Reader's Digest** study think that cheating is okay because the chances of being caught are slim. The Josephsen Institute for Ethics found that almost 40% of high school students had stolen at least once within a 12-month period. Worse, many justify such action because they feel it is necessary to *lie, cheat, and steal* in order to succeed. About a fourth of these youngsters agreed with the following statement: *It is not unethical to do whatever you have to do in order to succeed as long as others are not seriously hurt.*

Several years of data from an ongoing study by **Who's Who Among American High School Students** support these findings. Students claim they "have to" cheat to get good grades and be competitive for top-rated colleges. An overwhelming proportion admits to cheating, yet virtually all know it is wrong to do so. And these include some of our best and brightest students (See Figure 1).

This disconnect between understanding and behavior is not reserved for adolescents. In 1997, the Ethics Resource Center, in conjunction with the Society for Human Resource Management, conducted a survey of adults in their role as employees. In that survey, 35-45% of respondents report having witnessed lying to supervisors or falsification of information in correspondence or records. Almost 30% observed theft and about 25% had seen misuse of organizational assets. When asked if they reported their observations, almost invariably the answer was: "No!" When asked *why*, close to 60% justified their inaction by saying, "Nobody cares about business ethics." Well over half said that they did not *trust* the company to protect their identity and protect them from reprisal. These are people who see themselves as valuing loyalty and courage, but who are unable to follow through when tested. Rather than display their loyalty to their employer and demonstrate the courage to do the right thing, they turned away with rationalizations or in fear.

FIGURE 1. Academic Cheating:
Research Chronology — 1990 to 2004

High School
- Surveyed 20,000+ students at 65 schools

College
- Surveyed 75,000+ students at 125 schools

The U.S. high school cheating picture*

	Public	Parochial	Private
Test/Exam	76%	72%	49%
Plagiarism	61%	64%	47%

*Data collected from over 18,000 students at 61 schools across the country.

Motivations to cheat in high school
- High school never seems like that big a deal.
- Why do the work when you don't have to?
- There is no need to work so hard if everyone else is cheating.
- Courses weren't interesting enough to actually want to learn the material.
- Time — or lack thereof.
- The need for better marks.
- Pressure to get good grades.
- Cheating on tests and assignments not seen as big deal or bad thing.
- Peer pressure — or fact that in high school, the implications and consequences of cheating don't seem that bad (and to young minds, right and wrong is often dictated by the consequences).
- Desire not to disappoint teachers and/or parents.

Collegiate institutional factors associated with greater cheating
- Cheating is campus norm — there is a culture of cheating.
- School has no honor code.
- There is little chance of getting caught.
- Penalties are not viewed as significant.
- When students feel faculty support of integrity policies is low.

College students reporting greater cheating
- Business majors (Communication/Journalism)
- Males (especially test cheating)
- Students with low or high GPA's
- Younger students
- Fraternity/sorority members

Summary Collegiate Cheating Indicators

	1995	1999/00	2001/2
Test Cheating	30%-45%	23%-45%	23%
Written Cheating	42%-58%	45%-56%	50%
Serious Cheating	54%-71%	53%-68%	56%
All Cheating	62%-83%	68%-83%	73%
Repeat Test Cheating	7%-17%	6%-17%	8%

Plagiarism at college level

	1999	2002/3	2003/4
Written 'cut & paste'	40%	39%	38%
Written plagiarism	16%	7%	7%
Internet 'cut & paste'	10%	36%	36%
Internet plagiarism (e.g., paper mills)	5%	3%	4%

Some motivations for cheating in college
- Because I had more to do than time to do it in (specific course).
- Course load is too heavy to handle on your own.
- Fear of failure; pressure to do well.
- I have cheated in a course that was required. There was no other way that I could have gotten through it.
- Meaningless assignments that serve no purpose.

Some positive collegiate student views
- As best I can tell, the policies in place are quite good.
- The majority of students have high integrity. Yet, the majority don't understand the rules and might cheat due to ignorance.
- I personally do not see cheating as an issue in this university.
- I think the policy (on academic integrity) is fine right now.

Negative collegiate student views
- I'd say over 80% of students have cheated, especially 1st year science.
- It seems like so many cheat that you are almost left behind if you don't.
- With competition increasing for the top jobs and more specifically for entrance into professional faculties, cheating will continue to run rampant.
- Internet cheating is huge… getting papers off the net, especially the ones that are written for you.

The information presented above has been used with the permission of Donald L. McCabe, Ph.D., Professor, Management & Global Business, Rutgers, The State University of New Jersey and reflect his research and extensive writing on academic integrity. He is considered an expert on the subjects of Cheating in College, College Education and Ethical Development, and Ethical Decision Making.

Survey after survey, study after study, reaches the same conclusion. We all seem to know what our values *ought* to be and we profess allegiance to them. Yet, we do not *act* — we rationalize misconduct with an "ends justify the means" mentality that is a sure prescription for a complete breakdown in integrity. This frightening disconnect between our values and our behavior manifests itself in schools, family, government and business. We have a problem and it appears to be getting worse. As we embark on our journey into the 21st Century, we must be concerned that we do not destroy ourselves from within by moral and ethical decay. World leaders have fallen before — the history of mankind is an undeniable harbinger — unless we learn from the past, we are condemned to relive it.

So, what can we do? What can we do to reverse the trend and restore our ability to live ethical, values-based lives? The first step is awareness of the problem. The second step is a shared concern for our children and our country. The next step will require a determination, a sustained and solid determination and national will to effect a meaningful change in society's standards and behavior.

We are well on our way with step one. Surveys indicate that many Americans are worried about this state of affairs. Recent Gallup polls have found that by margins of almost 2 to 1, we believe that society is in a moral and spiritual decline. Similar proportions of respondents are unhappy with others' ethical standards and they deplore the state of the American family. Shearson Lehman Brothers surveyed "Life in America" and reports that 80% of us think the United States is on the wrong track. The *Futurist* reports that almost 85% of Americans think that modern Western culture fails to provide a proper sense of belonging, purpose and values. Similarly, *Newsweek* found that 80% of us think we are in a moral and spiritual decline and we tend to blame parents, political leaders, teachers, and the clergy for failing to set the proper example. Complementing this troubling finding are the results of a *Parents Magazine* survey that 90% of the readers who responded believe that we have lost track of our basic values and that it's harder to teach traditional values to children today. The Josephson Institute reports that even our youth fear the deterioration of national values as our greatest present danger.

So, we have a starting point. That's a good sign. Now, we must find a way to motivate ethical behavior. That is the challenge of leadership. We can all be leaders, because all of us influence others by our example, our mentoring, and our pursuit of truth. This is the key: we have to believe that ethical practices are really best for us and we have to teach this belief to our children. The best way for them to integrate values into their lives is to see us integrate them into ours. We can't just tell them, we have to show them. As parents and exemplars we have to live the life and practice the values that we want our children to emulate. And we have to do the same in our adult relationships — family, friends, business, government, service relationships. True success and happiness in life are possible only through the practice and implementation of ethical behavior. And all the faces of success are possible through the tremendous promise and power of character. In the end your character is your destiny and you are the architect of your own character.

CHAPTER TWO

THE MORAL BASELINE

I N ORDER TO FULLY APPRECIATE the interviews and conversations with the moral exemplars presented in the next twelve chapters, we should look at some key definitions, some selected notions of moral philosophy and lastly, some representative codes of ethics or statements of values.

The following dictionary definitions may facilitate your appreciation of this and succeeding chapters:

ETHICS — A system of moral principles; the branch of philosophy dealing with human values and moral conduct. The science of moral duty or the science of the ideal human character.

MORAL — That which is right and proper; conduct based on perceptions of what is right and wrong as determined by conscience. Pertaining to man's natural sense of what is right and proper.

PRINCIPLE — A fundamental truth, a comprehensive law or doctrine; a settled rule of action; a governing law of conduct.

VALUE — That which is worthy of esteem for its own sake; that which has intrinsic worth; a principle, standard or quality regarded as always worthwhile or desirable.

VIRTUE — An attribute; a moral quality; moral excellence.

INTEGRITY — Decision-making and conduct that is based on principle(s); rigid adherence to a code of behavior; probity; honesty.

CHARACTER — That which constitutes a person's nature and guides decisions and actions. A person of character seeks the truth, decides what is right, and has the courage and commitment to act accordingly.

If we take a look at the chronological history of moral philosophers we see names that go back nearly 500 years before Christ starting with Socrates, Plato, Aristotle, and Epicurus.

After Christ's birth the following names dot the Western philosophical landscape: Epictetus, St. Augustine, St. Thomas Aquinas, Niccoli Machiavelli, Sir Francis Bacon, Thomas Hobbes, John Locke, Rene Descartes, Benedict De Spinoza, David Hume, Immanuel Kant, G.W.F. Hegel, John Stuart Mill, Jeremy Bentham, Frederick Nietzsche, John Dewey, G.E. Moore, and Ludwig Withgenstein, among others. Although there are many more philosophers, this list represents many of the more prominent thinkers and writers of their time. What do they share in common?

It is well beyond the scope of this book to define or elaborate on the basic theses of each philosopher. There have been volumes written to describe their various points of view. However, the purpose of much of the thinking and writing on ethics is to help us to make the correct ethical decisions. This is no easy task and it is confounded when we face ethical dilemmas in our day-to-day encounters. So, before proceeding it may be useful to distill moral philosophy into principles for making ethical choices.

Even if you have not read or understood the thinking and writing of the moral philosophers you most likely have an intuitive feel for the following principles for resolving ethical dilemmas:

END BASED THINKING, or *utilitarianism,* is that approach whereby a solution is sought that maximizes benefits for the greatest number of people. (Stated another way — *Do what's best for the greatest number of people.)* The utilitarian theory was espoused by the British philosophers John Stuart Mill and Jeremy Bentham.

RULE BASED THINKING is the *categorical imperative* whereby a solution is based on a rule that everyone should follow in all such situations, regardless of consequences. Stated in a more colloquial way *"Follow your highest sense of principle."* Immanuel Kant is often considered the preeminent historical proponent for this mode of reasoning. Kant held that ethics are universal and inviolate and that it is our duty to adhere to these principles — thus creating the categorical imperative. Kant strongly adhered to the notion that motives, not consequences, are the important factors in making moral judgments.

CARE BASED THINKING in which a solution is sought that reflects the way a person would like to be treated in such a situation — or stated colloquially *"Do what you want others to do to you."* This concept is widely known as the Golden Rule. The Golden Rule is often thought of as a solely Christian doctrine because of its appearance in the book of Matthew. However, it appears in the Talmud as well as in the teachings of Islam. Moreover, Confucius, nearly 500 years before the birth of Christ wrote, *"Here is the golden maxim: Do not do to others that which we do not want them to do to us."* On closer inspection we find that the Golden Rule appears at the center of Hinduism, Buddhism and many of the world's major religions. The Golden Rule has played a major role in the moral teachings of nearly all cultures and religions and continues to play an important role in moral education.

These three perspectives for resolving dilemmas are very simple and they reflect common sense. If you had never heard anything about formal moral philosophy *you could intuitively use similar conclusions or similar rules to make values-based decisions.*

Now I want to carry this observation one step further. There is a school of thought that suggests ethical issues are relative to a specific culture. The ethical relativist believes that there are no universal cross-cultural ethical norms. An opposing point of view is asserted by the ethical absolutists for whom there is a single universal moral standard. However, suffice it to say that moral relativism or situational ethics, in the view of many, may partially explain the deterioration of our moral values. The debate between the relativists and the absolutists is theoretical and academic. The fact is, there are global values and global virtues. As I stated earlier, the Golden Rule has universal application and appeal and there is a growing body of evidence that suggests there are many values that have global acceptance.

In early October 1996, the Institute for Global Ethics conducted a survey with over 650 participants at the State of the World Forum's annual meeting in San Francisco. The 272 participants who responded represented 40 countries and more than 50 different faith communities. The participants had an average age of 51 years, were 57% male and 43% female and more than half had some graduate education. By occupation 32% were in business, finance or consulting and 36% were in education/research or in the nonprofit/volunteer segments. If you look at the participants from a religious standpoint there were those who were strongly religious and those who were not at all religious, with a leaning toward the former.

The survey asked the respondents to choose the five most important moral values from a list of 15 (See Figure 2). The most frequent choice TRUTH was chosen by 62% of the 272 respondents. The next four values chosen in order of frequency were *compassion, responsibility, freedom* and *the reverence for life*. The survey participants were also asked to select the single most important value. Compassion was the value that was singled out as the most important by 21% of the respondents, and truth and responsibility were tied for second place as indicated by 16% of the respondents. This is powerful and heartening evidence that we as humans are intrinsically caring and respectful people. Figure 2 summarizes the responses from the 272 participants attending the State of the World Forum.

Rather than get drawn into a statistical debate about the frequency and importance of respondents' reactions or judgments, I would rather

FIGURE 2. Most Frequently Chosen and Most Important Values

Please look at the list of 15 values carefully and check the five values that are most important to you in your daily life and choose the one value you consider to be most important.

Value	Chosen#	(%)	Most Important#	(%)
Truth	169	(62)	33	(16)
Compassion	153	(56)	44	(21)
Responsibility	147	(54)	33	(16)
Freedom	113	(42)	19	(9)
Reverence for Life	108	(40)	25	(12)
Fairness	100	(37)	12	(6)
Self-Respect	96	(35)	16	(8)
Preservation of Nature	92	(34)	5	(2)
Tolerance	86	(32)	8	(4)
Generosity	73	(27)	4	(2)
Humility	50	(18)	4	(2)
Social Harmony	43	(16)	2	(1)
Honor	31	(11)	4	(2)
Devotion	27	(10)	4	(2)
Respect for Elders	19	(7)	0	(0)

SOURCE: Survey conducted by IGE at the State of the World Forum in San Francisco, October 1996.

step back and present some of the general conclusions from the pilot IGE survey:

1. Seven of the values appeared to be the most significant or important in the eyes of the respondents. These seven values were:

   - Truth
   - Compassion
   - Responsibility
   - Freedom
   - Reverence for Life
   - Fairness
   - Self-Respect

2. There is a small group of core moral values that is cross-cultural and universal.

3. Concerning the three principles for resolving ethical dilemmas the survey revealed some interesting results. Of all the respondents who participated, 49% chose the utilitarian perspective (ends-based thinking), 39% chose the Golden Rule (care-based thinking), 12% selected the Kantian categorical imperative (rule-based thinking).

4. Individuals holding the same core values may use different decision rules to resolve their dilemmas.

5. Individuals may enjoy a variety of resolution principles as they move from dilemma to dilemma.

6. The Golden Rule is far more widely used than the *categorical imperative.*

7. The most powerful source of authority for knowing right from wrong is personal experience.

8. Television as it is seen today is generally unsuitable for providing moral instruction.

I am not at all suggesting that this pilot survey is the final word on these important questions but the survey is an indicator that there may be universality in shared core values. Certainly more research is in order. These hypotheses require further global research. Country specific surveys might indicate different results or they may reinforce the global commonality. Further surveys may shed more light on establishing a basis for conflict resolution. There are still some questions but the October 1996 survey on global values and boundaries conducted by the Institute for Global Ethics has provided some answers.

At the same time I was researching much of the extensive literature, interviews and surveys by the Institute for Global Ethics, I was also researching and reading everything else that appeared to be relevant to the subject at hand. In that regard I came across two books that proposed values for our consideration.

Bruce Hamstra in his book *When Good People Do Bad Things — How to Make Moral Choices In An Immoral World* presents what he calls The Incredible Seven: Key Values In Our Moral Universe. Here are Bruce Hamstra's incredible seven:

1. **JUSTICE:** Giving to each that which is their due. Equal, unbiased treatment, sharing, tolerance of legitimate, fair differences.

2. **CARING:** Kindness, compassion, humane treatment, cooperation, following the *Golden Rule: Do unto others as you would have them do unto you.*

3. **RESPECT:** Regard for the fundamental worth and dignity of every human being, including oneself, intending no harm, if at all possible. Respect for the rights and properties of others. Appreciation for other life forms and the environment.

4. **RESPONSIBILITY:** Keeping commitments, performing one's duty and fulfilling obligations, and exercising self-discipline.

5. **HONESTY:** Being truthful, forthright, and sincere.

6. **LOYALTY:** Keeping true faith with others and allegiance to one's values; maintaining trust and fidelity; respecting confidences; respect for legitimate authority.

7. **LIBERTY:** Self-determination with responsibility; freedom of political and religious choice and expression; freedom from oppression, and persecution.

If you look closely at these values you will find powerful consistency between core values flowing from two independent processes and derived by two separate methods. To further solidify my point, let me add one more source of core values on what Professor of Ethics Louis P. Pojman calls his basic objective moral set:

1. Do not kill innocent people.

2. Do not cause unnecessary pain or suffering.

3. Do not steal or cheat.

4. Keep your promises and honor your contracts.

5. Do not deprive another person of his or her freedom.

6. Do justice, treating equals equally and unequals unequally.

7. Show gratitude for services rendered, that is, reciprocate.

8. Tell the truth.

9. Help other people.

10. Obey just laws.

Professor Pojman goes on to say these ten principles are examples of the core ethical principles necessary for the good life. Fortunately, it isn't as though the ten principles were arbitrary, for we can give reasons why we believe these rules are necessary to any social order. Principles like the Ten Commandments, the Golden Rule, and values (e.g. justice, honesty, keeping commitments, etc.) are central to trust, civility and the peaceful resolution of conflicts. For example, effective communication itself depends on a general and implicit commitment to the principle of trust. Honest, candid expression is a critical element of truthfulness. Hence, every time we correctly describe something or share information, we are fostering trust. Without trust, communication is meaningless. Similarly, without trust contracts are of no consequence and cooperation is tenuous at best.

As we establish an ethical baseline we reveal that there is a great deal of commonality among the lists of core values as defined by different authors from different parts of the world. Said in other words, many people from many cultures hold dear the same values and ethical principles. Dr. Rush Kidder effectively discusses this observation in his book, *Shared Values For A Troubled World: Conversations with Men and Women of Conscience,* "No matter how hard we try to argue that different cultures and different segments of our society have different values, we continue to conclude that on close inspection there is, for the most part, a common moral baseline of shared values." The shared values that Dr. Kidder discovered are: *Love, Truthfulness, Fairness, Freedom, Unity, Tolerance, Responsibility, Respect for Life.*

Carrying our discussion one step further we can look at how various entities in our American society have codified their ethics and values.

THE BOY SCOUT LAW

A Scout is:
- Trustworthy
- Loyal
- Helpful
- Friendly
- Courteous
- Kind
- Obedient

THE GIRL SCOUT LAW

I will do my best:
- To be honest
- To be fair
- To help where I am needed
- To be cheerful
- To be friendly and considerate
- To be a sister to every Girl Scout
- To respect authority

- Cheerful
- Thrifty
- Brave
- Clean
- Reverent

- To use resources wisely
- To protect and improve the world around me
- To show respect for myself and others through my words and actions

WEST POINT HONOR CODE

Duty, Honor, Country
A Cadet does not lie, cheat, steal, or tolerate those who do.

ROTARY INTERNATIONAL FOUR WAY TEST

1. Is it the truth?
2. Is it fair to all concerned?
3. Will it build good will and better friendships?
4. Will it be beneficial to all concerned?

MCDONNELL DOUGLAS CORPORATION CODE OF ETHICS

In order for integrity and ethics to be characteristic of McDonnell Douglas, we who make up the corporation must strive to be:

- Honest and trustworthy in all our relationships.
- Reliable in carrying out assignments and responsibilities.
- Truthful and accurate in what we say and write.
- Cooperative and constructive in all work undertaken
- Fair and considerate in our treatment of fellow employees, customers and all other persons.
- Law-abiding in all our activities.

- Committed to accomplishing all tasks in a superior way.

- Economical in utilizing company resources.

- Dedicated in service to our company and to improvement of the quality of life in the world in which we live.

Decision-making that reflects integrity and high moral standards of behavior requires commitment and courage. Consultation among employees, top management, and the board of directors will sometimes be necessary to determine the proper course of action.

Ethics and morals may sometime require us to forgo business or other professional opportunities. In the long run, however, we will all be better served by doing what is right.

The following code prepared by the Institute of Global Ethics is reprinted here, word for word, from the Institute's Ethical Fitness Seminar's **Readings on Ethics**.

PERSONAL VALUES FOR THE 21ST CENTURY

Respect for Self

- Being self-disciplined enough to accomplish what we want to do and know we ought to do.

- Resisting peer pressure, especially when it would coax us into activities damaging to ourselves or others.

- Developing habits of study and reflection that allow constant self-discovery.

- Cherishing our own individuality and defending it actively from self-abuse by drugs, sex, or violence.

- Learning to trust our own intuitions, insights, and decision-making skills rather than relying blindly on others.

Respect for Truth

- Being honest in every aspect of our lives, even when no one is looking.

- Searching for and respecting reality, rather than yielding to self-deception, illusion, or counterfeits.

- Honoring promises, and being so trustworthy that others can rely on us to do right even when we haven't made any specific promise.

- Reporting as true only what we can verify, rather than gossiping about others or fudging data about the world around us.

- Observing clear distinctions between fact and opinion, both in our own minds and in communications from others.

Respect for Community

- Treating others as we want them to treat us, despite differences in gender, race, creed, or political persuasion.

- Being fair, even when we could gain personal advantage through partiality.

- Obeying the law as far as conscience permits, even when it deprives us of something we want, while recognizing that if civil disobedience seems appropriate, it may bring penalties that must be faced.

- Not stealing or defacing others' property, whether things or ideas, and whether owned by individuals or by larger, faceless entities.

- Being accountable for our actions, even in situations where there is no legal requirement for disclosure.

- Preserving the right of privacy for ourselves and others.

- Acknowledging the rights of others to hold, develop, and express ideas very different from our own.

- Having the courtesy to listen carefully to others' ideas without, however, accepting the validity of ideas that are trivial, corrupt, or damaging to ourselves or others.

- Recognizing the importance of the family in building solid communities, and abstaining from the physical and verbal violence, premature or abusive sexual experience, or irresponsible financial behavior that tends to destroy families.

Respect for Environment

- Understanding and appreciating the natural context in which every human action occurs.

- Consciously striving to use only our fair share of the world's resources, so that others around the globe can have their share.

- Protecting individual plants and animals from pointless destruction, and entire species from extinction, even when we can see no immediate reason to do so.

Respect for the Future

- Working to be sure that our individual actions, if universalized and done by everyone else, would contribute to a better future.

- Resisting waste and depletion of natural resources, human lives, and creative ideas and building instead a sustainable world of things, institutions, and concepts that can perpetuate itself.

- Greeting the future with enthusiasm and expectancy, and working to improve it.

- Acknowledging that the future will be determined by our individual actions within a global context, and taking responsibility for the consequences of those actions.

The above list, developed by the staff at the Institute for Global Ethics, draws some items from a list developed by Professor Reo M. Christenson, Miami University (Ohio).

In an effort to prepare you for the following chapters, we developed some definitions, looked briefly at selected philosophy, observed three concepts for resolving moral issues, and compared several sets of moral values. There is evidence that there is a moral baseline, a common vision of values, understood by the vast majority, that is at the heart of conscience.

There are rules — there are shared values — there are codes of ethics — there are guidelines for moral behavior — there is a moral baseline. How is our behavior, when measured against that baseline? In simple terms ***there is a major disconnect between the values we espouse and our actions***. There appears to be an alarming behavioral departure from our core values — an observation that is frightening when we consider the potential damage that even a few unethical people can inflict. The statement "*we will not survive the 21st century with the ethics of the 20th century*" should be a claxon, a harbinger. We have been forewarned! But with effort and commitment we can turn the tide. Let's focus on some beacons of light — some moral exemplars as we continue in our search of ethics.

SECTION II
THE MORAL EXEMPLARS

ETHICS SUCCESS STORIES THE MORAL EXEMPLARS

S
O FAR WE HAVE LOOKED at evidence for moral decay as manifested by our actions or perceptions and we have established the existence of a common ethical baseline — so what is next? One of the primary objectives of this book, simple and practical, is to identify and exemplify some moral heroes as some moral exemplars.

While I have been discouraged by the alarming erosion of moral values over the past fifty years, I remain hopeful that "we can overcome…." I firmly believe that there is latent goodness in most of us, if not all of us. However, good people sometimes do bad things especially when tempted by wrong situations or conditioned by the wrong stimuli, or if improperly influenced by unethical leaders.

The great thing about our American Democracy is that it is self-cleansing. Sometimes it appears to take forever to "clean up our act," but we do have the mechanisms to change our political leaders, to adjust our economy, and to commit to our values. To recommit to the shared core values that have made this nation great, however will not be a simple task.

Where do we start? Well, I believe we have already started. American industry has learned that ethics is good business and has initiated ethics training and ethics programs at an accelerated pace. Public schools are relearning that character development is part of education, and nonprofit ethics centers are focused on the essentiality of morals and ethics in all aspect of our lives. However, with one of every two marriages ending in divorce, with more single-parent homes, and with an increasing number of homes with both parents working, I am sure we have not made satisfactory progress in improving the overall family environment for developing character in our children. And, the family is *the* place where the most good can and must be done in instilling values in the next generation for the next century.

It is my conviction that as a society and a world community we are not morally bankrupt. Further the vast majority of people — albeit an often silent majority — are inherently decent. Moreover, essentially all of us want to raise our children to be good citizens and well adjusted ethical adults. As difficult as the task may be, we can do it. To support my optimism, this book is about role models — *moral heroes* to be exact. I have been inspired by what these people stand for, and how they have succeeded, and how they have led by example, doing so by living their values and their ethics. I conclude that they succeeded *because* of their lifelong commitment to values and ethical standards.

Let me elaborate with the following quote from Charles J. Sykes in: *A Nation of Victims, The Decay of the American Character*: "Put simply, character is formed by placing examples of virtue in front of young people. Ironically, the recent resurgence of interest in teaching values and ethics has too often ignored this basic principle. We must pay more attention to private decency, private morality, honesty, personal responsibility and honor. We are the product of our upbringing and we are the victim of our circumstances."

As we continue in our search of ethics, I offer for your consideration the following positive examples of individuals who live ethical lives:

- **BUSINESS ETHICS** — Norman R. Augustine, Retired Chairman and Chief Executive Officer of Lockheed Martin Corporation

- **HONOR** — General Fred Franks, Commanding General VII Corps — Desert Storm

- **IDEALISM** — James O. Freedman, Former President, Dartmouth College

- **SACRIFICE** — Bea Gaddy, "The Ghetto Angel"

- **VALUES** — Earl Hess, Ph.D., Founder and Retired CEO, Lancaster Labs

- **SERVANT LEADERSHIP** — General Charles C. "Chuck" Krulak, Vice Chairman MBNA America Bank

- **CHARACTER** — Mike Krzyzewski, Coach, Duke University Basketball Team

- **INTEGRITY** — Sue Myrick, Representative to U. S. Congress from North Carolina

- **TRUTH** — John Naber, U. S. Olympic Gold Medalist

- **MORAL COURAGE** — Dr. Nancy Olivieri, Professor Pediatrics and Medicine, University of Toronto

- **RESPONSIBILITY** — Rose Marie Strause, Medical Secretary

- **HUMILITY** — Monsignor James Treston, Pastor, St. Ignatius of Loyola Parish, Sinking Spring, PA

- **COMMITMENT** — West Point, The United States Military Academy

Because of the preeminent importance to our future, I have placed my interview with Rabbi Steven Carr Reuben concerning ethics and children in Section III as part of the ethics solution.

CHAPTER THREE

BUSINESS & ETHICS

NORMAN R. AUGUSTINE
Former CEO, Lockheed Martin Corporation

In the arena of human life, the honors and the rewards fall to those who show their good qualities in action

— Aristotle

I KNOW OF NO PRESENT BETTER example of one who has shown good qualities in action than Norman R. Augustine. As a son, a father, a husband, a student, a teacher, an engineer, a corporate executive, a government official and as a human being, Norm Augustine has demonstrated moral and ethical behavior. He graduated from Princeton with a BSE in Aeronautical Engineering magna cum laude, and he earned an MSE from Princeton with honors. Over the years, he has received Honorary Doctors Degrees from sixteen different universities or colleges.

He was chairman of the America Red Cross and a member of the Policy Council of the Business Roundtable. He is also a former chairman of the Education Task Force, a former chairman of the National Academy of Engineering, and a former president of the Boy Scouts of America. These are just a few of the important positions he has occupied.

In addition to his professional engineering and managerial duties, he serves on numerous boards of directors and boards of trustees.

He began his professional career in 1958 when he joined the Douglas Aircraft Company. During his tenure at Douglas he was a Program Manager and Chief Engineer. Beginning in 1965, he served in the Pentagon in the Office of the Secretary of Defense as an Assistant Director of Defense Research and Engineering. Joining the LTV Missiles and Space Company in 1970, he served as Vice President, Advanced Programs and Marketing. In 1973 he returned to government as Assistant Secretary of the Army and in 1975 as Undersecretary. Joining Martin Marietta Corporation in 1977, he served as President and Chief Operating Officer and then as the Chairman and Chief Executive Officer. He served as President of Lockheed Martin upon the formation of that company in 1995, and became Chief Executive Officer on January 1, 1996, after which he was elected Vice Chairman on April 23, 1996, and Chairman on January 1, 1997. He currently serves as Chairman of the Executive Committee of the Board of Directors of Lockheed Martin, having retired as an active employee on August 1, 1997, at which time he became a member of the faculty of the Princeton University School of Engineering and Applied Science.

For his accomplishments he was awarded the National Medal of Technology by the President of the United States and five times he was awarded the Defense Department's highest civilian decoration, the Distinguished Service Medal. Additionally, he received the Defense Meritorious Service Medal, the Army Distinguished Service Medal, the Air Force Exceptional Service Medal, the NASA Distinguished Public Service Award, the Department of the Treasury Medal of Merit, and Gold Medal of Merit. In September 1999, it is especially fitting that he received the West Point Sylvanus Thayer Award for exemplifying the ideals of West Point as reflected in its motto, "Duty, Honor, Country." Norm Augustine is the recipient of over 50 major awards from industrial associations, professional organizations, and national service organizations.

When you review the complete record of this distinguished citizen it becomes patently clear that Norm Augustine has devoted his life to constructive and productive service to his country, his family, and his fellow citizens. Make no mistake about it, Norm Augustine is a very successful person and a contributor to the welfare of others. He achieved his success by living his values. In all his endeavors in industry, in his Defense Department positions and in his public service roles he has conducted himself in an ethical and forthright manner. He has "talked the talk and walked the walk." He has gone on the record in support of moral behavior in our country and in strong support of business ethics in his profession. (See the Appendix for the Lockheed Martin Corporate Code of Ethics entitled *Our Values: Ethics Mission Success and Teamwork*. This code of ethics and the address "Ethics in America" presented at the end of this section provide additional insight into the character of this man.)

In summary, Norm Augustine has achieved success in his professional and personal life without deception, and without cheating.

Norm Augustine is what he appears to be and he has practiced and experienced his human virtues to a considerable extent. His effectiveness as the Chief Executive Officer of a major corporation, as a senior government official, as a public service leader, as a father, and as a husband has been greatly enhanced by this trustworthiness, his sense of honor, and his commitment to duty and service. If we can conclude that he is a positive role model, let us proceed in our search of ethics to determine what in Norman Augustine's background contributed to the development of his character.

Norm Augustine grew up in Denver, Colorado as the son of Ralph and Freda Augustine. The Augustines were hard working and honest people and were excellent role models for their son. Norm has stated that his father was the most honest person he has ever known. Ralph Augustine apparently didn't talk about honesty or character he just lived it and exemplified integrity by his daily actions. Norm's parents also practiced self-discipline and expected Norm to do likewise. They also expected their son to work hard and study hard and they had high expectations for him. Norm tells the story about how his father left a clipping for him on a mirror in his room when Norm was still quite young. The message simply stated, *Don't wait until you are a man to be great, be a great boy.*

It is no coincidence that many years later he became the National President of the Boy Scouts of America. It is also no coincidence that he has spent seven years as the Chairman of the American Red Cross. His sense of duty and dedication to the service of others are traits that were inculcated at an early age.

Norm Augustine speaks highly of several of his teachers during his early schooling. He singled out his sixth grade teacher, Mrs. Gleasner, who fifty years ago taught him the meaning of discipline and motivation. After all these years he remembers her as being *"tough as nails"* and noncompromising when it came to doing the harder right than the easier wrong. He insisted that she *raised the bar* and caused him to strive and stretch to get the most from his abilities.

Several years later Norm was accepted into a high school fraternity to which many Denver high school students aspired. Tau Sigma Fraternity in Denver was run by a spirited public citizen by the name of Fred Perkins. Fred allowed no smoking, drinking or drugs in the fraternity, he encouraged community service and would not tolerate lying. Obviously this fraternity and Fred Perkins had an influence on Norm's character development because here it is 45 years later and he can still easily recite the **Tau Sigma Prayer**:

Let us not be frightened by the problems that confront us, but rather give thee thanks that thou has given us the opportunity to show our worth. May we be part of the answer and not part of the problems of the youth of our age.

Norm Augustine is an avid sports fan and he uses many sports metaphors in his talks, in his writings and in his professional life. In my interview with him he admitted that as a sports participant he was good enough to compete but clearly not good enough to be great. Basketball, softball and tennis were his primary sports and he has positive memories of his days of sports competition. He also remembers many lessons in character development that came as a result of his willingness to compete in team sports and in individual sports.

NORMAN R. AUGUSTINE Q & A

In the course of our discussions and in an attempt to get a true measure of the man I asked him a number of pointed questions. Here are the questions and the answers:

Who were your heroes?
Winston Churchill, General Omar Bradley and Abraham Lincoln."

What values do you consistently try to uphold?
"Honesty, self-discipline, courage, selflessness, hard work, and respect for others."

Can you define your success for me?
"I will have considered my life to be successful if:

- I was a constructive participant in a happy marriage.
- I raised my children to be good citizens with moral value systems.
- I leave the world a little bit better than I found it.

- I have given my best to my profession and to my employers and employees.

- I leave behind a reputation of competence, trustworthiness and reliability."

Can you define the word courage?

"Ability to persevere in a worthy cause in the face of adversity."

Is a person's character formed at birth or can it be changed?

"A person's character can definitely be changed by training, experience and example. Many times I have heard a young student or employee say, 'I want to be just like so-and-so' or 'I really want to improve myself' or 'I really want to be a better person' and it can be done!"

What factors play a role in your decision making?

"I often ask myself two questions: is this decision in line with our objectives and will this decision result in the right thing being done?"

Have you ever had to adhere to a value in the face of difficult circumstances?

"Yes, indeed, not once but many times. I'll give you an example. Our corporation was bidding on a major contract, and we had spent months preparing our proposal. Just before we were to submit our proposal we anonymously received in the mail a copy of our competitor's proposal including its final bid data. No doubt a disgruntled employee of our competitor sent their proposal to us before it was submitted to the customer. After we saw our competitor's proposal we could have changed ours and assured our winning this major contract. But we didn't change our bid because we didn't think it was the ethical thing to do. We lost the contract and some would suggest that we were naïve, but I think in the long run we received more business because we developed a reputation for trustworthiness and ethical conduct in addition to our reputation for good engineering and hard work. After all, if you are developing missiles or rockets that are designed to put people or sophisticated technical equipment into space, a deserved reputation and performance based on competence and integrity are of paramount importance."

If you could express your gratitude for one or two things in your life what would it be and to whom?
"I will be forever grateful to my parents for the way they raised me, for the example, for the discipline and the work ethic. And I will be forever grateful to my wife for the family and support she has provided me."

How do you fight prejudice?
"I refuse to be a party to it."

Do you think America can still be the melting pot for all ethnic groups, races and religions?
"Yes, diversity can still be our greatest strength if we will all just treat one another with respect."

What would you like written on your tombstone?
"He did his best."

What was the biggest decision you had to make in your life?
"My most important personal decision was my marriage to Meg Engman, my wife now of 36 years.

My most difficult business decision had to do with the closing of a number of our plants. These downsizing decisions are, of course, intended to be in the best interest of the company and the shareholders, but can be quite devastating for the employees who are required to find employment elsewhere. When you consider that I have spent most of my adult life building teams and fostering teamwork, it is extremely difficult to downsize or rightsize or whatever you want to call it. The human price is immense, but so too are the consequences of failing to face the problems one confronts."

In your view what is more important in becoming a success in life — intelligence or social skills?

"They are both important but I think motivation is more important that either intelligence or social skills."

If a foreigner asked about your country, what three things are you most proud of? Three things you are ashamed of?

"On the positive side I am most proud of our democracy, our free enterprise system and our nation's general efforts to try to do the right thing.

On the negative side I am most disappointed in the deterioration of our moral values, the breakdown of our families, and the lack of true equality for all our citizens."

What advice would you share with the young people of our country as they pursue their goals in life?
"Preserve your reputation and work hard."

What is the duty of a parent?
"Give your children a set of values and an opportunity for a good education."

From your past experiences, what are some guidelines you would pass onto your children?
"Enjoy life and have the courage to do the right thing."

How can we help our youth bring pride and dignity back into their lives?
"By example."

IN HIS OWN WORDS

I think you will gain additional insight into the man from the following verbatim transcript of his 1992 address entitled *Ethics in America*.

ETHICS IN AMERICA

An address by Norman R. Augustine
Chairman and Chief Executive Officer
Martin Marietta Corporation, Bethesda, Maryland
At The Minnesota Meeting on April 3, 1992.
Carried on KSJN National Public Radio.

Thank you. It is indeed a pleasure to be here. I hope that I can live up to the expectations that have been created by that generous introduction.

It makes me feel a little like my friend David Roderick, the former chairman of US Steel, who was once introduced to an audience as the most gifted businessman in the country evidenced by the fact that he "had made a million dollars in California oil."

When Dave came to the podium, he was a bit embarrassed. Those facts, he said, were *essentially* accurate, but it wasn't oil, it was coal…and it wasn't California, it was Pennsylvania…and it wasn't a million…it was a hundred thousand…and it wasn't he, it was his brother. And he didn't *make* it, he *lost* it!

I have been asked to speak about ethics — the business of ethics and the ethics of business. Let me begin with two stories, both of which are true.

The first has to do with what is going on right now in universities across the country. More than 87% of business majors recently surveyed admitted to cheating at least once at college. The poll involved 15,000 juniors and seniors at 31 universities. Donald McCabe, a Rutgers

University business ethics professor who conducted the survey, speculates that "business courses attract students looking to make a quick buck and willing to cut corners to do it."

Those who never attended business school have no reason to be smug. Students in my own profession of engineering ranked second in the cheating league with 74%. Next came science students — 67%. Even those least likely to cheat — humanities majors — came in at 63%. And one wonders if that is simply because the format of humanities examinations lends itself less well to cheating.

The second story I would like to share with you took place more than 30 years ago, in 1959, when Ted Williams was 40 years old and closing our his career with the Boston Red Sox. He was suffering from a pinched nerve in his neck that season. "The thing was so bad," he later explained, "that I could hardly turn my head to look at the pitcher."

For the first time in his career Williams battled under .300, hitting just .254 with 10 home runs. He was at the time the highest salaried player in sports, making $125,000 a year. The following winter, the Red Sox sent him the same contract he had during his disappointing season.

When he received the proposal, Williams sent it back with a note saying that he would not sign it until they gave him the full pay *cut* allowed. "I was always treated fairly by the Red Sox when it came to contract," Williams said. "Now they were offering me a contract I didn't deserve. And I only wanted what I deserved."

The upshot was that Williams cut his own salary by 25%.

By the way, that year Williams had a great season.

I need to say at the outset I always feel awkward addressing ethics. There are very few absolute standards as to what constitutes ethical behavior — that's what makes the subject so difficult. I'm sure all of us here would agree that cheating is wrong. But how many of us would go so far as to practice Ted Williams' standard of ethics? Ethics is a highly personal matter, and I don't suggest for a moment any superiority of my personal standards.

There was a time when ethics was simple to explain. When a young school girl had been assigned a term paper on the subject, she went to her father for help on the meaning of ethics. Her father, who owned a dry cleaning establishment, told his daughter that he had settled an ethical question that very day. He had found $100 in the pocket of a coat that someone brought to be cleaned and pressed. "Now," he explained, "ethics is: do I tell my partner?"

We remember that Diogenes, lantern in hand, roamed ancient Greece looking for an honest man. If Diogenes roamed New York City today, he might be looking for a policeman to report his lantern stolen. A news clipping tells of a bookstore in Boston calling an affiliate in Washington, D.C., in search of the book *Some Honest Men*. Inquiring whether they had *Some Honest Men* in Washington, the clerk, momentarily taken aback, answered, "Perhaps two or three at the most."

I commend to you a recent novel by John Grisham called *The Firm*. It's been a best-seller. The book describes how young, 25-year-old attorneys fresh out of law school are recruited by a fictional Memphis law firm into what appears to be a dream job, a base salary of $80,000, plus such incidental perks as a BMW and frequent trips to the Caymans.

The only drawback for the rookie lawyers is that they lose their souls. They are gradually and inextricably trapped into crossing the ethical line — a line which they discover is incredibly difficult to walk back across in the other direction. Just as in the Watergate and Iran-Contra scandals, these were people with no record of wrongdoing who would seldom set out deliberately with the intent of breaking the law. They are drawn into it, almost as a boa constrictor consumes its prey.

I labored in the past under the impression that the boa constrictor drops out of a tree on its victims and quickly crushes them in the powerful folds of its body. A quick look in the encyclopedia reveals instead that "...the snake places two or three coils of its body around the chest of its prey. Then each time the victim exhales its breath the boa simply takes up the slack. After three or four breaths there is no more slack. The prey quickly suffocates and is then swallowed by the boa."

This deadly phenomenon of a victim becoming the unwitting accomplice of its own destruction is not confined to the world of reptiles. It's also around in the world of business, the world of politics, the world of athletics, the world of research and almost every place else. The boa we have to face and sometimes fail to face is following our ethical values; each lapse is another coil of the snake.

In the world of politics, we have the "Keating Five," in which United States senators, on both sides of the political aisle, were accused of ethical violations of their office.

In the world of athletics, we find that Pete Rose was involved in gambling; that Rosie Ruiz took a shortcut on the subway when she ran the Boston Marathon; and that numerous professional, Olympic and college athletes have taken steroids to boost their performance.

In the academic world, we find distinguished university professors falsifying their research to win new grants and fleeting prestige.

In the world of religious broadcasting, we have Jim and Tammy Bakker and Jimmy Swaggart.

In the world of hotel management, we have Leona Helmsley who is reported to have casually dismissed her tax violation charges with the statement that, "Only little people tax taxes."

In my own industry, we have "Ill Wind," a government investigation of wrongdoing that has put several formerly highly placed government officials in jail — one of whom had been a friend of mine.

On Wall Street, we have Ivan Boesky, who spoke at UCLA Business School six years ago, and told the students "Greed is a good thing." He ended up spending three years in a federal prison, where greed turned out not to be so good a thing.

In the movie *Wall Street*, Gordon Gekko says, "Greed is good! Greed is all right! Greed works!" In the Broadway play *Serious Money*, the American arbitrager Marylou Baines says, "Greed is all right. Greed is healthy. You can be greedy and still feel good about yourself."

As is often the case, art imitates life. Have we reached the point, in the words of the Washington Post, where "common decency can no longer be described as common?"

Go into book stores and you see best sellers with such titles as *Looking Out for Number One*, *Winning Through Intimidation*, and a book that came out in January, 1992: *Cheating 101: The Benefits and Fundamentals of Earning the Easy 'A'*. Recently I saw on the *Today Show* a manufacturer of sports trading cards who had just introduced a new line of trading material: a set featuring famous serial murderers. I really can't say if ethical lapses or collapses as the case may be are worse now than they were in the past. Martin Marietta keeps track of the numbers of calls to our Ethics Hot Line. When the number goes down, our Board asks me if we have lost interest in ethics. When it goes up, the Board asks me if we are less ethical!

On the other hand, the considerable public discussion about ethics could imply that more people are concerned about doing the right thing. And that really is what ethics is all about. It has been said if rascals knew the value of honesty they would be honest just because of their rascality!

Potter Stewart, the former US Supreme Court Justice, defines ethics as "knowing the difference between what you have a right to do and what is the right thing to do."

There are people who believe that if it's legal, it's ethical. Justice Stewart obviously doesn't agree with that. Neither do I. You have a legal right to burn the flag. But I believe it's the wrong thing to do. Racial discrimination was legal at one time. But is always was wrong. In business, hostile takeovers are legal but I think they are the wrong thing to do.

Others have stated it less elegantly but nonetheless insightfully:

"Ethics is being unafraid to give your pet parrot to the town gossip!"

Ethical behavior goes beyond merely complying with the law. Ethics requires some degree of voluntary compliance.

Another best-seller of a few years ago was written by Robert Fulghum: *All I Really Need To Know...I Learned in Kindergarten.* In that book, Fulghum gives us seven short sentences that you might call his rules for living the ethical life:

- Play Fair.
- Share.
- Don't hit people.
- Don't take things that aren't yours.
- Put things back where you found them.
- Clean up your own mess.
- And say you're sorry when you hurt someone.

Having thought about this issue a considerable amount, I have found no better test than the "Golden Rule" — *Do unto others as you would have them do unto you.*

When I was an undergraduate at Princeton, it was interesting to watch the evolution of students' attitudes toward the University's Honor Code — which was a very, very central part of the educational scheme of things. During an exam, the freshmen were afraid even to lift their eyes for fear they would be thought to be cheating. By the sophomore year, there was such great pride in the system that no one would have dreamed of violating it. By the upper-class years, it was just a normal aspect of everyday student life, and the possibility of cheating simply did not occur to most students. In fact, in four years I never saw anyone cheat.

At the University of Virginia, I am told that when a violation of the ethics code occurs, a small announcement surrounded by a black border is placed in the student newspaper simply stating that a student, unnamed, has left the university. In contrast, at ancient Olympia in Greece, where the original Olympic Games took place, the athletes' entrance to the arena is lined with statues, not of those having achieved great victories, but statues of those who had cheated. To this day, one is beset by a hollow feeling in the pit of the stomach when viewing those stone statues still shouting their message after some 27 centuries have intervened.

Ethics is not simple. Not only does one have to know the right thing to do, but one must also have the moral fortitude to do it. Not always easy. Ethical people, of course, believe in honoring their word, respecting the law, acting honestly, respecting other people's property, exhibiting loyalty, working hard.

But even these values can be misplaced. Optimism is not unethical. In fact, in most cases it's even admirable. But in business, misrepresentation under the guise of optimism is a crime.

Information is valuable, but it's ethical only as long as you have a right to have it.

Profit is valued, as long as you've earned it.

Loyalty is appreciated as long as it isn't misplaced. The Iraqis following Saddam Hussein could be said to have been loyal.

Pro-football teams labor all season to get into the play-offs and to get the "home-field advantage." Assuming this was what it was all about, I was surprised recently to see a letter to the editor in *The Washington Post* challenging the Redskins coach — a highly ethical man in my opinion — for being unethical in encouraging the crowd to make noise in the upcoming play-off game so that it would be difficult for the opposition to hear their signals being called. It probably never occurred to the 55,000 people in the stands that what they were doing might be considered by anyone to be unethical. Was it?

People sometimes adjust their ethical values to meet pressures of the moment. I am reminded of an incident involving one of my favorite cartoon characters, Charlie Brown. Charlie was doing some target shooting one day, practicing with his bow and arrows. He would pull the string back as far as he could and let the arrow fly into the fence.

Then he would run over to the fence and with a piece of chalk drawn a target around the arrows.

Of course it wasn't long before Lucy showed up, saw what he was doing and immediately became hysterical: "That's not the way to have target practice," she shouted. "You're supposed to draw the target first and *then* shoot at it."

But an unrepentant Charlie Brown dismissed the matter, remarking, "I know that, Lucy. But if you do it my way, you never miss!"

Ethics has to do with hitting the target the hard way. First you have to have ethical values. Then you have to live up to those values. You can't make up the ethics as you go along. That's the most common pitfall of all to rationalize one's ethics to meet the circumstances. That's when the boa gets its first grip.

At the same time, we have to recognize the enigma that ethical values are not absolutes — although they are hopefully absolute for any one individual. Countries spy on other countries. We apparently don't think there's anything wrong with that. But because it is regarded as acceptable behavior for countries to spy on other countries does not imply that it's acceptable for anyone else, whether it's spying on your neighbor or industrial espionage. There is, I believe, great irony in that observation. One might think we would hold our governments to a higher standard than individuals. But when it comes to spying, it's the other way around.

Henry L. Stimson, an attorney who had a distinguished career in government, serving twice as Secretary of War and also as Secretary of State during the early part of this century, once decided to close down the American counterintelligence and decipherment activities known as "the Black Chamber." He explained, "Gentlemen do not read each other's mail."

Those who do spy on others, of course, do so at their own risk, and sometimes punishment is swift. This is painstakingly true of government spies who may be revered in their own land but despised in another.

On a lesser scale, Frank Brady, in his biography of Aristotle Onassis, tells us that the Greek shipping magnate once installed a luxurious private bathroom adjoining his office. The door was a one-way mirror, so he could observe unsuspecting visitors from the privacy of the bathroom.

During a business meeting one afternoon, Onassis excused himself and entered the bathroom. Comfortably enthroned, he was horrified to see his own reflection staring back at him in the mirrored door.

It turned out that workmen making repairs earlier in the day had replaced the mirror the wrong way around...reflecting badly not only upon their workmanship but also upon Onassis' ethical standards.

Ethical standards, of course, vary from country to country and even within countries. Some years ago, I awoke one Thanksgiving morning to discover that a fresh turkey had been placed on the porch of almost every house except the one in which I lived and the one belonging to an airline pilot. Almost all our other neighbors were medical doctors. It turned out that a local mortuary had adopted the practice of delivering turkeys to the houses of all the doctors in our community. Needless to say, I did not find this a particularly reassuring practice!

Similarly, I once read of a man who went abroad on a mountain-climbing expedition. The first night in camp he put his sweater outside his tent before retiring for the night. Upon awakening in the morning, he found to his chagrin the sweater was gone. He assumed it was stolen until he noticed one of the local mountain porters in his party proudly wearing it as he went about his work.

Upon complaining to the head guide, the climber was told that it was the presumption of the mountain people that whatever you left behind had been discarded and thereby became the property of whomever took possession of it. It could be your sweater, your knapsack — even your shoes.

In some countries, the practice of "presenting gifts" to smooth the conduct of business is perfectly legal, even encouraged by custom. In our country, they're called bribes, at least in the eyes of our government.

Not only do ethical standards differ from country to country, they may also vary over the dimension of time. The great Daniel Webster, a leading political figures in the 19th century, was what we would now call "on the take" from Nicholas Biddle and Biddle's Second Bank of the United States. Webster, while holding public office, once wrote to Biddle to complain that "my retainer has not been renewed or refreshed as usual."

What was perfectly acceptable in the last century is not acceptable in this one.

On the other hand, in this century it is ethical for British members of Parliament to serve on the Boards of British industries. In our country, it's not only unethical, it's illegal. Foreign governments often give extravagant gifts to US diplomats; in our country it is illegal for the diplomats to keep them.

We regarded the Japanese sneak attach on Pearl Harbor as a "date which will live in infamy." In Japan, certainly in 1941, it was widely regarded as a brilliant strategic move.

Our country believed then — and still believes — that a sneak attack is immoral. We have been so affected by what happened at Pearl Harbor that when President Reagan decided to bomb Libya for its acts of terrorism, he publicly announced what we were going to do in advance. Newspaper accounts at the time made it clear that we did not want to be accused of doing to Libya what Japan had done to America at Pearl Harbor.

And before President Bush began the air war against Iraq, he announced the date it would begin, unless of course, Iraq previously withdrew from Kuwait. Iraq refused to withdraw and the bombing began right on schedule.

President Bush similarly announced the date the land battle would begin. Once again, Iraq refused to withdraw from Kuwait, and the attack began right on schedule.

In fact, there are ethics even in the conduct of war as codified under the Geneva Convention. Just because other countries may violate internationally accepted ethical standards does not free our country from the obligation to adhere to those standards we believe are proper.

And, just like countries, companies also have ethical standards. Employees are expected to know what they are and adhere to them. At Martin Marietta, for example, we have an ethics training program which virtually all 60,000 of our employees, both in this country and overseas, have attended, including me.

We also have a Corporate Ethics Office that's charged with responsibility for monitoring performance under our Code of Ethics, providing advice and resolving concerns raised by employees.

I can think of no commitment more important to the corporation or fundamental to its survival than its commitment to ethics. We, like any company, of course, intensely want to win business. But we even more intensely want to compete fairly and ethically for the business we win. And that means not only conducting our business affairs within the letter of the law, but also in the spirit of the law.

Sometimes the ethical choices faced are easy. Such was the case some time ago when we were in competition for a major contract, and the day before we were to submit our proposal we received in the mail a copy of our competitor's price sheet. It presumably came from a disgruntled employee.

We opened the package, not knowing what was inside. Once we realized what we had, we promptly handed the package to our attorneys, who informed the government and the competitor what had happened. We did not change our bid price.

Incidentally, we lost the contract, and some of our employees lost their jobs due to lack of work.

And that brings me to another facet of ethics. I wish I could say that ethical behavior always pays off. I truly believe that it does in the long term, but not always in the short term.

I can give an example from my own life. Some time ago my wife and I had dinner one weekend with a business associate who happened to be one of our suppliers. At the end of the dinner, as a thoughtful gesture, he presented gifts to my wife and me — attractive watches made by his corporation.

The following Monday, I asked my wife for her watch, explaining that since it came from a supplier, our company ethics code required that I turn both gifts into the company, which then would give them to charity.

But my wife *liked* her watch! She said it was a gift to her, not to the company; that she didn't work for the company; and furthermore, that our friend would be genuinely offended if he knew that the company had taken away from her what was intended purely as a thoughtful gift to her. Therefore, she informed me, I could do whatever I wanted with my watch, but she was keeping hers!

What to do! After a prolonged discussion, our corporation's legal counsel suggested I write a check to the company for the value of her watch and that amount would in turn be given to charity. Together, the attorney and I looked up the cost of a similar-appearing watch in a catalogue, the price: $120 — which I paid. All seemed well until a few weeks later, when our legal counsel mentioned to me that he had bad news: he had seen exactly the same watch which had been given to my wife in a jewelry store. I owed another $1,500!

I had the worst of all worlds. I was out $1,620 to buy my wife a watch, and my wife was mad at me for trying to take her gift away. She still thinks of the watch as a gift from my associate rather than from me. My wife is one of the most ethical people I know!

Let me give an example of a hard ethical decision. When I was managing Martin Marietta's Astronautics company, our space launch vehicle contract with the Air Force included a compensation clause rewarding the company with several million dollars every time we successful launched a spacecraft.

One day a representative in our insurance department brought to my attention that we could insure our launches for a very low premium cost. In other words, the Air Force would give us the incentive compensation if we succeeded, and the insurance company would give us nearly the same amount of money if we failed. This was the *best* of all worlds.

Now I should point out that I am absolutely certain no one involved in any of our launches tries one iota harder because there is an Air Force financial bonus for success. Nor do I believe for a moment that anyone would do less then their best if the launch were insured against failure.

Still, we seemed to have an ethical question before us. It clearly undermined the idea of the "incentive" intended by our customer if we merely went out and bought insurance to cover it. At the same time, our lawyers were quick to remind me that we also had a fiduciary responsibility to our shareholders to conduct our business on their behalf in a prudent fashion. Was it not sound business practice to purchase insurance which would in effect guarantee most of the reward to our shareholders?

How would you have decided?

Frankly, I struggled with that one. I eventually called the responsible Air Force general and explained the dilemma, noting that I was seeking advice, not guidance. But I did tell him that if the Air Force was indifferent to what we elected to do, it was my intention to buy the insurance. On the other hand, if the Air Force felt that the existence of the insurance policy undermined our customer's intent, we would weigh that factor in our decision.

After having thought about the matter for a few days the general telephoned to say that anything that would weaken the Air Force incentive for a successful launch did in fact undermine the government's intent. I eventually decided against purchasing the insurance to cover possible future failures. Certainly one could argue whether or not this was the proper resolution of the matter. But it seemed equitable.

As widely noted, there's no virtue in consistency if you're consistently wrong. What may be appropriate to do in one situation may be inappropriate in another. The world of ethics is, unfortunately, not often without an array of choices. In this spectrum of choices, honest people can honestly disagree on what is honest and ethical. As Yogi Berra might characterize the matter, "When you come to a fork in the road, take it!"

Let me offer the following scenarios which I often use to illustrate the point to colleagues in the aerospace industry. It is common in our business when you're in competition to build a new airplane that you take out ads in newspapers to display your new design. But the picture is always an artist's conception, and it never is the plane quite as it really looks.

Now, suppose that one of your competitors makes a mistake and publishes its real design in the newspaper and this becomes known publicly. Is it ethical to do some reverse engineering of their illustration and turn their mistake to your advantage? Most people I have asked would be ethical.

But what if we change the situation just slightly. Suppose you're at the airport and find the competitor's design laying on the top of a pile of paper in a wastebasket where it had been, perhaps accidentally, thrown? Is it ethical to dig it out of the garbage and use it to your advantage? We're told that some newspaper reporters go through discarded refuse to get leads for stories. So do government investigators. Is it ethical for one profession — say, the newspaper profession — to follow a fairly common practice but unethical for the engineering profession to do the same thing?

Now, suppose you're on an airplane, and two of your competitor's engineers seated in front of you are casually discussing their design in rather loud voices. Is it acceptable for you to hear them?

Or suppose you're on the same airplane and by chance are seated next to the competitor's chief engineer, who's openly studying drawings for the next plane. Or suppose the drawings carelessly remain on the engineer's tray while he gets up to use the telephone in the front of the airplane. Is it ethical to look at those drawings in that circumstance perhaps without even touching them? Certainly, the competitor was grossly negligent.

Suppose the plane lands, and your competitor accidentally leaves the drawings on his seat as he makes a mad dash to catch a connecting flight. Are you under an ethical obligation to run and catch him to return the drawings? Or would it be okay to take a look at the drawings, perhaps even make a photocopy of them, since he was so careless?

How about going to the local bar where your competitor's employees hang out after work and listening to their conversations? Or perhaps going one step further and buying everyone in the bar drinks? How about breaking into their plant and dynamiting the safe?

In this continuum of choices, I have found large numbers of people who consider themselves to be quite ethical yet disagree over the point at which the boundary of propriety was actually transgressed where the boa was lying in wait.

In the medical profession, the Hippocratic oath has been an ethical lighthouse since the time of the ancient Greeks. But what happens when that oath comes into conflict with late 20th-century medicine? A recent case in Florida tragically illustrates this problem. A baby is born without a brain. The parents want to donate the child's vital organs before she dies. A state law forbids declaring the baby brain-dead, because she does have the stem of a brain which is keeping her breathing and her heart beating. Her organs could save other babies' lives, but the courts have blocked donating the organs until her brain-stem stops functioning. By then, her organs will be unusable for transplants. *That* is a difficult ethical question, or at least in part an ethical question.

Turning to the legal profession, what of the case a few years ago where a court-appointed lawyer meets with the designated client, accused of murder, only to be told in confidence of two other murders and the location of the bodies? Finding bodies at those locations, the attorney later learns of the agony of two distraught families in the local community whose loved ones are missing but their fate is unknown. Should the lawyer reveal the location of the bodies, but in so doing violate professional confidentiality and possibly implicate the client he is sworn to defend?

Or what of the psychiatrist who is told, convincingly, by a patient of a plan to murder his spouse, and soon thereafter the spouse is found dead? Or suppose the patient indicates a pattern of murders and the intent to continue that pattern but indicates no specific individual as a future target?

I mentioned a moment ago that some newspaper reporters are known for digging through people's garbage as part of getting a story. Let me give you another example from the journalistic profession. The March 1992 issue of *Spy Magazine* contains an article describing how the magazine's editor, posing as an executive recruiter and claiming to have a client who might be interested in offering former White House Chief of Staff John Sununu a job, speaks to Governor Sununu over the telephone. The editor inquires about the salary range Sununu is interested in as well as a litany of other relatively personal questions. After publishing its story, the magazine represents its phone call, which it tape-recorded without Sununu's knowledge, as simply a hoax, a harmless prank.

Was it ethical for the editor to lie about his name, occupation and intent in order to get a story? And was it ethical to tape record the conversation secretly without Sununu's permission? Was it ethical to publish the article when Sununu was obviously under the impression that he was having a private conversation?

An even better question is: was it ethical for *The Washington Post* to carry a separate article reporting the incident without even questioning the ethics of how *Spy Magazine* obtained the story in the first place? *The Post*, in its story, did address one question of ethics: whether Gov. Sununu was himself behaving ethically in discussing a job in the private sector so soon after leaving a senior government position. That was it.

Let's look a little closer at some of the ethical dilemmas journalists face. A newspaper in Mankato, Minnesota, published a story about a one-year-old boy who needed a kidney transplant. Readers, greatly moved by the plight of the young boy, donated a considerable sum of money to pay for his operation.

But what if a similar care of genuine need comes up the next day? What if four or five cases come to the media's attention? Are newspapers and TV required to treat everyone equally? Should every needy case be offered the same public attention? Or can the news media simply say, "the first one was news, but we're not going to give the second child the same public attention — and opportunity — as the first?"

What are the ethical issues involved? In the words of *The Washington Post* ombudsman, "Was the family you helped the most needy? Were the donations properly spent? Do you become a fund-raiser for every needy family in town? Do you 'play God' and say one fundraiser a year is your limit? Or are you morally obligated to treat all comers alike?"

Another case of journalistic ethics involves a newspaper that, based upon some old newspaper clippings, identifies a candidate running for office as a Ku Klux Klan member. The reporter calls the man, who admits he was a member some 10 years before but asks that the paper not print the information, saying it would mean his certain defeat in the election.

So far, it's easy for the reporter to run the story. Before that happens, a representative of the Anti-Defamation League tells the reporter that the "Klansman" was really an FBI informer. If that fact were published, the man could well be killed. Then the reporter hears rumors that another paper has the story and may publish it. The reporter doesn't want to be scooped. Is a reporter relieved of any ethical responsibility merely because of a rumor that another paper may publish the story? One public magazine, *The Armed Forces Journal*, withheld its knowledge of the enormous military breakthrough of "stealth" for several years because of its concern that to do otherwise might undermine national security.

In contrast, *USA Today* revealed former tennis pro Arthur Ashe's closely held secret that he had AIDS, explaining that "it was news."

Is it ethical for reporters to use information that they know was received in an unethical manner, perhaps even stolen? During Clarence Thomas' Supreme Court confirmation hearings, confidential FBI information — called "raw information" because its accuracy had not been validated — was leaked to the press. Is it ethical for someone to leak information? Or is it more ethical to be public with your accusations rather than hide behind the anonymity reporters would promise to their confidential sources?

A few years ago, the well-known reporter Peter Jennings was presented with a hypothetical scenario wherein he was told that the era was during the Vietnam War and that he was traveling with a group of Viet Cong who had agreed to take him with them so he could see how they lived in the jungle. He was told he could report anything he wished, but only on condition that he report it after the fact and that while with them he was to do nothing to interfere.

As the group is traveling through the jungle the Viet Cong unexpectedly observe a group of unsuspecting American soldiers whom they prepare to ambush. If Jennings warns the American soldiers, he violates his ethical commitment to the Viet Cong. If he does not, the soldiers die.

What, Jennings is asked, would he do? Without a moment's hesitation Peter Jennings answered that he would warn the soldiers. "I am an American," he explained, "before I am a reporter."

We all face ethical dilemmas from time to time in our lives — hopefully less consequential than Peter Jennings' hypothetical predicament — but still critical in our own scale of affairs. Such great decisions are sometimes described as "crossing the Rubicon." The phrase, of course, comes from Julius Caesar's crossing of the Rubicon River more than 2,000 years ago and committing himself irrevocably to war against the Roman Senate. "The die is cast," in the words of Caesar.

For most of us, there is a personal Rubicon that, sooner or later, we have to cross. Our personal Rubicon may not be matter of life or death, as was the ethical situation posed to Peter Jennings. But, like him, we have to recognize that ethical comportment comes before business, before winning, sometimes even before individual loyalty.

W. C. Fields, the occasionally rude, heavy-drinking comedian of the 1930's and '40s, once was deeply immersed in a book just before he was about to begin a performance. A friend saw him and, to his amazement, noticed Fields was reading the Bible!

"Bill, what are you doing reading the Bible?" the friend asked. To which Fields replied, "I'm looking for loopholes!"

When it comes to ethics, there are no loopholes. There are no compromises. There are no back doors. But to be regarded as an ethical person may be the ultimate reward.

CHAPTER FOUR
HONOR

GENERAL FREDERICK M. FRANKS, JR.

Don't Worry, General, We Trust You
— 3rd Armored Division Soldier to General Fred Franks

THE WORDS ABOVE were spoken by one of the soldiers in the 3rd Armored Division just before the division launched its attack into Iraq during Operation Desert Storm.

For those of you who don't know about General Fred Franks or what he did in Operation Desert Storm, let me set the stage. General Franks was the VII Corps Commander during Operation Desert Storm, the code name for the campaign initiated by President Bush in 1990 in response to Iraq's invasion of Kuwait. Saddam Hussein, Iraq's authoritarian leader, had destabilized the Middle East by invading Kuwait and threatening Saudi Arabia. The United States formed and led a United Nations coalition to thwart further aggression and to restore the national integrity of Kuwait. The U.N. coalition, after several diplomatic warnings to Iraq, deployed a sizable military force into the region with the intention of forcibly achieving what diplomacy had failed to do. Iraq did considerable saber rattling and promised to annihilate the U.N. coalition in the "mother of all battles." General Frederick M. Franks, Jr. commanded the armor and infantry elements of the VII Corps, the main attack on the ground that was part of the U.S. coalition force that ultimately decimated Iraq's Republican Guard in a matter of days. Clearly, the Gulf War was a very successful campaign, and General Fred Franks played a major role in the success of the military mission.

So what does all of the above have to do with ethics and the stated objective of this section of the book, which is, to identify heroes who have succeeded in an ethical manner? There can be no doubt that Operation Desert Storm was a successful military campaign and that General Fred Franks' role in the campaign was significant and that this success was just one of the many memorable events in a long distinguished career. The successes and the career are important but the way General Franks lives his life and the way in which he achieved his success are worthy of emulation.

General Fred Franks is a "soldier's soldier." Throughout his career, which included duty in Vietnam, the Persian Gulf, and in Europe along the Iron Curtain, he gave proper attention to both the mission and the readiness and welfare of the troops under his command. He was firmly committed to the goal that the troops should have the best leadership that we, as a nation, can provide. He also understood that generals can lose battles, but only the soldiers win the battles. He sincerely believed that to lead is to serve, and he considered command an awesome privilege and responsibility. General Franks' character, competence, and genuine concern for the well being of his troops enabled him to inspire confidence, tenacity and trust. So it comes as a true tribute to a distinguished leader when one of his young soldiers offers this testimony as he was getting ready to go into battle — *"Don't worry, General, we trust you."*

Let's take a closer look at this man who fought in two wars. This man who loves his country, who loves his wife and daughter, and who loved his soldiers. These were the men and women who selflessly responded to the call of duty when their nation needed them. He is not a complex man; he is a straightforward, humble leader with a solid value system. He never forgot his roots and, although he rose to the rank of four-star general and had the responsibility to work with numerous high-ranking distinguished leaders, he never lost the common touch. The reason he had such great rapport with his troops is because he respected and trusted them; and he earned their respect and trust.

Despite his vast experience as an armor officer and the quiet confidence he displayed he seldom overlooked an opportunity to listen and to learn from his noncommissioned officers and his soldiers. He earned the trust of his soldiers and of his colleagues and senior officers because he was trustworthy. He spoke the truth, he respected the dignity and worth of every member of his command, and he gave due concern to his mission and to the welfare of his troops. This meant that he paid special attention to the preparation of his battle plan as well as the troops' readiness to execute the plan. His sense of personal responsibility to see every task through to its successful conclusion, his sense of loyalty to his friends and his troops, his intellectual honesty and his moral and physical stamina, are attributes worthy of emulation by all of us. In all of his successes he insisted on putting the spotlight on the followers and not on the leader. General Fred Franks is the personification of West Point's Motto — *Duty, Honor, Country*. Moreover the values of the United States Army: integrity, honor, respect, duty, loyalty, service and courage would be manifest in any accurate biography of this man.

General Sir John Hackett once said, *"The very efficiency of the Army depends upon fortitude, integrity, self restraint, personal loyalty to other persons and the surrender of the individual to the common good."* He could very well have been describing General Fred Franks.

At another place and another time General George Washington observed, "*War must be carried on systemically and to do it you must have men of character activated by the principle of honor.*" Although General George Washington spoke those words over 200 years ago, his words could also have been describing General Fred Franks.

And if we go all the way back to the 6th Century B.C., Lao-Tzu proclaimed: "*A leader is best when he is neither seen or heard. Not so good when he is adored and glorified. Worst when he is hated and despised. 'Fail to honor people, they fail to honor you.' But of a great leader, when his work is done, his aim fulfilled, the people will all say, 'We did this ourselves.'* Perhaps General Franks said the same thing when he stated, "*Put the spotlight on the led not the leader.*"

In a career that spanned over three decades he has been true to the ideals upon which the country was founded. He has been a faithful and loving husband to his wife, Denise, a dutiful and attentive father to his daughter, Margie, and a soldier who willingly put his life on the line to protect the freedom and rights we all take for granted.

GENERAL FREDERICK M. FRANKS, JR. Q & A

Let's get another snapshot of the man by looking at the responses to the questions I posed to him in a personal interview.

Where did you grow up?

"I was born in West Lawn, Pennsylvania in November of 1936 and spent most of my formative years within several miles of my birthplace although we did live in Stroudsburg, Pennsylvania in 1939-1946. I attended grade five through twelve in the Wilson School District in Berks County, Pennsylvania and spent one year at Lehigh University before acceptance into the United State Military Academy in 1955. I got a great start in life from my mom and dad and from growing up in West Wyomissing. The values learned at home, in school, in the community and on the athletic fields of Berks County prepared me well for a lifetime as a soldier.

Who were your heroes?

"Although I come from a large, tight-knit family with plenty of meaningful role models, I would have to say that my parents were my early heroes. I don't think my mom ever had a bad day. She was always there for us as we were growing up. I particularly admired my dad who, with only a high school education, rose to the position of senior vice president of a major shoe corporation.

Outside of my family and growing up in the 40s and 50s, I looked up to many national leaders and sports stars. I came to respect and admire President Harry Truman. His willingness to face tough problems and take stands on difficult issues, even when the outcome was not assured, were unique qualities. He made some tough decisions under trying circumstances, and in the end, history may judge him to be one of our more effective presidents. There were also military leaders, such as Bradley, Eisenhower, and Patton, as well as sports heroes like Ted Williams and Jackie Robinson."

Are there any values that you consistently try to uphold?

"I guess that my family upbringing and my participation on sports teams in high school and college taught me to think about the team before self. Teamwork always does more for an organization than a few individual stars. I carried that feeling into my military life, where teamwork on the battlefield is vital to mission success. In addition, when you ask others to put themselves in harm's way to achieve an objective or mission, it is of paramount importance to accomplish that mission at least cost to them. American soldiers have proven to be effective in combat if we properly equip and train them and if we truthfully keep them informed on the mission and the situations, in other words, establish trust.

Here are some of the principles I have tried to live by:
- Be honest with yourself and your soldiers.
- To lead is also to serve
- Maintain a sense of personal responsibility for your organization and your conduct
- Put the spotlight on the led not the leader
- Create a climate wherein everyone can succeed
- Maintain a sense of loyalty to your friends, colleagues, the troops and your boss
- Maintain a sense of integrity in being and in action

I have tried to live these qualities in my professional life and my personal life. Even during those time when I failed to measure up to those standards, I picked myself up and went right back to trying to live those values."

In your opinion what are the three most important family values, in order of importance?
- Unconditional love between family members
- Sense of loyalty and responsibility to each other
- Honesty and integrity as a family; stand up for what you believe

It is difficult to maintain your values and your integrity while receiving so much admiration and attention?

"I try not to get too carried away with the attention and kudos I sometimes get. We have had some terrible lows in our life, so together with my wife, Denise, and daughter, Margie, we try to keep it all in perspective. I feel fortunate for what success I have had in life and I am grateful to the many people and the circumstances that have created that.

Most people know that it is more difficult to maintain your faith and your values when you lose children or when you are confronted with a major illness or major medical hardship or handicap. Meeting those challenges is hard for anyone, and we are no different. Yet, I believe you can gain wisdom and strength by how you handle those situations. You either grow from all that or you die a little bit as a person. Fortunately for me, during the low periods in our life, my wife, daughter and I grabbed hold of the steel that we knew was within us and we moved forward determined to be thankful for what we had and not focus on what we did not have.

And thanks to a lot of determination, support and assistance from medical professionals and former commanders, I was able to remain on active duty in the Army and go on to a lifetime as a soldier. All in all I consider myself a fortunate man with a wonderful wife and daughter. I am thankful for what I have."

How can we improve upon the values and morals in our country?

"That is a tough question and I certainly do not have the only answer. I think each of us contributes in our own way. First, each of us in our own circle of responsibility needs to have the courage to be who we really are. We need to stand for something good and right, to make our actions connect with the values we profess to believe in, or said in another way, make what we do equal to what we say or believe. One act of moral conscience can turn the tide in our own circle of influence."

Define your success for me and how did ethics, honor or integrity contribute to or detract from your success?

"Success for me is to use whatever God-given talents I have to make my small part of the world a little better than I found it. It is extremely important to take actions to assure that what you say and what you do are consistent with the internal code of ethics to which you profess to believe. Integrity and honor have a clarity and a steel all their own — they need no explanation, and they will stand the test of time."

Who is the most ethical and moral person you know?

"My wife, Denise, and daughter, Margie, have a purity of motivation. They are who they appear to be. There are no hidden agendas nor motivations. They both have an unbelievable sense of empathy and compassion for others and delight in making people feel better about themselves. They are honest and straightforward; they are simply what they are and make no pretense to be anything else. I admire and respect how they live their lives. They are my angels."

Who was your best teacher? What did you learn from him or her?

"Mrs. Hemmig, my 5th grade teacher from West Wyomissing grade school, was one of a kind. I never encountered another teacher quite like her. She opened a new world of reading and history for me. She was very positive, very encouraging, and really committed to her students. She made learning fun and exciting. My mom was also a great teacher at home."

Did you ever truly go beyond the call of duty?

"The word duty is hard to put limits on. It is a wonderful value and I wish I heard it discussed more in public life. Duty transcends self. Duty is limited only by your sense of responsibility for the people you are responsible for and your given mission. Some define that very narrowly; others do not. Seeing the possibilities of what you and your people can achieve and your sense of obligation to get that done expands your vision of duty. One's sense of duty to soldiers in battle and to the mission in combat defines one's behavior and actions. And in wartime a commander's duty to his troops is endless."

Do you think a person's character is formed at birth or can it be changed?

"We are not at the mercy of the genetic lottery. Character can be taught and character can be molded. In my own case, I am convinced that my character was formed by my immediate family, by my extended family, by some of my school teachers, by exercises in sports, by my church, by my wife and family. The Honor Code at West Point was a continuation, formalization and refinement of an ethical process that began at an early age.

I also believe that our character is also affected by role models and the heroes we choose to admire and emulate."

What can you say about character and integrity as they relate to your life and your career?

"In my career and especially in command and leadership positions I found the following three fundamental principles to define command:

CHARACTER — Yes, character does count. Actually it is the foundation for everything you do in an organization especially a military organization wherein you may be asking your troops to put their lives on the line. Trust is the vital link and basic bond between a leader and his troops. Trust is earned continually by word and action. In the final analysis the ultimate alignment of the leader and the led is based on trust. When it comes to developing bonds of mutual trust to motivating people toward extraordinary performance, character in the leader is vital.

COMPETENCE — As important as character is, there is more to command. When your stakes are high such as human lives or the financial viability of a large organization leaders need to know their business or their profession. Character develops trust and competence develops confidence. If members of your organization truly believe you know what you are doing, that you have a vision and worthy achievable goal and a well-thought-out tactical plan coupled with the necessary material and people resources they will confidently follow you anywhere; that is, providing you have earned their trust.

LEADERSHIP — Is in my view the ability to motivate and challenge the organization to achieve its goals. Leaders give purpose, motivation, and direction. They challenge the status quo. They lead the organization and stay out in front. Leadership is the glue that synthesizes character and competence into a working entity. It is the catalyst that makes it all happen."

Define the word courage.

"In my view the word courage is the willingness to do and say what is right. There are two parts to courage; a physical part and a moral part. Physical courage is the most obvious because it is immediately visible and the physical courage of a leader and/or his troops is an essential ingredient for winning battles.

The second part of courage is moral courage — the willingness and ability to do what is right when faced with all intense scrutiny of your troops and of the world. There are extraordinary pressures as you go up the hierarchy of command and responsibility. You will be required to make judgements and decisions in compressed time frames and with uncertain or incomplete information. Success is not always assured when commanders make choices. Leaders have always faced some of these pressures but in the current time frame your statements and actions are subject to immediate historical judgement and criticism. Accordingly, leaders can be tempted into giving themselves an escape in case things don't work out as they planned. They must have the courage to assume both public and private responsibilities. It is at times like this when moral courage faces its biggest test. It is at times like this when leaders must have the courage to be who they really are and what they stand for.

But make no mistake about it, the higher the position the greater are the pressures and the greater are the consequences. And it is for these reasons that moral courage is essential."

What factors play a role in your decision making?

"As a soldier, my oath to uphold and defend the Constitution and accomplishing our assigned mission at least cost to my troops. Other factors are, how does this decision fit into our vision for our organization, can the decision be better made by subordinates, and what are the cost/benefit/risk tradeoffs?"

Can you give a specific example of a time you chose to act on a value even though it seemed the most difficult path to follow? What was the outcome?

"I had a section on this in my book with Tom Clancy, *Into the Storm.* In Operation Desert Storm our military success caused considerable displacement of Iraqi refugees. There were thousands of refugees as an aftermath of our successful military attack into Iraq. There was a policy that we not do anything in occupied Iraq that would look like a long-term occupation since the anticipation was we would be out in weeks. After the XVIIIth Corps left Iraq, I was the senior American Commander on the scene, and the sanction arrangements with Iraq were not yet completed. We were going to be there awhile, and despite the policy we needed to do some things as an occupying force. My feeling was that we are Americans and we stand for something and that we had an obligation according to law and to who we were to do what was right.

So, not only did we feel compelled to establish law and order and to clear out all of the unexploded ordinance around populated areas but we also felt that we should provide water, food and medicine and medical treatment to the refugees and establish refugee camps for those without homes. So we opened hospitals, schools and medical clinics and established refugee camps during our over seven-week stay in occupied Iraq. I was aided in this by my staff judge advocate, who drew up a list of those things we should have accomplished by the time we left — whenever that might be.

Because there was a high probability that the government of Iraq would punish many of the refugees and claim they were traitors or defectors, we all wanted some way to ensure there would be no retribution to the refugees after we left. Since the UN Commander would not help us, the solution was to give the refugees a choice to stay in Iraq or leave. The only question was when they would go. General Yeosock, who was the Third Army Commander and my immediate boss, talked the Saudi leadership into building a camp to take care of those refugees who wanted to leave. Almost 20,000 chose to leave. This was a case that as Americans we chose to do the harder right rather than the easier wrong.

From where have you drawn your inner strength?

"I guess I draw strength from a clear conscience and from trying to do the things that are right. I enjoy responsibility and working with teams to solve tough problems and the satisfaction that comes to the whole team from that success. I do believe that to lead is also to serve and so I also enjoy making others feel good about themselves and seeing them go on and be successful."

How would you like to be remembered?

"I would like to be remembered as a soldier's soldier."

What has given meaning to your life?

"My wife, Denise, our daughter, Margie, and our two grandsons and granddaughter.

The other thing that I think about often is of soldiers feeling good about their service to our country. The one aspect of Operation Desert Storm that I am so grateful for is the pride and respect given to our soldiers who once again stepped forward when our nation called and did their duty with great skill, courage, and at great personal sacrifice.

One of the most discouraging happenings in my life was the treatment given to our soldiers when they returned from Vietnam. For the most part they responded to the call from our national leaders to go to Vietnam and most went willingly, and they gave of themselves selflessly. They also did their duty with great skill, courage, and at great personal sacrifice. Yet when they returned home they returned to an ungrateful nation, and the leadership that called them to duty was not there to acknowledge their sacrifices or say thanks for their service."

What are your strengths and weaknesses?

"People tell me my strengths are my ability to quickly size up a situation; to understand my troops and my assigned mission and then to get the most out of the people who must accomplish the mission.

On the negative side I tend to overcommit myself. I can't say no to good causes and good people, and therefore I find myself sometimes spread too thin. But I have been that way a long time and am happy with myself over committing rather than passing up a chance to serve."

Was there any particular experience or event in your life that influenced your philosophy of life or your management style?

"Yes, during the Vietnam war I was wounded in Cambodia and spent 21 months in the hospital. Toward the end of my hospital stay, I finally told my doctors to amputate my leg below the knee after over eight months trying to save it. Those tough days in the hospital and the final decision to amputate forced me to do some serious introspection. With the support from my wife and daughter, I was able to gradually turn that adversity into the positive notion of being thankful for what I had and not worry about what I didn't have. It was not easy and did not happen overnight. That whole process influenced my behavior as a person and my sense of duty as a soldier, reinforcing many things but also changing my perspective on many things. Fortunately, the Army saw fit to say yes to my request to remain on active duty, thus giving me the opportunity to continue to serve."

What were the major turning points in your career, and how do you feel about your choices now?

"The prolonged hospital stay caused by the wounds I sustained in Cambodia during the Vietnam War was for me and my family a trying experience. The turning point came when I decided to take one of the choices my doctor gave me and elect to have them amputate my left leg below the knee rather than endure the probability of constant physical pain and limited activity.

Once I made that decision and focused on the positive things in my life I was able to move on. At that decision point, I had no idea that the Army would allow me to continue as an active duty military officer, and I certainly had no idea that I would be able to again command troops in combat and, ultimately, be given the opportunity to serve as a four star general. To this day I am grateful to our Army as an institution that allowed that opportunity and to those who helped me along the way. Something like that could only happen in American."

If you could express your gratitude for one thing in your life, what would it be and to whom?

"In a word — Denise. She has been and is now my special angel.

I had inscribed on the inside of her engagement ring (a miniature of my own West Point Class ring) the words of that old love song I'll get by...The rest of it is 'as long as I have you.' How true that has been for me."

Describe the time in your life when you experienced the most fear?

"The low point in my life and the time when I experienced the most fear was during my 21 month stay in the hospital. The fear of the unknown, the future, and the concern about the possible loss of one of my legs were frightening and depressing days for me. Much soul searching went on during that period and had it not been for the loyal and loving support of my family the ultimate outcome might have been quite different.

Getting shot at in combat also has its fearful moments especially when you are wounded or exhausted because your body tells you one thing and your mind tells you something else. But in the end you remember that you have a mission to accomplish and some troops to look after and just forge ahead and do what you have to do."

Describe yourself in one word as a child!

"Soldier. For as long as I can remember I wanted to be a soldier."

If you had been the President in 1945, would you have dropped the Atom Bomb?

"Yes, because that decision brought a quick end to the war and undoubtedly saved many lives."

Would you march on Washington for a cause? What would the cause be?

"No, that is not to say that there are not important causes because there are. But I would go about supporting an important cause in a different way."

How do you fight prejudice?

"By doing something to combat it every time we see it. I am proud of the Army's record of equal opportunity and intolerance of any manifestations of prejudice."

Do you think America can still be the melting pot for all ethnic groups, races and religions?

"Yes — I believe in the notion of E Pluribus Unum i.e., One from many."

Was there a speech or presentation that you consider the very best you ever heard?

"President John F. Kennedy's Inaugural Address and Dr. Martin Luther King's speech at the Lincoln Memorial in 1963."

If you could sit down to dinner with one famous person, who would it be?

"General Colin Powell. He is a man I admire and respect."

If you could have one wish granted, what would it be?

"I would ask for good health and the opportunity to grow for my family, especially my daughter and grandchildren."

What quote of yours would you want carved in granite or bronze?

"To lead is also to serve."

What is your best personality trait?

"Tough on being uncompromising to meet standards while remaining sensitive to others. Tom Clancy called me the "Quiet Lion" in his intro to **Into The Storm**. I like that."

What does it take to be a great leader?

"Character, competence and the ability to motivate others."

What is the nicest compliment ever given to you?

"I have always felt that my troops' judgment of me was more important than how my superior officers rated me. If I had to pick one, it would be: '*Don't worry, General, we trust you*.'"

What is more important to be a success in life?
Intelligence or Social Skills?

"Although I think intelligence is important, one does not need to be a genius to get most jobs done. So working with people and motivating people and building mutual trust and respect with people are more important in my mind."

Do we really learn from history?

"We learn if we look at events in the context in which they happened."

What makes you smile?

"Family. Tough jobs well done. Success of subordinates."

Do you think there will truly ever be world peace?

"It is a noble goal and we must pursue it, but it has proven to be an elusive goal over the centuries."

If a book would be written about you in the future who would you like to be the author?

"Tom Clancy."

If a foreigner asked about your country, what would you say would be three aspects you are most proud of and the ones you are most ashamed of?

"I am most proud of our Constitution, our system of government and rule of law, the United States Army, and the freedom of opportunity for life, liberty and the pursuit of happiness.

I am most ashamed of past inequities, such a racial discrimination or lack of a chance in life for our citizens, leaders who let things distract them from doing the right thing and the poor treatment of Vietnam veterans."

What are your hobbies?

"Reading, writing, baseball, golf and family get-togethers."

What are the most important human traits?

Honesty and integrity."

Do you have to be aggressive and cutthroat to get ahead in life?

"Aggressive and competitive are OK, but cutthroat no."

Do you believe the good guy always finishes last?

"No, I believe that may be a myth perpetrated by the bad guys."

What advice would you share with the young people of our country as they pursue their goals in life?

"My advice to them would be:

- Be all that you can be
- Take advantage of your talents
- Establish and live by a meaningful value system
- Give something back
- Be and make a positive difference where you are

What is the duty of a parent?

"My view of what parents can and should do for their children:

- Help them develop a sense of values about their lives, their country and their religion and live by those.
- Help them and give them increasing opportunities to make choices in their lives and to live with the consequences.
- Help them to develop their talents and their own identity and way in life.
- Teach them to give proper consideration to others and treat others as they want to be treated."

If you could select a role model for your child, who would it be?

"Dr. Carl Hassler, who recently passed away because of cancer, was my high school football teammate, best man in our wedding, and my life-long friend. His courage, personal dignity, selfless friendship and community service are worthy of emulation by anyone.

I also have a tremendous admiration for the personal qualities of my wife and daughter and anyone who modeled his or her life after them would not be disappointed.

I gather from the question that you were looking for a famous person for me to offer up as a role model. These are the famous people in my life."

From your past experiences, what are some guidelines you would pass on to your children?

- "Be thankful for what you have and build on that and don't worry too much about what you don't have.

- Build a future every day and don't mortgage your future with an *instant gratification mentality*.

- Don't compromise your values; have the courage to be who you are.

- Be honest with yourself and others.

- Work hard because there are no real shortcuts in life.

- Take responsibility for your actions."

How can we help our youth bring pride and dignity back into their lives?

"Many already have it. We need to give them the opportunity and the challenge to demonstrate their adherence to a value system that is positive, noteworthy and meaningful. We need to spend more time looking for the good in people. It is my thought that we should accentuate the positive and give young people the opportunity to fulfill their unlimited potential in terms of their talents and their values. Give them a chance. Young people are our future."

Are we as a nation guiding our children to be honorable good citizens?

"One of the last things I did before I retired from the Army was to go and visit our initial entry soldiers in basic training at Ft. Jackson, South Carolina and ROTC Cadets at Hampton University. I wanted to see and listen to the future of the Army. What I found is that the future is in good hands and it is up to all of us to provide them the right environment and give them a chance to live up to their potential and, 'To be all they can be.'

"I think our nation can be proud of our continuing work to 'form a more perfect union.' There is much left to be done, however, especially with our young people to help them and give them all the opportunity to 'be all they can be.' It is harder to grow up now then it was for me, so we have our work cut out for us. But there is no alternative."

C H A P T E R   F I V E

IDEALISM

JAMES O. FREEDMAN
Former President of Dartmouth College

The final index to a nation's destiny is within its people, in their commitment to principles and ideals and their willingness to sacrifice for the common good.

— President Dwight D. Eisenhower

IN MAY OF 1998 SUZANNE FIELDS, a syndicated columnist for the *Los Angeles Times* presented an article entitled, *Liberalism Today Suffering From Its Lost Morals, Ideals*. In this article Ms. Fields states, "Today liberalism suffers from a moral crisis that exasperates serious men and women who have long memories. Some are conservatives; but contemporary liberals also express a desire to reinvigorate their lost idealism. These men and women lament the loss of legitimate debate that enabled liberals to take the moral high road against conservative arguments of tough-love realism. It kept both sides intellectually honest in a constructive engagement of ideas." She also goes on to quote Richard Rorty, the author of the book, *Achieving Our*

Country: Leftist Thought in the 20th Century wherein Rorty states, "Reform movements require champions of moral and patriotic nationalism which are demeaned by tenured teachers who reduce literary excitement to dry, dogmatic analysis: The academic left has no project to propose to America, no vision of a country to be achieved by building a consensus on the need for specific reforms." I have taken excerpts from Suzanne Fields and Richard Rorty to make a point. That point is the important issue; we are all, left or right, liberal or conservative, suffering from a fleeting or diminishing sense of morality and idealism.

This all serves as an introduction to James O. Freedman who, at the time of my interview with him, served as the President of Dartmouth College. James O. Freedman is an interesting man described by some as a shy scholar, but to me is morally courageous and worthy of emulation. President Freedman would no doubt take serious exception to the notion that the Academic Left is morally bankrupt. If one talks to him, hears his speeches, reads his book *Idealism and Liberal Education*, or looks at his heroes, one would have to draw the conclusion that James O. Freedman's view is quite different from Richard Rorty's position concerning the contribution of the Academic Left to the national value system.

President Freedman speaks directly to the subject. In the section of his book entitled, *The Teaching of Values*, he asks the question:

"Why cannot colleges just educate students, without seeking to impose any particular set of values, whether institutional or personal, liberal or conservative, on their students?"

"The answer in my judgment is that any mode of instruction, in any classroom environment cannot escape the teaching of values. The pursuit of a liberal education is inseparable from the acquisition of values, that is so today, even as it was long ago, found to be true at Padua and Bologna. There is simply no such activity as value-free teaching.

Colleges do inevitably teach values and they do so by example. Students learn values by observing how professors perform inside and outside of the classroom — professors who are passionate in their search for truth, careful in their weighing of evidence, respectful in their toleration of disagreement, candid in their confession of error, and considerate and decent in their treatment of other human beings."

From the above quotes you can readily discern that James O. Freedman believes that a liberal education and the idealism associated with such an education effectively teaches values.

"Indeed professors may teach most effectively about such values as integrity and honesty precisely when they admit to their own doubts or ignorance. There is no more important event in the moral development of a student than that quiet, suspended moment when a professor responds to an unexpected question by saying, 'I don't know.'"

The morality of a professor's example is perhaps the most powerful force in the teaching of values. By the power of their example, professors engaged in liberal education convey the humane significance of such values as inquiry, integrity, empathy, self-discipline and craftsmanship. These are values that inform the academic process.

My purpose in presenting moral exemplars such as James O. Freedman is to show that one can be an honest, forthright, moral person and succeed in life. One does not have to lie, cheat and steal in order to be successful in life. Let's take a closer look at James O. Freedman in an effort to get a better understanding of the idealism and character of the man and his contribution to academia.

James O. Freedman was born in Manchester, New Hampshire on September 21, 1935. He received his B.A. cum laude from Harvard College in 1957 and his L.L.B. cum laude from Yale Law School in 1962. Before moving on to the law firm of Paul, Weiss, Rifkind, Wharton and Garrison in New York he spent one year (1962-1963) as the law clerk to Justice Thurgood Marshall. In 1964 he joined the faculty of the University of Pennsylvania Law School. Over a period of eighteen years he held the following positions at that school:

Assistant Professor of Law	1964-67
Associate Professor of Law	1967-69
Professor of Law	1969-82
Professor of Political Science	1980-82
University Ombudsman	1973-76
Associate Dean of the Law School	1977-78
Associate Provost of the University	1978
Dean of the Law School	1979-1982

After his distinguished service at the University of Pennsylvania, he served as the President of the University of Iowa from 1982 until 1987, at which time he became the President of Dartmouth College.

His academic tenure and longevity at three prestigious American universities speak for themselves. What I would have you focus on are the courageous stands that he has taken concerning racism, bigotry and cultural diversity. Keeping in mind that President Freedman was the first Dartmouth President since 1822 who was not a graduate of the college or a faculty member, and his plans to change the Dartmouth culture were noteworthy and not necessarily popular with all of the Dartmouth alumni.

He made his mission quite clear in his inaugural address when he spoke to the Dartmouth trustees, alumni, and faculty members assembled on the lawn adjacent to the Baker Library: "*We must strengthen our attraction for those singular students whose greatest pleasures may come not from the camaraderie of classmates but from the lonely acts of writing poetry or mastering the cello or solving mathematical riddles or translating Catullus.*" His inaugural address woke everyone up. The faculty had never heard a Dartmouth President make that type of commitment — some would say he raised the intellectual ethos.

There obviously were those students and faculty members who had reservations about the new Dartmouth. Some were apprehensive about President Freedman's approach. They were concerned that too many creative loners would come and that too much emphasis might be placed on intellectualism. For a long period of time, Dartmouth College had the reputation of being male-oriented, "jock"-oriented and fraternity oriented. Enter James O. Freedman, whose vision for Dartmouth emphasized diversity, intellectualism, and the value of a liberal education. To this day some Dartmouth alumni have trouble swallowing those goals, especially since they were promulgated by the shy scholar who was educated at Harvard and Yale and taught at Penn. But the proof of the pudding is in the eating, and Dartmouth appears to be all the better having embraced diversity and intellectualism. Notwithstanding these new thrusts, "Dartmouth, in some fundamental ways, is still Dartmouth," according to Mr. Freedman. Dartmouth didn't give up its jock reputation. In 1996, the college won the Ivy League Football Championship and finished the season with a 10-0 record. Interestingly enough, President Freedman and his wife did not miss a single home game. At the same time, "President Freedman has made Dartmouth a place where intellectuals feel comfortable, where athletes feel comfortable." This comment was made by Monica Oberkofler, who graduated summa cum laude with a degree in history and was headed for Oxford University. Sara Rimer published an excellent article in the *New York Times* on January 4, 1997, outlining how a shy scholar transformed Dartmouth into a haven for intellectuals.

All of this didn't happen without a few bumps or potholes in the record. Tensions on the Dartmouth campus were high when President Freedman arrived. The existing tensions were fueled by the ***Dartmouth Review***, an off campus ultra right wing student newspaper. The ***Dartmouth Review*** took aim at a black music professor and described him as a "used Brillo." At nearly the same time the newspaper published a confidential list of gay students and also ran a front page cartoon showing Mr. Freedman, who is Jewish, in a Nazi uniform and wearing a Hitler mustache.

President Freedman defended the right of the Dartmouth Review to publish and even be provocative, but he also insisted on civility. He was very clear in speeches before the faculty and students that, "Racism, sexism and other forms of ignorance and disrespect have no place at Dartmouth." President Freedman stated that he had a responsibility for protecting the college's "moral endowment no less than its intellectual and financial endowment." The President's overt and public stance on these issues appeared to have had a dramatic impact on the policies of the Dartmouth Review, because the off campus newspaper has since kept a much lower profile. President Freedman courageously faced head-on the issues of racism, sexism and anti-Semitism. Here is how the *New York Times* described the incident:

Donald Pease, an English professor, recalled: "That was a moment of great moral courage. Everything turned on that moment."

Looking back, Mr. Freedman said that he had felt compelled to act after meeting with a group of black students. "Those kids just felt vulnerable," he said. "They felt defenseless. They felt alone. There were some who said, 'Who is going to defend us? Who is going to speak up for us?'"

"Defending them," Mr. Freedman said, "was a personal liberation of sorts." The Review incident forced me to display a side of myself I had never displayed before," he said. "I had to face someone down. I had to attack someone. It is just not who I am fundamentally."

He spoke out again two years ago, making his struggle with cancer the theme of his commencement address. "He lost all his hair, but that made no difference," Professor Penner recalled. "He taught us all what it is to be courageous."

Mr. Freedman said that he had never thought of himself as brave. As a young man growing up in Manchester, N.H., he had worked at *The Union Leader* as a copy boy and, briefly, as a reporter. As for a career in journalism, "I didn't dare," he said.

"I was scared to death," he added. "I didn't think I was good enough. I just really lacked confidence in my ability to do things, to compete in the larger world."

He said that he was driven as a young man by, what Virginia Woolf called, the pressure of convention. That drive got him to Harvard, he said, but because he was loath to take risks, he believed it also kept him from being a brilliant student. He blossomed at Yale Law School, but it was at Dartmouth that he truly emerged on a public stage.

"I've been drawn out of myself necessarily," he said. "I'm pleased that events pushed me in that direction."

Another way to look at the entire episode and President Freedman's response is to consider the words he spoke on October 4, 1990 at what was called: the Dartmouth United Against Hate Rally.

"This has been a week of infamy for the Dartmouth community. It began on the Holy Day of Yom Kippur with the masthead of a student newspaper brazenly quoting from Mein Kampf. Those who published Adolf Hitler's words as their own must have been surprised when this community rose up in anger and fury. What kind of people did they think we were?

Throughout the week, students have come to my office and home — outraged at the egregious expression of anti-Semitism, filled with anguish at the latest in a decade of attacks on blacks because they are black, women because they are women, homosexuals because they are homosexuals, Native Americans because they are Native Americans, and Jews because they are Jews. Those who signed their names to this grotesque defamation must have thought they could intimidate us into silence. What kind of people did they think we were?

For the last ten years, these same shameless voices have ranted that Dartmouth is for some people but not for others. These voices have preached exclusion from the Dartmouth family and have expected us to heed their words. What kind of people did they think we were?

Acts of such appalling bigotry have no place at this college. Dartmouth is a commonwealth of liberal learning, united in celebrating the dignity of the individual, joined together in seeking an understanding of the human condition.

An organizing principle of this commonwealth is inclusion, not exclusion — inclusion of every member of this community. Diversity is the very best substance of our human wealth.

The maintenance of a commonwealth of liberal learning at Dartmouth depends upon the principle of inclusion. If Dartmouth is to continue to educate men and women who will be leaders of American society, the practice of inclusion is essential.

I am immensely proud of your action and those of our community during the past week; by our presence here today we affirm that Dartmouth is a commonwealth of liberal learning, devoted to the principles of inclusion and individuality. We testify to Dartmouth's fundamental commitment to diversity and human dignity. And we renew our pursuit of the glories of liberal education.

I assure you that it will be ever thus."

It was Walter Lippman who said, "He has honor if he holds to an ideal of conduct though it is inconvenient, unprofitable or dangerous to do so." President Freedman honorably and courageously held to an ideal, and he made a difference.

If you were to ask James O. Freedman who or what shaped his idealism, his character and his career he would most likely say:

- "The gentle learning of his father.
- The powerful ambition of his mother.
- The Jewish values of his youth.
- The stimulating academic environment of Harvard, Yale, and Penn.

- The exemplary influence derived from the heroes he chose to admire."

One could legitimately ask the question — what role do heroes play in shaping one's character or idealism? The clear and unequivocal response is and properly should be — a significant and lasting role. In that regard, let us take a brief look at just a few of the people whom James O. Freedman held in high esteem — such as Václav Havel, Thurgood Marshall, Alexander M. Bickel, George F. Kennan, Harry S. Truman, and Ralph J. Bunche.

Václav Havel was a Czechoslovakian idealist whose achievements and courage during the Cold War made him one of President Freedman's heroes. Havel was a playwright, an intellect, a patriot and an idealist —not necessarily in that order. In 1968, when the Soviet tanks invaded Prague, Havel broadcast from his underground radio station pleas for resistance. Although many Czech intellectuals chose to collaborate with the Communist regime, Havel resisted and did so for two decades. As a consequence of his overt and vigorous criticism of the Communist authoritarian regime, Havel's plays were banned, his passport was revoked, and he was repeatedly imprisoned. Freedman wrote of his hero:

Despite this persecution, Havel became the principal spokesperson for a coalition of intellectuals, artists and underground poets. In 1977, the coalition issued Charter 77, a human rights declaration that called on the Czech government to comply with the Helsinki Covenant on Civil and Political Rights, to which it was a signatory. Soon after the document was issued, Havel was sentenced to prison for 'subversion of the Republic' — the crime of questioning the official dictum that the state can do no wrong.

By December 1989, when the so-called Velvet Revolution succeeded in throwing off Communist rule, Havel's long-time status as a dissident had given him the moral stature that stamped him as a symbol of civic courage and fresh ideas. As a result, he was catapulted

into the presidency. Some saw him as a Platonic "philosopher-king."
Although Havel had not sought the office, he agreed to assume the
role that events had written for him: he became the leader who
would establish a pluralistic democracy in Czechoslovakia. He
encouraged the nations of the Warsaw Pact to support the reunifica-
tion of Germany. He denounced anti-Semitism in a visit to Israel to
correct an historic wrong.

The manner in which Havel reacted to his new prominence is
morally instructive. From the very outset of his presidency, Václav
Havel spoke as an idealist, as an honest man with the courage to tell
unpopular truths. He told his fellow citizens, for example, that they
must accept responsibility for the moral illness that infected the pub-
lic discourse of the Czechoslovak nation. He said that Czechs had
become accustomed to saying one thing and thinking another and
have learned not to believe in anything, not to have consideration
for one another, and only to look after themselves. Notions such as
love, friendship, compassion, humility, and forgiveness have lost
their depth and dimension.

Central to Václav Havel's life — both as a private and public
person — has been a commitment to personal responsibility: the
moral obligation of individuals to serve others and to recognize the
special radioactive power of the truthful word. In an arresting speech
to a joint session of the United States Congress in 1990, he argued
that politics was ultimately about the choices that individual men
and women make — not choices to accept individual rights, but
choices to accept individual moral responsibility.

Much can be said about Václav Havel and his moral courage, and
James O. Freedman' admiration of Havel speaks volumes about
Freedman. And the same can be said about Freedman's admiration of
Thurgood Marshall, Justice of the Supreme Court. James O. Freedman
aptly describes Thurgood Marshall as a man of character. Thurgood

Marshall was a living manifestation that character counts and that the power of example is intoxicatingly persuasive. Exemplary lives do matter. Freedman writes, *For me — as for thousand of people, young and old, White and Black, from all walks of life, who filed through the Great Hall of the Supreme Court when the justice's body lay in state in January 1993 — the example of Thurgood Marshall as person of character does truly matter and carries extraordinary power. By living the law, Thurgood Marshall transcended it and thereby became as inspiring exemplar of civic virtue.*

Freedman further describes Thurgood Marshall as a person who changed the lives of all with whom he worked. *They all were marked indelibly by Justice Marshall's idealism and courage, his compassion and humanity, his craftsmanship and wit. The force of his moral example changed our lives utterly and in ways that have made us better citizens and more reflective lawyers.*

Alexander M. Bickel was James O. Freedman's teacher at the Yale Law School. Freedman claims that Alexander Bickel was, along with Thurgood Marshall, a source of vision and an inspiration to his future. Freedman describes Bickel "as a teacher and a scholar, a man of the book, an elegant intellectual who challenged and deepened our understanding of the functions of law in a democratic society." Alexander Bickel taught James O. Freedman and his Yale Law School colleagues the importance of process — or what Bickel called "the morality of conscience" and the importance of the procedures by which public decisions are reached. Bickel emphasized that adherence to the time-tested processes of the legal order is more important than the achievement of any momentary political result. Professor Bickel, along with Thurgood, taught by their example that the managing of a democratic society and the living of a moral life are both dynamic processes. *They require a continuing dialogue about our inherited values which are bedrock and which are merely convenient and conventional; a dialogue between the generations that have come before and our own generation; a dialogue between our own generation and the generations that will come after; a dialogue between any public selves and our private selves.* Modern philosophical thought might describe their debate as moral objectivity versus moral relativism. It is obvious to me that Professor Alexander Bickel had an important impact on James O. Freedman and conditioned him to accept or be open to the guidance of future mentors and exemplars.

Another of James O. Freedman's exemplars or heroes was George Kennan. Freedman truly admired George Kennan's accomplishments as a Russian historian and as an architect of postwar American foreign policy. Freedman describes Kennan as being one of those people who was truly great. Before I expound on Kennan's greatness, let me explain how Freedman defines truly great. *People who are truly great are important to us because their lives embody abundance and possibility. They are exemplars of the best that individuals can seek and achieve. They are emblems of the moral substance of personal resourcefulness, and of intellectual growth. They are talismans for inspiration and rejuvenation at those hollow moments when we feel depressed and defeated, captured by life's pettiness, wearied by the dreaded fear that, in the end, life comes to naught.*

Kennan was born in Milwaukee in 1904 and had a relatively undistinguished academic experience at Princeton. Upon graduation from Princeton, George Kennan joined the State Department and was immediately posted to a number of European cities and then to the University of Berlin, where he immersed himself in Russian studies. When the United States recognized the Soviet government in 1933, Kennan, who had not yet reached his thirtieth birthday, accompanied America's first ambassador to Moscow. During World War II, Kennan served in the American embassies in Moscow and Lisbon. He returned to the United States and served as Director of the State Department's Policy Planning Staff. From 1946 to 1950, Kennan, who was an acknowledged expert on Soviet affairs, became directly involved in the formulation of foreign policy at the highest levels in the State Department.

In July of 1947 George Kennan wrote an article in Foreign Affairs that *expressed reservations about restoring American foreign policy on the hope of building trust with the Soviet Union.* Keenan argued that conciliation and appeasement would not work because of Russia's sense of insecurity and its commitment to world domination. Kennan suggested a containment policy that should be based on *"the adroit and vigilant application of counterforce at a series of constantly shifting geographical and political points."* George Kennan's containment policy became the cornerstone of the Truman Doctrine, the Marshall Plan, the North Atlantic Treaty Organization, and the Berlin Airlift. For forty years, Keenan's policy of containment provided the basic underpinning of America foreign policy. After his State Department days were over Kennan joined the Institute for Advanced Study at Princeton, where he wrote more than twenty books, including his memoirs, which earned him a Pulitzer Prize. His influence on American foreign policy and international relations was significant, and he certainly earned the right to be called truly great. Freedman summarized his exemplar's greatness in the following way:

> *In the end, George Kennan's inestimable effectiveness and influence stemmed from his daunting integrity, his refusal to trim his views to fit the fashion of the moment, and his willingness to relinquish the heady satisfaction of power that were his as an insider in order to preserve his moral authority as an outsider.*

> *We live today in a society of self-promotion and networking, a culture obsessive with who is in and who is out, who is hot and who is not, a country mesmerized by the meretricious tinsel of fame. If our society truly cares about excellence, we must celebrate those heroes and heroines who achieve the disciplined dignity of intellectual independence. The life of George F. Kennan provides an elevating example of such heroic achievement.*

Two more of James O. Freedman's exemplars are: Ralph J. Bunche and President Harry S. Truman. Freedman characterized these two gentlemen as extraordinary men derived from ordinary backgrounds. There was little evidence in their childhood days to suggest that either would achieve greatness. To the contrary they faced early personal failure, tight economic conditions, and, in the case of Ralph J. Bunche, racial discrimination. Yet each helped the United States and the United Nations into an era of vast and unprecedented responsibilities.

Ralph Bunche was born in Detroit in 1903 and raised in Albuquerque and Los Angeles. Bunche graduated from the University of California, Los Angeles, in 1927 as the valedictorian of his class and went on to Harvard for his master's and his Ph.D degrees. He began his career as a professor of political science at Harvard University and proceeded from there to assist Gunnar Myrdal, the Swedish social economist, in conducting a comprehensive study of the Negro in the United States to be undertaken in a wholly objective and dispassionate way as a social phenomenon. After this scholarly pursuit, he moved into the field of diplomacy with the United Nations. His career as Undersecretary of the United Nations was dedicated to peacemaking. He undertook diplomatic efforts around the world, and in 1950 he was awarded the Nobel Peace Prize for his work in negotiating an armistice agreement between Israel and Egypt. His biographer, Brian Urguhart described the sources of Ralph Bunche's professional success:

His stamina, his charm, his capacity for inspiring personal confidence and respect, his unwavering honesty, his ability to keep things going in critical situations, his understanding of the preoccupations and fears of the negotiators, his unique knowledge of the situation on the ground, and his brilliance, originality and speed in drafting, all combined to make an extraordinary impression on those he dealt with.

Harry S. Truman came from ordinary beginnings and early on no one would have predicted that someday he would become President of the United States. But against all odds, Harry Truman, the failed haberdasher, the nearsighted artillery officer, the politician from Independence, Missouri, rose to the challenge of the most powerful office on earth. When he became president he didn't even know about the Manhattan Project and our efforts to develop the atomic bomb.

Shortly after he became president, he had to make the decision to drop the atomic bomb on Japan.

Harry Truman faced the challenge of replacing a legend in Franklin Delano Roosevelt. Initially he was not a popular president and some thought he was inept. Circumstances and events, however forced him to make some tough decisions and he never backed away from that responsibility. History most likely will be very kind to Harry Truman. Here is how James O. Freedman described President Truman's record:

> He had not even been told about the Manhattan Project until he had been president for twelve days; shortly thereafter, he had to make the decision of whether to use the atomic bomb against Japan.

> Truman's achievements as president were formidable. In foreign affairs, he devised the doctrine of containment toward the Soviet Union. He formulated the Truman Doctrine, which committed the United States to assist anti-Communist forces in Greece and Turkey; and, after an invasion by North Korean forces, he sent American forces into battle in South Korea. He implemented the Marshall Plan for rebuilding Western Europe, ordered the Berlin Airlift, and created the North American Treaty Organization. He recognized the State of Israel — making the United State the first nation to do so — and firmly committed the United State to support of the newly born United Nations.

> On the domestic front, Truman's Fair Deal sought to continue the work of Roosevelt's New Deal. Although his origins were in a border state where Jim Crow still prevailed and Confederate nostalgia lingered, Truman knew from historical reflection and humane instinct that racial discrimination was wrong. He desegregated the armed forces and the civil service by executive order, and, at great cost to his political fortunes, he advocated the nation's first meaningful civil rights program, seeking legal protection against lynching, poll taxes, and employment discrimination.

The heroes of James O. Freedman demonstrated idealism, intelligence, and character. He admired their courage, both physical and moral, during times of challenge and stress. He admired their decisions in crisis situations and their commitment to world peace and world progress. Their collective contributions were truly significant; they made or positively changed the policies that affected the entire world. The common denominator among them was their idealism and their moral fiber. With such role models, it is no coincidence that President James O. Freedman demonstrated moral courage and steadfast adherence to his values when he was faced with momentous decisions during the crises he faced. That is why he advocates that we choose our heroes with care.

C H A P T E R   S I X

SACRIFICE

BEA GADDY
"The Ghetto Angel"

"Character is the indelible mark that determines the only true value of all people and all their world."

— Orison Swett Marden

B EATRICE FRANKIE GADDY WAS BORN in Wake Forest, North Carolina, on February 20, 1933 and has traveled a long, arduous journey in her 67 years of life. She is affectionately referred to as "The Ghetto Angel" or "The Mother Teresa of Baltimore"…titles that were earned and not merely bestowed upon her.

For nearly nineteen years Bea Gaddy has worked as a humanitarian who has served over 500,000 families in Baltimore, Maryland, from 1981 to the present. On October 1, 1981, the city of Baltimore celebrated the opening of the Patterson Park Emergency Food Center, thanks to Bea Gaddy. On August 24, 1989 she opened Bea Gaddy's Women's and Children's Center. Ms. Gaddy presently runs three homeless shelters, the latest of which is a renovated warehouse and this latter facility will ultimately provide a hundred beds and a commercial kitchen. Bea keeps an unofficial tally of the homeless people served, and the average monthly total is approaching 8,000 people.

Bea Gaddy is a true humanitarian who is much more concerned about the homeless people who need assistance than about her own needs. An interesting story about her selfless service concerns her special efforts to feed the homeless and the hungry on holidays. For Thanksgiving in 1981, Bea invited 39 of her friends and neighbors for dinner. At the time she had no income and had just moved into a two-room apartment. As she was cleaning her furniture, she found fifty cents in coins in the upholstery. Since fifty cents was all that she had, she bought a lottery ticket and, as fate would have it, won two hundred and ninety dollars with which she purchased food to feed her Thanksgiving Day guests. That was the start of Bea Gaddy's traditional Thanksgiving meal for the homeless. In 1981 she served thirty-nine people, and in 1991 Ms. Gaddy served 21,000 families at her annual Thanksgiving Dinner. In 1992, 23,467 families were served dinner on the grounds of Dunbar High School. In 1997, 49,000 people were served Thanksgiving Dinner. These numbers would be impressive if the city or a corporation were behind them, but we are talking about the initiative of one woman. Granted, by 1997, Bea had many volunteers helping her, but it was her initiative and her commitment to help the homeless that made these accomplishments possible. Thousands of people in Baltimore are ready to thank Bea Gaddy, not only for offering a helpful hand but also for lifting their spirits.

In addition to providing food and shelter, Bea's works are encouraging and motivating her homeless friends to pick themselves up and to move forward to be all that they can be. Bea has repeatedly reminded them: "You've got to start loving yourself, motivating yourself. You don't have to be beat. You're God's child, you have to be your best." And I suspect Bea has to repeat those words, from time to time, to herself to keep her motivated to do her work.

It hasn't been an easy life for Bea Gaddy. She was born in the middle of the Depression in 1933. She never knew her father; her mother and grandmother raised her in conditions of poverty and with a stepfather that Bea intensely disliked. Bea's early school days were not fun because her mother struggled to provide decent clothes and food for her family. It wasn't until Bea was in the seventh grade that she felt comfortably dressed because one of her aunts took a special interest in her. Bea married Lacy Gaddy and gave birth to five children, three daughters and two sons. All five of Bea's children grew up in a tough environment and ultimately all five forged ahead to become productive citizens.

Bea will tell you that on many occasions she has been broke but she has never been "broken." She came to understand that, oftentimes, there is a fine line between a homeless person and a homeowner. She also understands that it is easy for a homeless person "to get down on himself or herself," and those negative feelings really undermine one's sense of self worth or self esteem. Bea experienced all of those negative feelings at various times in her life, and she finally realized that low esteem breeds negative attitudes which, in turn, cause people to become frustrated and disheartened. Accordingly, in addition to providing food and shelter, Bea is a spirit lifter, a motivator, and an encourager. She helps people identify their strengths and encourages people to live and work up to their God-given potential. Her goal is to make people independent and to have them strike out on their own, to be all that they can be and to develop pride in their accomplishments and in their perseverance.

Bea well knows the meaning of the word perseverance. She struggled through her childhood and school years. She struggled through poverty and through raising five children. She took jobs and positions wherever she could and took advantage of every educational opportunity that presented itself. And finally, after much nighttime schooling, Bea Gaddy finally received a college degree. She earned a B.A. in Human Services from Antioch College in 1977 at the age of 44. Her choice of Human Services as her primary course of study was a prediction of her future. Human Services is what she studied, and human services is what she practices. Bea Gaddy has taken on every challenge to help others; she has single handedly put together programs, services and groups of volunteers to reach out to help the homeless and disadvantaged. She has used every ounce of her creativity, compassion and optimism to serve others, asking little or nothing for herself. She has earned the title "Ghetto Angel," with the emphasis on the word "angel."

My visit to and interview with Bea Gaddy started out as one of the unique, interesting and inspiring stories in my life. When I called Bea to set up a time for my visit and interview, she sounded a bit uncertain but she said "come ahead — we'll work it in somehow." In that I was visiting a center for the homeless, I thought they might be able to use some serviceable clothing. This was just the motivation I needed to finally look hard in my closets and chests to separate myself from the shirts, jackets, trousers and sweaters that I did not need, and with the help of my wife and daughter, we filled up a van with those unneeded clothes and headed for Baltimore to spend as much time with Bea Gaddy as she would give us.

When my daughter and I arrived at Bea Gaddy's Family Center on Collington Avenue in Baltimore, I immediately understood why Bea had sounded a bit uncertain when I first tried to schedule the interview. Bea reminded me of traffic cop directing traffic at a busy intersection. The phone was constantly ringing and people looking for direction, guidance and encouragement continuously interrupted our interview discussion. Bea seemed unfazed by the interruptions and gave my questions the same personal attention that she gave to the score of volunteers and her homeless friends. She seemed to be juggling a dozen balls at a time, and as each ball hit her hand she gave it the concentrated attention and focus it deserved. It was a tough way to conduct an interview, but we got it done and did so with only a minimum distraction from Bea's efforts to help the people for whom she obviously had a genuine concern.

In the course of the day, Bea made sure that we met and talked with some of her volunteers and homeless friends. I met a young, single mother of two young boys who Bea was helping to get her life back on track. This young lady, who was not only quite intelligent but had two young sons was recovering from a drug problem. To see the encouragement Bea gave her and her two young sons to lift them to a position of independence and productivity was truly remarkable. She not only fed and housed the homeless, she also inspired, encouraged and "cajoled" them to move forward and make something of themselves.

I also met one of Bea's most dedicated volunteers, a former Army cook who served in one of the Army's toughest infantry divisions. He did a lot of the cooking in the shelters and was getting ready to organize the commercial kitchens that would be an integral part of Bea's new converted warehouse 100-bed shelter. This army veteran undoubtedly had other employment opportunities but he remained committed to help Bea Gaddy accomplish her mission of sheltering and encouraging the homeless.

In the course of a short day, I visited all three of Bea Gaddy's shelters, talked with her volunteers and homeless friends, conducted an interview, and watched her disseminate food, clothes, and encouragement. All of this came from a slight, 67-year-old widow who had fought a serious bout with cancer. She makes things happen, and many people in Baltimore are better off because of her. When I asked Bea if there was anything I could do for her for allowing me to visit with her and to interview her, she simply said, "I would greatly appreciate an orange soda." In the time it took to go to a pizza restaurant to purchase an orange soda for Bea and some pizzas for her volunteers, she had laid out all of the clothes that we and others had donated onto clothing stalls on the front pavement in front of her shelters. During the course of the day, people who needed the clothing would come by and select what they needed and/or wanted. Bea kept a watchful eye on this process, along with everything else that was going on.

BEA GADDY Q & A

My personal interview with Bea Gaddy was so interesting and so revealing that I felt compelled to present to you verbatim the following questions and answers:

Was church a big factor in your early life and in molding your character?

"I feel it is a must! As you get older you get away from it. I was ashamed to have people hear me pray. I thought they'd laugh. My faith is back now and it's everything. I will be ordained as a Minister for the Methodist Church. My sermons are about self worth and loving themselves."

Who coined the name "The Ghetto Angel?" Do you like it?

"I don't know exactly where it came from. It fits me, works for me, and it doesn't bother me. People tend to exaggerate it a lot. There are so many Bea's out there. So many good people who are ready and willing to help."

What did you do before you became "The Ghetto Angel?"

"I worked in social services as an aide, however, they did not care for me because I spoke up for the rights of the underprivileged. I went to night school and graduated from Antioch College. I graduated from college the same day my daughter graduated from high school."

What prompted you to become involved in working with the homeless?

"My hunger and my children's hunger. It was not planned. I prayed and asked God what to do. I got some clean garbage cans and went to stores for their old food. People laughed at me, but at night they ate the food.

I have been running ever since and will never forget the feelings I experienced as a starving person."

You just won a seat on the city council. In your campaign you said
you wanted to make sure that the homeless are better represented
in city government. What specifically do you hope to accomplish?
"The homeless need representation. Government officials are making decision about things they have not experienced, mainly hunger. Some officials think we are not smart enough to sit on boards."

What do you see as the greatest problems facing the black community
in Baltimore (and the US) in general and the homeless you work
with in particular?
"This is not a black and white issue. Poor has no color. We don't care what color they are. We have wasted too much time being racial. We need to care for each other. Everyone should have three meals a day and medical coverage. Out greatest problem is not having access to these resources."

What are the greatest concerns of the men and women you work with?
"I hope to always teach people to love themselves. This will bring on motivation. Letters pour into me about how terrible and useless some feel. The community does not accept them, so they tend to isolate themselves. They are not always accepted in schools, and how then can the children learn? There is a general attitude of hopelessness. Thankfully, there are also a lot of success stories."

We've heard a lot about the "missing father," especially in the black
community. What is your view about the role of black men in families?
"Welfare is a big part of separating families, and especially welfare screeners, who tend to run men out. They should tell the fathers to stay at home with their family and we will support you. They are instead

locking the men up in prisons versus teaching them to be stable. There is nothing to believe in anymore."

What are your greatest concerns about the next generation?

"Children are learning and developing very bad habits because they are being bounced all over while their parents work. They need to learn modern technology. Education for all should be demanded and always stayed on top of."

Do you feel that children are being instilled with ethical values?

"We all need to do a better job in this area. We need to form partnerships. Poor people are very proud. Sometimes they teach values much better than rich folks, because they want to instill pride of self into children. Parents also need to be active and part of the educational system."

Do you think that ethics are in decline in the US?

"Yes! Children have no manners, no respect for authority, no limits. People just do not care. Some people don't give a hoot about anything. We are going through a moral downsizing."

Is there some standard or guide for ethics?

"Learn from each other first, and then be kind to each other. Stay clean — ask for it, don't steal it. The Bible says, "Ask and you shall be given. Don't steal and don't covet. Live by the Golden Rule. We are not being true to ourselves."

Do you feel that women ought to spend more time at home with their children?

"The government should subsidize families until children are in elementary school. Then mom should fly and blossom after the children are in middle school. We need to go to neighbors and ask for help. I did. I told my neighbor that I was hungry. We need to help each other."

Do campaign contributions — so called "soft money" — corrupt influence?

"My goals from a city position will be as follows:

- Receive a salary — one half will go to run the centers.
- Pull people together with rules and laws. I want to make sure each person receives two meals a day and blankets.
- Make one effective program that will come back to fruition."

How well do you think ethical values are being taught to children in school (or by their families?)

"Ethical values should be taught in depth. They are not being taught at all right now."

Both political parties are advocating that religious organizations and charitable institutions assume responsibility for distributing funds to the poor and needy instead of the Government. Do you agree?

"The national government should get it off the ground. They need to trust someone, and that should be the people doing the groundwork. We have sound record. Let us take care of it. We cannot keep letting the city dictate to us. They should monitor us, and let us do it."

Do you think that compensation for executives is out of line with what other employees are paid?

"Anyone who makes more than I do and is not sharing it is out of line!" (She smiled and winked.)

In the last couple of years we have seen a tremendous outpouring of grief for Princess Diana and more recently for JFK, Jr. Yet the death of Mother Theresa, who certainly accomplished far more than either figure, did not inspire such sadness. To what do you account this phenomenon? Are people projecting certain unsatisfied needs and desires on celebrities?

"This is all so sad. I met Mother Theresa. She really cared about the people. Princess Diana's workings were not even publicized while she was alive. We hear about all these wonderful things now that she is no longer with us. They were both wonderful ladies in their own special worlds."

Recently the House of Representatives passed legislation permitting the display of the Ten Commandments in schoolrooms. Do you think it is anything more than a symbolic gesture or can it help encourage students to lead better lives?

"Prayer should have stayed in the school and so should have religion. We let our values slide in the country. The Ten Commandments should be hung in every school."

If this chapter and Bea Gaddy's example have inspired you in such a way that you want to render assistance, you can contact Bea at:

Bea Gaddy's Family Center
140 North Collington Avenue
Baltimore, Maryland 21231
(410) 342 - 3570

VALUES

EARL H. HESS, PH.D.
Former CEO, Lancaster Laboratories, Inc.

Of all the properties which belong to honorable men, not one is so highly prized as that of character

— Henry Clay

I F THERE EVER WAS AN AMERICAN success story it is personified in the lives of Earl H. Hess and his wife, Anita. Earl and Anita trace their lives back to modest beginnings. It is a true tribute to Earl to recognize how he started his business, the Lancaster Labs, with just three people, minimum startup capital, and a dream. He developed it into a profitable, value-oriented, company with revenues over 30 million dollars and well over 500 employees. The physical and financial growth of his company was noteworthy, but it is significantly more important to recognize the manner in which he grew the business and the commitment he made to his employees, his customers, and his vendors.

Earl Hollinger Hess was born on June 26, 1928, on a farm in Lancaster, Pennsylvania, just about two miles from his present home. Earl began his formal education at age five in a one-room school called Mill Creek but often referred to in later years as *corn cob academy*. One half of the students in his elementary school were Amish, and when Earl was in the first grade he was the only pupil. At first, he was so bashful that he couldn't bring himself to talk to the teacher for nearly a month. When he got over his shyness, however he progressed rapidly through elementary, junior high, and senior high school and graduated from Upper Leacock High School in 1944 at the age of 15.

From 1944 to 1948, Earl was his dad's right hand man on the farm. In 1948 he decided to go back to school and enrolled in Franklin and Marshall College as a chemistry major. Earl commuted to college and earned his way by milking his father's cows each morning and evening and working full time on the farm each summer. At the end of his junior year at F&M College he married Anita.

In the fall of 1952, Earl and Anita moved to Urbana, Illinois, where he became a doctoral candidate and part-time teaching assistant. In Urbana, the Hesses lived in a small co-op apartment with no private bath. He completed his doctoral course requirements and thesis work in two years. Earl claims that this third year at the University of Illinois at Urbana was one of the most enjoyable of his life, because he had a fellowship which supported exploratory research under one of the finest professors in the country.

Athletically, Earl never got beyond intramural sports. In high school he was much younger and smaller that his classmates, and in college he didn't have much time for sports because of his work and study schedule. In college, he maintained a sufficiently high grade point average to stay on the Dean's list and to graduate cum laude with election into Phi Beta Kappa. At Illinois, many of his classmates arrived with master's degrees from prestigious schools, such as MIT and Harvard.

Many of them were still working on their theses when Earl earned his degree. Earl loved the sciences and mathematics, but he also enjoyed the humanities. He is the first to admit that he tried to steer clear of the philosophy and ethics courses in college. As his interest in chemistry grew, he gravitated toward the biological and analytical aspects of chemistry, although his thesis was in classical organic chemistry.

If Earl was not enamored by philosophy and ethics courses in school, where did he develop his deeply rooted value system and the ethical principles that have guided him throughout his adult life? Earl Hess' response to that question and others that were posed to him are most revealing:

"My father — Abram M. Hess, was one of 13 children and so his farming startup was without much assistance from his parents. In the midst of the struggle to get established came two events — the Great Depression, which hit him so hard that his entire income for one year did not pay to replace a horse that died that year, and a call to the ministry by his church. (At that time the Church of the Brethren was served by *free* ministers called by the church to serve without professional credentials.) My father had only an eighth grade education and, therefore, needed to work very hard to gain the basic skills necessary for ministry. He burned a lot of midnight oil and became self-educated in theology. He also ministered in very practical ways. Non-farm parishioners, many of whom lost their jobs and had no income, became dad's workforce during the summer and went home with apples and garden produce. A ninety-year-old widow in our church still likes to tell me how products from dad's farm sustained her family through their darkest hours when her husband could find no work at all. But we made it through the depression. After buying the farm, he generated modest wealth but continued his spirit of generosity, especially in supporting relief efforts in post WWII Europe. Each year he donated an acre of potatoes (A Lord's Acre) for Church World Service. Dad wanted me to go into the ministry, offering me a free college education if I chose to, but he never applied pressure.

My mother, Ruth S. Hess, was born and reared most of her life before marriage in a poor farm family. She was well prepared to assume the role of a hardworking frugal wife of a startup sharecropping farmer at the onset of the Great Depression. She managed the household well with very limited resources, by gardening, drying and canning fruit, butchering hogs from the farm, canning the meat, making sausage, etc., all of which provided basic food necessities and more. Sunday, family and church gatherings were the end result of her hard work and commitment to her homemaking skills. Although her work was mainly in the house, it was not unusual to find her in the field with a team of horses, helping out during the press of summer farming activities. She loved horses to the extent that, when our last two horses wore out and were replaced by tractors, she insisted that they go directly to the scavenger so that no one would abuse them. There were several days of mourning for Bob and Jim.

Although I felt my mother's love from the beginning, my awareness of it was at age seven, when I was seriously ill for most of the winter. I was hospitalized for a period of time, and she stayed with me constantly, sleeping in a cot in my room, standing by through the painful moments while my father and brother kept the household intact.

Mother and Dad followed my career at Lancaster Labs with strong moral and financial support in the early years of struggle and with a sense of pride as the company grew. They were both especially proud of the ventures we took into the areas of social responsibility and ethics. One of my dad's last meaningful experiences, before dementia took him away from me, was a visit with Rush Kidder, the President of the Institute for Global Ethics."

EARL H. HESS, PH.D. Q & A

Dr. Hess, who were your heroes?

"I had many, but undoubtedly my most significant hero and role model was my father. I must also give credit to Miss Stauffer, my first grade teacher, a compassionate and loving person who saw potential in me. Later, there was my high school principal, who was also my algebra teacher. Another important influence in my life was Mr. Evans, my science teacher in high school. In my community and church, there were those adults who patiently tolerated the mischievousness of junior high boys. I could propose several for sainthood, because the lives they lived personified what exemplary ethical conduct was all about. In college, several professors became heroes to me. The Chairman of the Chemistry Department, Dr. Weisgerber, had a real love for science. He made it come alive and challenged me to think both analytically and creatively. There was also Dr. Moss, my Religion Professor during my sophomore year. At a time when the simple faith and practices of my small country church seemed irrelevant to the world of science, he showed me a side of religious inquiry that was both scholarly and devotional. His influence combined with that of Dr. Sievert, my organic chemistry professor, who often spoke in chapel and the classroom about the compatibility of science and religion and encouraged me to sort things out for myself. These role models during my years in college were critical in keeping me connected to the Christian Church and thus to the foundations of my values. Finally I would mention the influence of men like Kierkegaard and Martin Luther King, who modeled the kind of courage necessary when one's conviction come into conflict with popular opinion."

Are there any values that you consistently try to uphold?

"Yes, there are two that stick out in my mind, integrity and compassion. *Integrity* — I mean that, not as a synonym for honesty, but with the meaning it has in integral calculus. It means that there is a completeness

— a consistent wholeness to the honest and fair way that one deals with every situation. It means that I will deal with a used car salesman with the same openness and fairness and respect that I would in my relationship with my pastor. And the other central one to me is *Compassion.* To practice the reversibility principle and always look at another person's situation as if I were in his/her place. We have been studying John's Epistles in Sunday School lately and trying to comprehend the depth of God's love and then reflect it in our relationships with others is a real challenge."

What values have played a major role in your life?

"The values that have played a major role in my life are complete honesty and unconditional love. Additionally, I would include the concept of trust, a trust that allows me to show trust in another person even before that person has proven himself trustworthy. Another way of stating it is making yourself vulnerable by being the first to show trust.

Is it difficult to maintain your values and integrity while receiving so much admiration and attention?

"Each of us has a certain vanity about us. It feels good to be admired and to be in the spotlight. But when I sense that feeling, I think of an expression my dad used to make in jest when someone expressed admiration for my accomplishments. He said, "I taught him everything I know." It reminded me of my tremendously rich heritage, and the fact that I have simply had the wisdom and humility to build upon it using the opportunities that life has afforded me. There simply would not have been a Lancaster Labs, in its present form, had I not had the examples of hard work and absolute integrity lived out in my home and community as I grew up."

How can we improve upon the values and morals in our country?

"Mainly by exemplifying them in our own lives — walking the talk. My dad preached some pretty good sermons over the years, but I was impacted more by his manner of living as he related to me as a parent and as I witnessed him dealing fairly as a farmer businessman."

Define your success for me and how did ethics, honor or integrity contribute to or detract from your success?

"My success is not measured in dollars accumulated, although financial success allows us to be supportive of causes in which we believe. I think that my greatest satisfaction in life is to realize that my success in both material wealth and public recognition was achieved without having to lie, cheat or steal. I was fortunate because I was able to adhere to my core values. We built a model business, one of the most profitable in its industry, but also one that set new standards in its honest and caring relationship with employees, vendors, the community, and all its stakeholders.

The success of the business provided the foundation for my extensive volunteerism in both business and personal endeavors and allows me in retirement to continue my usefulness to various segments of society."

Who is the most ethical person you know?

"I don't know anyone today who seems to have it all together in the same way that my dad did. My dad was hewn out of a rock of granite whose primary constituents were character and integrity."

Did you ever truly go beyond the call of duty?

"Yes, I think I did and still do. That's part of being ethical — going beyond what is required. I've done it by giving an employee a second or third chance when I would have had justification for firing. Some paid off, others took advantage of my good nature. It's the kind of action that some people refer to as "second mile religion" — going beyond what is required. I'm involved in just that way with a number of people presently, not always successfully, but rewarding. When I do not succeed in such efforts, I need to remind myself that God does not call us to be successful, but to be faithful."

Do you think a person's character is formed at birth or can it be changed?

"Although genetics may have something to do with personality (outgoing vs. introvert), I don't think that character is passed on that way. I am like my father and mother in certain mannerisms, etc., but they instilled in me my values. I believe such happens in early childhood, so as to lead some people to believe that character is born into a person."

What can you say about character and integrity as they relate to your life and your career?

"Without them, life would have no real meaning, no matter how rich or famous."

Define the word courage?

"Courage is what it takes to do what you know is right when such action is not popular. I will give you an example. Recently, I promoted a code of campaign conduct in the mayoral election in Lancaster. I was accused of meddling in the affairs of politicians by asking that they conduct their campaigns in an upright manner and was not so politely told that "election ethics" is an oxymoron. In recent months, Anita and I have been publicly accused of having an ulterior motive in the gifting of the family center (childcare, adult care and fitness) which we had built for our business to a non-profit group for use as a community center. It's at times like these that one's character is tested."

What factor most contributed to your success?

"I really don't know what to call myself — chemist, business leader, husband, father, community leader, or some of each. However, in whatever role I find myself at any given time, I try to provide some leadership and some visionary focus."

What factors play a role in your decision making?

"Integrity, as defined earlier, fairness and application of the care-based decision rule. By that I mean, how would I want to be treated if the role was reversed? What I describe as the care-based decision rule others might call the Golden Rule."

From where have you drawn your inner strength?

"I draw my strength from the inner peace that comes to me when I know I have given my best effort toward lifetime goals without sacrificing my core values."

How would you like to be remembered?

"As one who lived in an imperfect world, visualized how it should be and then worked toward those goals."

What has given meaning to your life?

"Experiencing God in this life through the many fine people that I can claim as friends — my lifetime partner Anita, our family, brothers and sisters in my church fellowship, business associates (that includes persons from the third shift maintenance staff to presidents of large corporation clients). Then, too, there are a host of associates in public life.

Over many years, I developed a really close relationship with a builder who did a lot of our construction. Over lunches we would not only talk about building but share our personal joys and challenges. Written on a greeting card which I received from him on the occasion of my retirement were words something like this: *'If I were able to name the day that our business relationship turned into the personal relationship that we now enjoy, I would mark that day on my calendar and celebrate it as an annual holiday.'* Three years later, while having no business reasons to be together, Nick and I still have lunch together.

What are your strengths and weaknesses?

"A stubborn commitment to do what it takes to make a thing happen can be a strength or weakness. Also my interest in helping other people out of predicaments. Currently, I have at least four of those brewing. Some people consider me a sucker for getting involved in too much when I could be out playing golf. I acknowledge that as a perceived weakness, but I am not working too hard to change it!"

Was there any particular experience or event in your life that influenced your management philosophy or style?

"My heart condition, which first made itself evident when I was only 36 (half a lifetime ago!). It put me into a state of depression that lasted for about three years. God, why me? I have so much to offer! A few years later, I became aware of the fact that my health problems had slowed me down enough to be more reflective and smell some roses along the way. I became a much better person. I became a visionary in building the Lancaster Labs organization that exploded during the 1980s. Two open-heart surgeries along the way barely broke my stride, whereas minimal illness was nearly catastrophic earlier. But the question really asks about management style. I think that the Earl Hess who emerged from his facing health challenges was a kinder, gentler, more empathetic person that the previous one."

What were the major turning points in your career, and how do you feel about your choices now?

"Here are what I consider five major turning points in my career and my life: My choice of a life partner and the family which resulted from that union, my decision to utilize my education in chemistry in a private practice, the struggles we had in getting the business off the ground, my illness at a critical stage of the business development, the positive impact of that physical ailment on my emotional, psychological and spiritual development, and, in retrospect, I feel quite good about the choices."

If you could express your gratitude for one thing in your life —
what would it be and to whom?

"My heritage — to my family."

Describe a time in your life when you experienced the most fear?
How about the most courage?

"Fear — my first episode of heart problems which were minor rhythm problems. Courage — facing my first open heart surgery at a time when open heart surgery was not quite as routine as it is today."

Describe yourself, in one word, as a child?

"Sensitive."

What is your favorite novel? Magazine? Newspaper?

"I read very little fiction. I read trade magazines and periodicals focusing on business issues, especially leadership, ethics and social responsibility.

What is the one personality trait you would change about yourself?

"I would like to concentrate on less time talking and more time listening — I'm working on it!"

Would you march on Washington for a cause? What would the cause be?

"Yes, I would march on Washington if I thought I could in any way help restore integrity in government and in our society, in general."

Do you think America can still be the melting pot for all ethnic groups,
races and religions?

"It is and there is nothing we can do about that fact. The question is whether we are going to let that be the cause of our eventual downfall or recognize that cultural diversity can be a powerful positive force in our society.

Does religion play an important role in your life? How?

"Religion — no; faith — yes. I'm defining here religion as humankind's attempts to figure out God, while faith means being open to God's revelations of Himself to us. Among other things I'm still trying to comprehend God's love as expressed in the gift of his Son. Each Christmas and Easter I grow a bit in that understanding. Then, too, Faith and Ethics, are in my opinion inseparable, my relationship with God being in dynamic equilibrium with my relationship with other persons."

Was there a speech or presentation that you consider the very best you ever heard?

"Martin Luther King's Letter from a Birmingham Jail."

What would you like written on your tombstone?

"He gave his best."

Did you ever have an adverse experience that taught you a great lesson?

"Yes, all the time one learns from his mistakes. In the area of firing — don't do it too soon, but also don't do it too late. The time to let a person go is when you have reached the decision that is in the best interest of both parties."

What is the name of the issue that you think will be the most important in the next election?

"I think it will be the economy, and what to do with the projected budget surpluses, but it should be restoring integrity to Government."

If you had one wish granted, what would it be?

"I would like very much to get more out of this tired heart so as to have sufficient strength to be able to put full energy behind my desire to make this a more ethical world."

What quote of yours would you want carved in granite or bronze?
"Borrowed from the Prophet Micah — '*What does the Lord require of you but to do justice, love, mercy and walk humbly with your God.*' "

If you had unlimited funds, what area of science research would you put it into?
"Medical Research."

What does it take to be a great leader?
"I could write a book on that subject, but in a nutshell you might start with a spirit of servanthood."

What is the nicest compliment ever given to you?
"After my business had grown to the size where I was no longer serving an old client directly, he stated that the people who now served him reflected my values and personality in their relationship with him."

What is your most prized possession?
"The host of persons I can call true friends."

What is more important to becoming a success in life: Intelligence or Social Skills?
"Intelligence certainly doesn't hurt, but if by social skills you mean the ability to relate to others, then I would name the latter. There's nothing more offensive to me than a smart snob who constantly has to show off his/her intelligence."

Do we learn from history? Why do we repeat our mistakes?
"We should, but we don't. It seems like each new generation has to learn some things for itself."

If a foreigner asked about your country, what are the three things you are most proud of? Three things you are ashamed of?

"Most proud — our basic freedoms — of expression, of religion, of property. Least proud — our intolerance of diversity, our obsession with materialism."

Do you have to be aggressive and cutthroat to get ahead in life?

"Assertive, not aggressive."

Do you believe the good guy always finishes last?

"Quite the opposite! Did Jesus finish last? It may have appeared so on Good Friday but not ultimately."

What is the duty of a parent?

"To be a role model of responsible behavior."

If you could select a role model for your child, who would it be?

"Gandhi."

From your past experiences, what are some guidelines you'd like to pass onto your children?

"Keep your mind open to new possibilities, act upon them with discretion."

How can we guide our children to be honorable, good citizens?

"First and foremost, be an example. It is imperative that we establish solid value systems, teach better parenting, reverse the spiraling divorce rate and be held accountable for our actions."

During his active business career and since his retirement Dr. Earl Hess has contributed his time and energy to a broad spectrum of volunteer activities that reflect his commitment to society at large. Over the span of two decades he worked at all levels in his national trade association (ACIL) and in the local, state and US Chambers of Commerce as an advocate for small business. He served as either chair or vice chair of each of the four organizations. He was recognized by his peers as an "ACIL Fellow" in 1992 and by the PA Chamber of Commerce as its "Business Leader of the Year" in 1998. Until Earl's death in 2001, he worked essentially full time as a volunteer, coaching many start-up small businesses, leading an organization devoted to microenterprise development for the economically disadvantaged and teaching and lecturing extensively on the subjects of leadership and ethics to both business and church related groups.

CHAPTER EIGHT

SERVANT LEADERSHIP

GENERAL CHARLES C. KRULAK
Former Commandant of the Marine Corps

"The first responsibility of a leader is to define reality. The last is to say thank you. In between the leader is a servant."

— Max DePree

THE LATIN WORDS SEMPER FIDELIS or the shortened version "Semper Fi" has special meaning for every person who has ever worn the uniform of a United States Marine. The Latin words translate to mean: Always Faithful. General Charles C. Krulak, the Commandant of the Marine Corps from 1995 to 1999 and currently Vice Chairman of MBNA America Bank, provides an expanded definition of Semper Fi. He will tell you that "Semper Fi" means;

- Always Faithful to your God
- Always Faithful to your Country
- Always Faithful to the Marine Corps

- Always Faithful to your family
- Always Faithful to your spouse

On this latter point he has gone so far as to tell his marines that any marine who removes his wedding band when he or she crosses the International Date line is not truly a marine. This admonishment to the troops one would expect from a chaplain. In this case the admonishment came from the Commandant of the Marine Corps, a seasoned combat tested veteran with 35 years of Marine Corps Service. In a military service that has a tradition of toughness, dedication, integrity and patriotism, General Krulak raised the bar several notches higher by his leadership and example.

General Krulak is an amazing man. His physical stature presents him at 5'6" but my perception of him is that he is 10 feet tall in character. I must confess that I am greatly impressed and greatly inspired by the genuine and authentic goodness of this leader and this human being.

The obvious question to be asked is what makes this man tick and/or what training or life experiences allowed General Chuck Krulak to take on the challenges that he encountered in his life. Let me start with his upbringing. He was raised in a military family. His father, Victor H. Krulak, or "Brute" as he was better known, retired as a Lieutenant General from the Marine Corps and at the age of 92 will be recognized as a Distinguished Graduate of the United States Naval Academy. So General Krulak grew up in a disciplined household with a father who exemplified leadership and character. His mother, Amy C. Krulak, raised three boys primarily by herself from 1942 to 1952 while his father was deployed to wartime assignments. From what I can determine, Amy Krulak was a wonderful woman and mother who gave her sons a strong sense of values. It appears that General Krulak received good solid guidance on ethics, respect, responsibility and patriotism from day one by both of his parents.

Like many military families, the Krulak's lived and were schooled in many parts of the world. General Krulak capped his high school years with a scholarship to Phillips Exeter Academy in New Hampshire prior to going to the Naval Academy. After graduation from the Naval Academy he attended the appropriate military schools in addition to earning a Masters Degree from George Washington University. He applied himself as a student but he revealed during our conversation that his life experiences taught him more than any school could ever teach him. Let me enumerate some of these life experiences. He served as a leader at every level within the Marine Corps — from infantry platoon to Commanding General of Marine Forces Pacific — and then ultimately the Commandant of the Marine Corps. In addition to all of the above, he also served as Assistant Deputy Chief of Staff for Manpower and Reserve Affairs, Commanding General, Marine Corps Combat Development Command, Deputy Director of the White House Military Office and in the Office of the Secretary of Defense. All in all, an impressive array of challenging assignments.

As I searched for words to describe this man's character and sense of integrity, I came across a biographical sketch of General Krulak in an MBNA document entitled, *Who We Are*. Let me quote what was written in that release:

> *"In a time when integrity and courage have become rare qualities in our nation's public and private sector leaders, General Krulak is a prominent stand out. Having led a Marine Corps platoon and a company during two tours of duty in Vietnam and having commanded the 2nd Force Service Support Group during the Gulf War, General Krulak is a leader who has been tested in the most severe environments. In a time when going along with the political whim-of the-day is the key to success in Washington D.C., General Krulak never wavered in upholding the correct course of action in the face of every level of political pressure. In a time when cynicism and apathy run rampant in our nation, General Krulak sets an example for us all, that honor and virtue are a way of life."*

During the course of my conversation with General Krulak the importance of integrity in a leader continually surfaced. When I questioned him on the subject he was very quick to remind me that integrity is the only possession that we truly own and no one can take it from us without our permission. We can give it away and once we do that it is very difficult to recover. As I researched the subject further I made note of some remarks that General Krulak made about this subject in a speech he gave at the Naval Academy in January 1997:

"We study and we discuss ethical principles because it serves to strengthen and fortify our own inner value system…. it gives direction to what I call our moral compass. It is the understanding of ethics that becomes the foundation upon which we can deliberately commit to inviolate principles. It becomes the basis of what we are….of what we include in our character.

Based on it, we commit to doing what is right. We expect such commitment from our leaders. But most importantly, we must demand it of ourselves.

Sound morals and ethics cannot be established or created in a day…a semester…or a year. They must be institutionalized within our character over time…they must become a way of life. It goes beyond these walls and beyond our ranks: it cuts to the heart and to the soul of who we are, what we are…men and women of character. It armors us for the challenges to come and imparts to us a sense of wholeness and unites us in the calling we know now as the professions of arms.

Of all the moral and ethical standards and responsibilities that we have been brought up with, one of those — at least for me — stands out above the rest. It is the one I have kept in the forefront of my mind…it is my ethical and personal touchstone…it is INTEGRITY.

Integrity as we know it today stands for soundness of moral princi-
ples and character — uprightness — honesty. But there is more,
integrity is also an ideal...a goal to strive for...and for a man or
woman to "walk their integrity" is to require constant discipline and
usage."

So far I have given you a lot of Krulak talk on the subject of integrity and character but where is the walk? Let me cite a few examples. As
I present these examples try to envision yourself in General Krulak's
position and ask yourself what you would have done in a similar situation.

The first example has to do with a memo that was sent to the Joint
Chiefs of Staff from the Secretary of Defense during the Clinton
Administration. The memo appeared to be a trial balloon and it suggested that perhaps adultery should be removed as a punishable offense
under the Uniform Code of Military Justice — unless the adultery
occurred among people in the same chain of command. As
Commandant of the Marine Corps and a member of the Joint Chiefs
of Staff, General Krulak was sent a copy of the memo for his comments.
General Krulak strongly opposed the memo and replied that if this line
of reasoning continued from the Secretary of Defense or the White
House they would have his uniform in the morning. Whether you agree
or disagree with General Krulak on this matter you have to agree that
he had the courage of his convictions and put it all on the line. He
talked the talk and he walked the walk. He put his career on the line in
support of a principle.

In another example when he was testifying in front of the Senate
Armed Services Committee he was questioned and challenged concerning his decision that the marines would not have gender integrated
training as did the other services. General Krulak was not convinced
that was not in the best interest of the Marine Corps to throw men and
women together for their recruit training. He insists that his decision
had nothing to do with the physical capabilities of men versus women.

He simply did not believe it was prudent to put young men and young women together in a pressure cooker environment in situations where close and intimate and lengthy contact was part of the training. A Senator on the Senate Armed Services Committee admonished him and wanted to know why the Marine Corps didn't follow the practice of the other Services and conduct gender integrated training. The Senator pressed on with her line of questioning and finally arriving at a point of frustration or exasperation she asked General Krulak if there was any condition or situation where he could envision the Marine Corps conducting gender integrated training. According to the information I have, he replied "Yes Senator, over my dead body." Some might construe that as a career ending move and General Krulak took some flak and "dressing down" from his boss. But once again, as he had done many times during his career, he did what he thought was right. He talked the talk and he walked the walk. He remained true to his principles.

As far as I can determine this is a man who in all phases of his life — as a husband, father, marine, businessman or friend has remained steadfast to his values. He has, on several occasions, told me that his life is simple and his decisions are easy because he adheres to a basic tenant which states just do the right thing. When I asked him to name his heroes he stated that

Ronald Reagan was one of them. When I asked him what he admired about President Reagan he said the President surrounded himself with good people; he listened to what they had to say; he used his moral compass to assess their input and then he just tried to do the right thing.

In a nutshell whether General Krulak was defending the Marine Corps budget before Congress or expanding and toughening marine basic training, or defending the Marine Corps position on gender integrated training or enforcing adultery provisions in the Uniform Code of Military Justice or leading troops in combat, he remained faithful to his principles. "Semper Fi" is not only a motto for General Chuck Krulak, it is a way of life…"Always Faithful."

I hope the following verbatim reprint of a speech given at Pepperdine University on 14 October 1998 will give you an additional measure of the man:

GENERAL KRULAK'S COMMENTS ON CHARACTER

Remarks for Pepperdine University Convocation Series
14 October 1998

Gen. Charles C. Krulak Commandant of the Marine Corps

I am happy to be here this morning — to have an opportunity to talk to the leaders and thinkers of tomorrow and, more importantly, the day after tomorrow.

I considered a few different topics to talk to you about this morning: The importance of my Christian faith in guiding my personal and professional life, the Marine Corps' intensive efforts to develop values in our newest Marines, or even my thoughts about our Nation's role in humanitarian missions around the globe…I will do that if you would like-but during the Q&As.

There is another topic that I would like to talk about today--one that is critical to each of us, our nation, and our world-as we move toward the 21st Century … A topic that rarely gets talked about in forums such as this, which makes it all the more important to discuss. It serves as the foundation for all that we are, all that we do, and all that we will be … I will talk about the importance of character.

I can tell you from personal experience that combat is the most traumatic human event. It strips away an individual's veneer, exposing their true character. If a character flaw exists, it will appear in combat — guaranteed.

This morning, I will tell the story of an American whose true character was tested and exposed in the crucible of war. I will then draw some conclusions that are applicable to how the rest of us should live our lives ... lives where combat will hopefully never play a role. He was a 19 year old Lance Corporal Marine-about the same age as most of you in the audience this morning. He was a man of courage ...a man of character ... and this is his story ... Vietnam ... It was 0600, the third of June, 1966. I was a First Lieutenant at the time, and had been given this command because the previous commander had been killed about one week earlier. My Company had been given a simple mission that began with a helicopter assault. We would land in a series of dried-up rice paddies about 6 football fields in length, and three football fields in width. These paddies were surrounded by jungle-covered mountains, with a dry stream bed running along one side. We were supposed to land, put on our packs, and do what all Marines do: find the largest mountain, and climb to the top. There we would put ourselves in a defensive perimeter to act as the blocking force for an offensive sweep conducted by two battalions.

The helicopters landed, unloaded my company of Marines, and had just started to leave when the world collapsed. Automatic weapons, mortar fire, artillery — it was hell on earth. Fortunately, a good portion of my Company had managed to move into the dry stream bed where they were protected from most of the fire. However, one platoon had landed too far west to move immediately to the cover of the stream bed. As they tried to move in that direction, the fires on them became so heavy they had no alternative but to hit the deck. One particular squad found itself directly in the line of fire of a North Vietnamese 12.7mm heavy machine gun. In a matter of seconds, two Marines were killed and three were seriously wounded.

As I watched what was happening from my position in the stream bed, I knew that it was just a matter of time before that machine gun would systematically "take out" that whole platoon--squad by squad. If I didn't act immediately, they would be lost in just a matter of minutes. I made a call to the commander of the first platoon that had made its way into the stream bed, directing him to move up the stream bed so he could attack across the flank of the gun position — not having to assault it directly from the front. At the same time, I directed another platoon to provide suppressive fire that might diminish the volume of fire coming from the machine gun position. All this was happening in the midst of smoke, multiple explosions, heavy small arms fire, and people yelling to be heard over the din of battle.

Suddenly, my radio operator grabbed me by the sleeve and pointed toward the middle of the rice paddy where a black Marine — a Lance Corporal — had gotten to his feet, placed his M-14 rifle on his hip, and charged the machine gun — firing as fast as he could possibly fire. He ran about 40 meters directly toward the machine gun and then cut to the side, much like a running back might do during a football game. Sure enough, the machine gun, which had been delivering heavy fire on his squad, picked up off of the squad and began firing at the young Marine. Seeing the fire shift away from them, the squad moved immediately to the cover of a small rice paddy dike — thick ground, about a foot high separating each paddy from the other. Both they, and the other two squads were able to drag their casualties and gear to the position of safety behind this dike.

This young Marine didn't look back. He didn't see what happened. He kept on fighting. He dodged back and forth across these paddies, firing continuously. He would run out of ammunition, reload on the run, and continue forward — dodging back and forth as he ran. BAM! Suddenly he was picked up like a dishrag and thrown backward — hit by at least one round.

The rest of the platoon charged. My radio operator grabbed me again, but saying nothing, he just pointed to the middle of the rice paddy. That young Marine -- had gotten to his feet. As he stood, he didn't put the rifle to his hip; he locked the weapon into his shoulder...took steady aim — good sight picture, good sight alignment — and walked straight down the line of fire into that machine gun.

About four minutes later, my command group and the rest of the unit finally arrived at the now-silent machine gun position. There were nine dead enemy soldiers around the gun... This young marine was draped over the gun itself. As only Marines can do, these battle-hardened young men tenderly picked up their friend and laid him on the ground. When they opened his "flak jacket" he had five massive wounds from that machine gun. FIVE...

About seven months later, I traveled back to Headquarters Marine Corps in Washington and watched the Commandant of the Marine Corps present this Lance Corporal's widow with the nation's second highest decoration for valor — the Navy Cross. In this woman's arms was the baby boy that the young Marine had only seen in a Polaroid picture.

This leader displayed great physical courage. Somewhere in his character was another kind of courage as well — moral courage — the courage to do the right thing. When he had the chance to do something else, he chose to do the right thing. His squad was in mortal danger. He had a choice to make, and he did what was right, at the cost of his life. Let me remind you, this was 1966. This was a black Marine from the deep south, who couldn't even buy a hamburger at the McDonald's in his hometown.

Moral courage ... personal courage ... character ... So, what of your character? Who are you? No, not the way you look in the mirror or in photographs ... but who are you really? What do you stand for? What is the essence of your character? Where is your moral compass pointing? Which course do you follow?

Everyday we have to make decisions. It is through this decision-making process that we show those around us the quality of our character. The majority of the decisions we have to make are "no brainers." Deciding what we are going to have for breakfast is not going to test your character ... Judgment maybe, but not character. The true test of character comes when the stakes are high, when the chips are down, when your gut starts to turn, when the sweat starts to form on your brow, when you know the decision you are about to make may not be popular ... but it must be made. That's when your true character is exposed.

The associations you keep, the peers you choose, the mentors you seek, the organizations you affiliate with-all help to define your character. But in the end — you will be judged as an individual — not as part of a group.

Success in combat — and in life — has always demanded a depth of character. Those who can reach deep within themselves and draw upon an inner strength, fortified by strong values, always carry the day against those of lesser character. Moral cowards never win in war — moral cowards never win in life. They might believe that they are winning a few battles here and there, but their victories are never sweet, they never stand the test of time, and they never serve to inspire others. In fact, each and every one of a moral coward's "supposed victories" ultimately leads them to failure.

Those who have the courage to face up to ethical challenges in their daily lives will find that same courage can be drawn upon in times of great stress, in times of great controversy, in times of the never ending battle between good and evil ...

All around our society you see immoral behavior ... lying, cheating, stealing, drug and alcohol abuse, prejudice, and a lack of respect for human dignity and the law. In the not too distant future, each of you is going to be confronted with situations where you will have to deal straight-up with issues such as these. The question is, what will you do when you are? What action will you take? You will know what to do-- the challenge is--will you DO what you know is right? It takes moral courage to hold your ideals above yourself. It is the DEFINING aspect ... When the test of your character and moral courage comes — regardless of the noise and confusion around you — there will be a moment of inner silence in which you must decide what to do. Your character will be defined by your decision ... and it is yours and yours alone to make. I am confident you will each make the right one. When that moment of silence comes and you are wrestling with your decision, consider this poem:

THE EAGLE AND THE WOLF

There is a great battle
that rages inside me.

One side is a soaring eagle
Everything the eagle stands for
is good and true and beautiful.

It soars above the clouds.
Even though it dips down into the valleys,
it lays its eggs on the mountain tops.

The other side of me is a howling wolf.
And that raging, howling wolf
represents the worst that is in me.

He eats upon my downfalls and
justifies himself by his presence
in the pack.

Who wins this great battle?...
The one I feed.

May God bless you and Semper Fidelis!

GENERAL CHARLES C. KRULAK Q & A

I. BACKGROUND

Where did you grow up?

I lived in many places. My father served 35 years in the Marine Corps and had numerous assignments around the world.

Where did you go to school?

I went to various schools while growing up. Prior to going to the Naval Academy (class of 1964) I went to Philips Exeter Academy in New Hampshire and later on, during my military days, I acquired a Masters Degree from George Washington University.

What were your scholastic or athletic achievements?

I excelled at wrestling and was inducted into the National Wrestling Hall of Fame. While at the Naval Academy I also played Lacrosse.

Who were your heroes?

My father and my mother laid the keel and set the standards. Lieutenant Colonel Dutch Shultz, my battalion commander in Vietnam, was someone I admired and respected.

Tome Draude, now a senior executive at USAA, was truly an exemplar for me. He had all of the attributes of an exceptional leader. I learned much from him and from President Reagan.

Tell me something about your parents

I was raised in a disciplined household with my two brothers. My mother pretty much raised us by herself because my father was a career Marine Corps Officer (class of 1934 USNA) and from 1942 to1952 he spent much of his time at war or training. My mother provided us a strong sense of values that were reinforced by my father who was a giant of character.

II. VALUES

Are there values that you consistently try to uphold?

Selflessness, Moral Courage, Integrity

In your opinion, what are three most important family values, in order of importance?

A. Love of God — this is needed to be an anchor for a nuclear family

B. Trust — which comes from being a person of character. Trust greatly facilitates the leadership process.

C. Unconditional Love — go 100% of the way and if your spouse and children will go 100% of the way you can meet somewhere in the middle.

Is it difficult to maintain your values and integrity while receiving so much adoration and attention?

I am aware that everything is fleeting and I also know that when you are gone you are gone. People tend to adore the office or the position more than the person. Nevertheless, I have always tried to stay humble. For example, I don't always fly first class; I frequently drag my bags and me into the back of the aircraft.

How can we improve upon the morals in our country?

First we must understand and respect authority, responsibility and accountability. We must also know which of these we can delegate and which ones we can't.

Define your success for me and how did ethics, honor or integrity contribute to or detract from your success?

Integrity had a great deal to do with my success. The people that I worked with believed that I was selfless — that it was never all about me but about us. They also knew that I had the courage of my convictions and that I had the moral courage to do the right thing regardless of the consequences. I put my career on the line many times because I believed the position I had taken was absolutely the right thing to do. To me my integrity was everything but you can't just talk. Your actions must be meaningful and honest.

III. MORALS AND INTEGRITY

Who is the most ethical & moral person you know?

Tom Draude is the most ethical and moral person I know. He is a remarkable man and he should have been the Commandant of the Marine Corps. I pale to insignificance when compared to him.

Who was your best teacher? What did you learn from him/her?

My best teacher is Christ. He taught me the Golden Rule; He is my model for servant leadership and He inspired me to place my country, my family and my troops well before myself.

How do you define integrity? What does it mean to you?

It is an important possession and the only possession that each of us truly owns. Nobody can take it away from you; only you can give it away and once you do it is extremely difficult to regain.

IV. CHARACTER

Do you think a person's "character" is formed at birth, or can it be changed?

No I don't think a person's character is formed at birth and yes character can be learned and changed. The learning process however requires discipline and in many ways it is akin to developing good habits. It takes time, commitment and discipline, and a little inspiration also helps.

What can you say about character and integrity as they relate to your life and your career?

Character and integrity have made my life and career very easy. Decisions have been easy to make because my moral compass is calibrated to "true north." My faith and my integrity allow a "peace of mind" and what I stand for is very important to me.

Define the word "Courage"

There are two facets to this word; physical courage and this aspect is easy for a well trained marine and an a scale of 1 to 10 I place physical courage at a 1 and moral courage, in my view, is more difficult to achieve but on the scale of 1 to 10, I would place it at an 11.

V. INNER STRENGTH AND INSPIRATION

What factors most contributed to you success as a General, executive and a parent?

The factors that I consider important to my success: My faith, my family and the great support from my wife, children and parents. I also consider my energy level and sense of humor to be important factors.

What factors play a role in your decision making?

Only one — DO THE RIGHT THING.

What I admired about President Reagan was that he surrounded himself with good people. He listened carefully to what they said and then he used his moral compass to do the right thing and make the right decision.

IV. PERSONAL

How would you like to be remembered?

Someone who tried to do his best for his God, his family, his country and his beloved Marine Corps.

What has given meaning to your life?

My religion, my family and the Marine Corps.

What were the major turning points in your career and how do you feel about your choices now?

I went to Vietnam several times and was deployed to other places a number of times and in every instance I went willingly and learned something each time. More specifically in 1972 the Marine Corps was in crisis, beset with drug problems and race problems. Pessimists left the Marine Corps and the idealists remained and corrected the problem and made the Corps stronger than ever.

If you could express your gratitude for one thing in your life – what would it be and to whom?

My wife, Zandi — the fact that this wonderful woman consented to marry me, bear my children and follow me all over the world for over 40 years. I am a very fortunate person.

What is the one personality trait you would change about yourself?

Emotional spikes

How do you fight prejudice?

Expose it for what it is — a cancer in our society and if not excised it will metastasize and kill us.

What job would you like to have now? Other than your own?

Either Secretary of Defense or President of the United States so I could help set the moral compass of the nation. But the reality is — I'm happy doing what I am doing right now.

What major event (or events) inspired you to pursue the career you did?

My father and the people he brought into my life inspired me to follow in his footsteps and pursue a career in the United States Marine Corps.

Does religion play an important role in your life? How?

Yes, my faith plays an extremely important role in my life. Although I was raised as an Episcopalian. I really was "born again" and truly inspired by an Army Chaplain who had been a war hero and a charismatic leader. From that time on and up to the present I conduct a morning prayer session in my office and any member of my team is invited.

What was the biggest decision you had to make in your life?

My decision to become a Christian.

Did you ever have an adverse experience that taught you a great lesson?

I think I have learned from a lot of small lessons taught one at a time.

If you could sit down to dinner with one famous person, who would it be?

Jesus Christ

What is your best personality trait?

My sense of humor

What does it take to be a great leader?

Be a man or woman of integrity.

What is the nicest compliment ever given to you?

That my wife consented to marry me.

What is your most prized possession?

My integrity

What is MORE important to be success in life? Intelligence or Social Skills?

Social skills

Do you think we are put on earth to fulfill a purpose? What is yours?

Yes. I don't know if I have determined mine yet?

If a foreigner asked about your country, what would you say would be three things you are most proud of? Three things you are ashamed of?

The things I am most proud of are:

— The remarkable resilience of the American people

— Our democratic way of life

— Our toughness

The three things I am ashamed of are:

— Our arrogance

— Our decreasing morality

— Our softness in our physical condition

Do you have to be aggressive and "cutthroat" to get ahead in life? Why or why not?

No. If you are energetic, smart and honest you need not be cutthroat!

Do you believe the good guy always finishes last?

No. A good guy — a truly good guy will never finish last.

CHAPTER NINE

CHARACTER

MIKE KRZYZEWSKI
Head Coach, Duke University Basketball Team

Every great institution is the lengthened shadow of a single man.
His character determines the character of his organization.
> *— Ralph Waldo Emerson*

THE DUKE UNIVERSITY BASKETBALL program is truly the lengthened shadow of its coach, Mike Krzyzewski. At this writing, he has taken the Blue Devils to ten NCAA Final Four appearances and led them to three National Championships (1991, 1992 and 2001). In 2001 Mike was inducted into the Naismith Basketball Hall of Fame. He has also been named National Coach of the Year twelve times in eight different seasons and has the highest NCAA Tournament winning percentage among all active coaches. In his collegiate coaching career, he has amassed over 700 victories — a number which in time will grow to a point where he will no doubt surpass the records held by Dean Smith and Bobby Knight. Mike was selected as the Coach of the Decade (for the 1990's) by the NABC. *Time* and *CNN* honored Coach K as "America's Best Coach (which covers all sports, at all levels) in 2002. Off the court the coach has become an author with three books under his belt. The story of his 2001 National Championship is told in 5 Point Play. He also authored the *New York Times* bestseller *Leading with the Heart: Coach K's Successful Strategies for Basketball, Business and Life.*

While he has proudly produced All-American basketball players, he can be doubly proud that these young men have also become productive and successful citizens. The Duke basketball team gives true meaning to the term *student-athlete,* because Coach Krzyzewski's players finish college and, with few exceptions, graduate on time. The 1997-1998 Duke basketball yearbook has best summarized what the basketball world thinks of Mike Krzyzewski and his program:

> *Such accomplishments have not gone unnoticed by his peers in coaching. In 1991, on his way to guiding the Blue Devils to the title, with a 32-7 record, he was named the Kodak/National Association of Basketball Coaches (NABC) National Coach of the Year. In all, Coach K has been named National Coach of the Year in five different seasons by major organizations including Chevrolet (1986), Naismith (1989), the Sporting News and Naismith (1992) and Basketball Times (1997).*

In 1992, the *Sporting News* named him Sportsman of the Year, becoming the first college coach ever to win the honor. The magazine reported: *"On the court and off, Krzyzewski is a family man first, a teacher second, a basketball coach third and a winner at all three. **He is what's right about sports.**"*

Leadership by example is one way to view the life of Mike Krzyewski. And in 2004 his actions spoke louder than many would have possibly imagined. In July he choose a 25th season at Duke University over a reported $40 million offer to coach the Los Angeles

Lakers. Krzyzewski said. "It's like I did something. They may be thinking that I'm nuts. But for whatever reason, it has had a very good impact." It did have a major impact and his decision to stay at Duke instead of moving to the NBA drew praise from the college community and fans across this nation.

With all this performance and all these records we only have one half of the story of Coach Krzyzewski. The victories are important but more important is how he achieved these victories. The late, renowned sportswriter Grantland Rice is credited with this quote:

"When that great scorer comes to mark against your name, he'll mark not if you won or lost, but how you played the game."

Mike Krzyzewski was born and raised in Chicago. His mom and dad were the children of Polish immigrants, and they worked hard and sacrificed considerably to give Mike and his brother Bill the best possible upbringing they could provide. Mike's parents, Williams and Emily Krzyzewski, were good people — hardworking, honest and determined to provide a solid ethical foundation for their children. In the 1930's and 1940's, the tradition of families like Mike's was to work hard and make whatever sacrifices were required to provide their children a greater opportunity to succeed in the world. The senior Krzyzewskis were no exception. They grew up in an ethnic neighborhood and experienced their share of discrimination but were determined to raise responsible, educated, honest, successful children. They afforded the Krzyzewski children a marvelous combination of discipline and unconditional love. Coach Krzyzewski speaks admiringly of his mother when he says, "My mom is the best person I ever knew."

So when his parents sent him to Catholic school and encouraged him to be a good student, he reacted the way one would expect given the sacrifice and example his parents provided. That is, he was not only an honor student, but he also turned out to be an all-state basketball player. As an outstanding high school student athlete, a number of scholarship opportunities became available to him, including a request from Coach Bob Knight for Mike to apply to West Point. There are easier ways to get a college education and play basketball than enduring the rigors of academics and the disciplined life of the United States Military Academy. And, were it not for his parents, Mike Krzyzewski probably wouldn't have considered West Point. Mike's folks, however, were proud that their son had the opportunity to attend a school that had such a proud tradition and reputation for Honor. So, in a nutshell, Mike opted to go to West Point to please the parents who had worked so hard and sacrificed so much to get him a good education and provide him decent clothes to wear and put wholesome food on the family table. Upon reflection Mike's mom and dad, despite their lack of a formal education, knew exactly what was in the best interests of their son. Just as his Catholic education experience had provided character and academic education in the form of structure, discipline and role models, Mike's decision to attend West Point also played a major role in his moral and intellectual development. In retrospect, Mike is the first to admit that going to West Point was a turning point in his life.

The natural reaction or a rational question is, "why was going to West Point such an important move in Mike Krzyzewski's life?" The answer is simple — Mike grew up in a family and school system where respect, discipline, ethics, structure and example were the cornerstones for his development. His parents showed him the value of hard work, discipline and love. And the structure and doctrine of his Catholic schooling and upbringing reinforced the values he was taught at home. West Point reinforced the principles he has learned as a youth. This strengthened his commitment to these timeless values.

He felt right at home with the motto of the Military Academy — DUTY, HONOR, COUNTRY. Mike had always had a sense of duty — that is to do what is right to the best of his ability. Honor at West Point is reflected in the famous code: "*A Cadet will not lie, cheat, steal or tolerate those that do.*" This prescription is a natural extension of his upbringing. To this day, Coach Krzyzewski sincerely believes that telling the truth, at all times, in matters large or small, is of paramount importance. It is the basis of credibility and trust. Trust is the primary foundation of leadership, and it is a major factor in Coach K's success. So, West Point reinforced Mike's sense of duty and honor. It also fostered a patriotic awareness, love of country, and all that it stands for.

If I had to sum up the essence of Mike Krzyzewski in two words, they would be "honesty and consideration." When I arrived at Duke University to interview Coach K, he had to postpone our interview for a couple of hours because of a Coaches and Cancer TV Charity he was participating in. I took the extra time to briefly interview his secretary, Gerry Brown, and the Duke University Sports Information Director, Mike Cragg.

The coach's secretary was a reluctant interviewee — she didn't want to intrude on the coach's spotlight. But when I asked if she would simply answer one short question, she agreed. The question simply stated was — why do you like working for Mike Krzyzewski, and the answer was simply stated:

"He is a perfectionist; he truly cares about his athletes; he runs an up and up clean program; he is a great family man; he is active in his church; he doesn't forget the little people; and he is successful, but he is also humble."

When I asked Mike Cragg, the Duke University Sports Information Director, what he thinks of Coach K he responded:

"Mike has been a successful coach at Duke for 18 years, and he is the same person now that he was when he arrived. He treats everyone with respect, from the President of the University to the custodian who sweeps the floors on the basketball court. He does everything with the big picture in mind — how to run a successful major college basketball program and do it in a way that reflects favorably on the University and his players. He is a teacher and a coach, and for some of his players, he is like a father. He tries to recruit good basketball players who are student-athletes and young men of character. The graduation rate of his basketball players is well over 90%; and

he strives to prepare his players for life, not just basketball. He insists that basketball is just a part of university life and not bigger than the University. Coach K is a celebrity and does not know it and certainly doesn't act it! He is a class act and represents everything that is right about college sports."

MIKE KRZYZEWSKI Q & A

The following questions and answers reveal the essence of my conversation with Coach Krzyzewski:

Are there any values that you consistently try to uphold?

"It is my intent to be truthful and honest in everything I do and with everyone I deal. I believe it is important to be honest — I want very much to be trustworthy so that everyone will accept my work at face value. It is so much easier to tell the truth consistently and not have to remember or worry about the lies you told last month or last year.

It is important to be honest and forthright with my players. To be truly effective, one needs to be trustworthy and to be trustworthy one must earn that trust. That can only happen if you are honest, truthful, and dependable. I tell my team that to win by cheating is not to win at all. I want us all to be responsible and accountable for our actions. Very simply, I subscribe to the notion that people should not lie, cheat or steal. Sometimes this is easier said than done, but that doesn't mean we should stop trying."

In your opinion, what are the most important family values?

"I view the family as a team — a team of interdependence. In my view it is important for a family to be willing to depend on one another and to be a support system for whomever in the family needs support. In this regard there needs to be an openness and truthfulness which facilitates loyalty and mutual support.

It is also important for a family to provide unconditional love to one another. Close bonds are essential and the knowledge that family members can be open with one another to discuss their problems and their vulnerabilities is important.

Is it difficult to maintain your values and integrity while receiving so much admiration and attention?

"No, it is really easier because success gives one a little more breathing room — in a way success gives you a platform to do good things and sponsor good causes."

Can you define your success?

"Let me say right up front that if you let other people define your success you may never have it. Success is a journey and a process not an event. Success for me has been the opportunities that I have had to do my part as a responsible son, husband, father, friend and coach. Success is derived and defined for me as giving it your best shot, whatever you are trying to accomplish. People are surprised when I tell them that although winning is important, you can't always define success as winning — you can have success in a loss. Often times we learn more from our losses and failures than we do from our successes.

For example from 1988 to 1992 our basketball team made it to the final four of the NCAA Tournament, but we didn't win the NCAA Tournament Championship until 1991. The sports media asked me in 1991 how it felt to get the 'monkey off my back' by finally winning the tournament after three final four appearances without winning the big game. In 1988, 1989, 1990, we had excellent programs, and in no way did I view those teams as unsuccessful. Those teams worked hard and gave it their best shot and were recognized as one of the four best teams in the country. So I never viewed them as unsuccessful and I never sensed that there was a 'monkey on my back.' That 'monkey on my back' comment is what I mean when I said we shouldn't let other people define our success."

What do you tell your new players when you first meet them?

"I tell them that they should not be afraid to fail. People who worry about failing are tentative, and I don't want my players to be tentative. I want them to energetically and vigorously apply their talents to the task at hand and let the chips fall where they will. There is more to lose from tentativeness that comes from halfhearted application than the patented failures associated with a vigorous effort. Failure is part of the growth process."

Who were your heroes?

"The people who most influenced my life are my parents and the teachers and nuns who taught me. My ambition was to be a teacher and coach in high school. Although I am reluctant to single out one teacher or coach, I do distinctly remember my high school geometry teacher who really was a mentor for me. I really respected how he related to me as a teenager and I admired his ability to empathize with me and how he helped me and others to solve our problems. He was a true model for consideration and respect for others."

What are some of the qualities you look for when you are recruiting your basketball players?

"I essentially look at three factors — basketball talent and skills, academic performance and potential and character. The first two factors are relatively easy to ascertain but the last one, character, is not so easy to determine. One revealing indicator to me is how the basketball recruit treats and respects his parents and coaches."

Do you think a person's character is formed at birth or can it be developed?

"I definitely believe that character and leadership can be taught and exemplified — although it appears that some people may have a greater propensity to learn and be developed than others."

From where have your drawn your inner strength?

"I am fortunate in that I have a tremendous support system in my wife, family and friends. When I fall, they catch me and prop me up again. My religion also provides me strength — I do believe in God and I pray regularly for strength and guidance. I believe there is a life after death and that I will be judged someday. And that judgment will not necessarily be about how many wins I have been a party to but about how I have played the game — the game of basketball and the game of life."

How would you like to be remembered?

"As an honest and considerate person. If they write on my tombstone: good son, good husband and father, loving grandfather, good teacher and coach, I would be happy with that."

What one thing in your life are you most proud of?

"My reputation — I am proud of my whole life — I don't want one deed in my life to define my reputation or my success or my shortcomings."

What are your strengths and weaknesses?

"Most of my strengths come from the example of my parents and my upbringing. My father taught me about the dignity of work, so I am a hard worker. What I learned from my athletic experiences is the importance of teamwork and not to be afraid to fail. I truly believe that if you have a great fear of failure you will never perform to the best of your ability. I also have learned the value of surrounding yourself with good people and not worry about who gets the credit and accolades. There are many intelligent and effective assistants out there from whom each of us can learn something. And last, but not least, I truly believe in telling the truth. I want and need to be dependable and relied on and credible and for me that only comes with telling the truth.

As for my shortcomings, I suspect my wife, Mickie, could make quite a list. I will mention just a few. I have a short fuse, and I am very impatient. I am not cutthroat, but I am aggressive, and I am very competitive by nature. I have a passion for perfection, and although winning is not the only thing, I prefer winning over losing. I also prefer that my teams play as a team and not as a collection of individuals. I also prefer that we take high percentage shots and my players find ways to pass to the open man. I do get impatient and sometimes quite angry when all the things we teach and practice don't materialize in a positive way. On occasion I find myself being envious of another person. It is a trait that I am not proud of and I hate myself whenever I find myself envying someone else."

How do you fight prejudice?

"I simple refuse to allow it in situations on which I have some control." You cannot produce truly effective teams by tolerating racial or ethnic prejudice. When I discriminate I do so on the basis of effort, execution, and commitment. I discriminate against the player who misses the open man or who takes a dumb shot, and it doesn't matter if he is white, black, polka dot, Polish or Irish."

Do you think America can still be a melting pot for all ethnic groups, races and religions?

"Yes I do — if we can get away from judging people by color or language or religion. Diversity in our country is a strength."

What is the issue that you think will be the most important in the next national election?

"There are two issues that I think are important, but I am not sure they will get the national attention that I think they deserve. The first one concerns learning how to truly educate our young children, because I truly believe that a broadly educated populace would go a long way toward eliminating poverty. And I also believe we need to do a better job of taking care of the elderly and better utilize their talents and experience."

If a foreigner asked about your country, what three things would you be most proud of?

"America is still the land of opportunity — this country still rewards hard work; there is still opportunity for upward mobility.

There is also freedom of speech and freedom of choice — and many freedoms. However in the end the freedom that is the most relevant is the freedom to discipline ourselves and that latter freedom sometimes is lacking."

Do you have to be aggressive and cutthroat to get ahead in life?

"Aggressive yes — cutthroat no. This goes back to my statement about not letting someone else define your success. I believe in aggressively and ethically pursuing your goals and your dreams, but you don't have to cut someone else's legs off to help you succeed."

Do you believe good guys always finish last?

"To the contrary. I believe that good guys always finish first. By good guys I mean people who know themselves, believe in themselves, who aggressively and ethically strive to do the best they can without undermining or disparaging others. Good guys, and generically that includes boys and girls, men and women, are those people who strive to be the best that they can be in the pursuit of success as they define it and do so without lying, cheating and stealing their way to success.

In that context, good guys or good people always finish first."

Coach K, what advice would you share with the young people of our country as they pursue their goal in life?

- "Don't be afraid to fail — pursue your dreams vigorously.
- Never stop educating yourself.
- Keep learning about yourself.
- Never be afraid to change direction.
- Never make a decision based solely on money.

- Nobody can tell you what you love, except you.
- Never let someone else define success or failure for you.
- Love your work, and success and money will follow."

CHAPTER TEN

INTEGRITY

SUE MYRICK

Representative from the 9th District
North Carolina House of Representatives
Congress of the United States

Reputation is what men and women think of; character is what God and angels know of us.

— *Thomas Paine*

S OME PEOPLE ARE BORN INTO POLITICS, and others have aspired to high political positions since they were children, but as a youngster Sue Myrick never dreamed of a life in the political arena. For the first 40 year of her life politics was the farthest thing from her mind. It was only when she and her husband Ed tried to buy some property in downtown Charlotte, North Carolina, and were unjustly denied the property, that she decided to run for political office. So, in 1981, without any prior experience she ran for the Charlotte City Council, losing by a mere 200 votes. In 1983, she ran again, won, and served on the City Council of Charlotte for two years during a period of major confrontation between large developers and city neighborhoods. In 1985, she ran for the office of Mayor of Charlotte and lost the primary by 58 votes. In 1987, she ran again and won, despite the fact that her opponent was a popular incumbent. So, in six short years, Sue Myrick rose from political obscurity to be mayor of one of the nation's most progressive cities. She served two terms, from 1987 to 1991, and counts among her accomplishments the building of a large homeless shelter and the passage of a $100 million bond referendum for roads. She also supported and helped to assure the acquisition of the Carolina Panthers Football Team for the City of Charlotte. Significantly, she managed the budget for the city of Charlotte for four productive, progressive years without a tax increase.

In 1987, Sue Myrick was persuaded to run for the U.S. Senate and was barraged with negative publicity from what some people alleged was a "smear campaign." To set the record straight in 1970, while she was separated from her first husband, she had a relationship with another man. It was a brief and unhappy chapter in her life. She still feels considerable regret and remorse and wishes it had never happened. But, it did happen, she accepts responsibility, she has learned from it, and has turned that negative experience into a positive commitment. Notwithstanding her candor and regret, that incident was publicized and used to undermine her political base. She not only lost the election, but it also left her feeling that she really wanted nothing more to do with politics.

In 1994, however, upon the retirement of Alex McMillan, the North Carolina Representative to the U.S. Congress, Sue Myrick's friends and colleagues urged her to run for the U.S. House of Representatives. She accepted the challenge and, despite a strong array of primary candidates and strong opposition in the main election, won the seat. The irony in this campaign was that the front runner displayed very questionable ethical behavior, but the voters forgave Sue Myrick's earlier indiscretion because she openly admitted and apologized for it. When asked why she ran for the House in 1994 after the distasteful campaign in 1991, she simply and sincerely says, 'My hope is that I can make things better for my grandchildren."

Discussions with Ken Moffitt, Sue Myrick's Legislative Director at the time, reveal some special insights into Sue Myrick. He told me that Sue is a genuine, straight-forward human being who develops a special rapport with her constituents and her colleagues because of her honesty. Ken respects Sue because of her sense of duty and her drive to truly serve her constituents. She votes in a manner that addresses her constituents' needs. She is not without tact, but sometimes her direct manner catches people off guard, but they always know where she stands. She is not ego driven, but she is motivated to make America a better place for those young people who will follow her. Those who know her well speak of her integrity and her dedication. She played an important role in the Congress' effort to balance the budget and reform the welfare system. She is also quite concerned about organized crime in Russia and the control of a number of Russian banks by a criminal element. She is also focused on redressing the immorality and breakdown in ethics in America. Her worry is that there is an incremental, gradual tolerance for unethical social behavior. We might destroy ourselves from within if we don't reverse this condition. Her attempts to introduce a code of ethics into the Congress in 1997 met with indifference, if not passive resistance. It is still her plan to introduce such a code, and she is working hard to muster enough support to get it off the launch pad.

By way of background, Sue Wilkins Myrick was born on August 1, 1941. She grew up in Northwestern Ohio and attended Port Clinton High School. She entered Heidelberg College in Tiffin, Ohio, with the intention of becoming a teacher but chose to move on after one year. In 1962, she married Jim Forest, a sports announcer. They were together for 13 years. She and Jim had two children, but in 1970, the marriage ended in divorce. In 1977 she married Ed Myrick, and they have been married for 23 years. Today, Sue Myrick serves in the U.S. Congress committed to raising the standard for ethical government, committed to basic values and focused on addressing the needs of her constituents. She has vision, but no great political aspirations — except to make a positive difference and to leave things better than she found them.

SUE MYRICK Q & A

In my conversation with Representative Sue Myrick, we discussed some of the same issues I raised with the other interviewees.

What can you tell me about your parents?

"My dad and mom worked together at their nursery and on the farm. They were straightforward, hardworking people and money was not a primary focus in their lives. They were Lutherans who were active in their church. They loved people and always had friends visiting them at our home. My dad was the most ethical and moral person I've every known, and he set a marvelous example for me and my three younger brothers. My mother was extremely compassionate and nurturing. I am truly thankful to my parents for all that they taught me and for all the sacrifices they made for my brothers and me.

In your opinion what are the most important family values?

"If family members can be honest with one another and practice the Golden Rule and look after each other's best interests then each family member should be able to achieve his or her goals. And if you can add a sincere measure of love to the above equation then success and happiness should follow. The short answer to your question is, that honesty, the Golden Rule, and love are the most important values for a family."

What values have played a major role in your life?

"The answer is the same as the previous question — honesty and truth are the foundation of trust and credibility. Trustworthiness and credibility are the cornerstones of effective leadership. So I hold honesty and the Golden Rule in the premier positions in my hierarchy of values."

Is it difficult to maintain your values and integrity while receiving an inordinate amount of attention and admiration?

"No, this is not a big problem for me. I am Sue now, and I'll be Sue later, and I view myself as a public servant. I don't focus on the congresswoman title. Also, I prefer being at home in my jeans and sneakers rather than in a cocktail gown at a fancy political party. I take my job seriously, but I don't take myself too seriously. But, just in case, I still pray each day for humility."

Who was your best teacher? What did you learn from him or her?

"There were a number of good teachers in my life, but two stand out. Mr. Rofkar taught me English, and he also taught life's practical lessons. Katherine Gross was my elementary school principal, and she was a positive encourager. Sometimes we all forget to go back and thank those people who have major influences on our life."

Do you ever go beyond the call of duty?

"As much as I treasure the privacy of my family life, I never turn away a constituent in need. Regardless of the time or the day, I respond to constituents' needs on their schedule, not on mine."

Do you think a person's character is formed at birth or can it be changed?

"I definitely believe character can be taught and exemplified. One's environment can have an effect on one's character."

What factors play a role in your decision making?

"I simply ask myself two questions. Is it right? What do people in my district want? And then I vote my conscience."

How would you like to be remembered?

"I tried!"

What has given meaning to your life?

"My faith and my family."

What are your strengths and weaknesses?

"On the strength side of the ledger, I am not afraid to take a stand when needed, and I can bring people together from diversity to consensus. On the weakness side of the ledger, sometimes I feel I lack the self confidence to maximize my effectiveness on the job. I am a bit of an introvert, and I don't feel comfortable at big social gatherings with strangers."

What were the major turning points in your career, and how do you feel about your choice now?

"In 1981, I ran for the city council in Charlotte because of what could have been an unfair real estate transaction, and although I lost that election, it got me started in politics. In 1983, 1987, 1989, and 1994, I won elections and each time some unique event or some special people encouraged me to run and fortunately in each position I was able to make a positive contribution. But, it all started when my husband Ed and I tried to buy that piece of property in Charlotte, and we lost the property because of political shenanigans despite the fact that we made the highest bid on the property."

If you could express your gratitude for one thing in your life, what would it be and to whom?

"My gratitude goes to my mom and dad for the solid upbringing they provided me. I was lucky enough to have a solid childhood and now I am lucky enough to have a very supportive family group."

Who are your heroes?

"Margaret Thatcher and Ronald Reagan — because of their conviction and their ability to communicate their convictions."

If you had to choose one thing in your life and could go back and change, what would it be?

"My affair in 1970. I will regret that indiscretion until the day I die. But it did happen and I was at fault. I accept responsibility for it. I truly wish it hadn't happened, but I learned from it and I grew from it."

What are your most proud of about your life?

"I am extremely proud of my two sons — Greg, who is a Federal Probation Officer, and Dan, who is an architect."

What was the biggest decision you had to make in your life?

"Running for Mayor of Charlotte."

What is the issue you think will be the most important in the next election?

"I think social security will be the most important issue in the next election. I am also concerned about the standard of ethics and morality that I see in our country. I fear a deteriorating trend could eventually destroy us from within, if we don't turn the tide."

What does it take to be a great leader?

"Not being afraid to fail. Pursue your vision vigorously and honestly and let the chips fall where they may. Vision, courage, reality, communication and bold execution are primary ingredients for effective leadership, but in the end you have to go for it and not be afraid to fail. Failure is only a part of the journey; it is a means to a successful end."

What is more important to be a success in life, intelligence, or social skills?

"I think they are both important, but if you force me to pick one, I'll pick social skills."

*If a foreigner asked about your country, what would you say would be
three things you are most proud of? Three things you are ashamed of?*

"This is still the land of freedom and opportunity and I am proud of
that. However on the negative side, I see problems with crime and
drugs and a lack of respect and deterioration of moral values."

*What advice would you share with the young people of our country
as they pursue their goals in life?*

"I would tell them to keep their moral bearings and don't be afraid to
fail."

Do you have to be aggressive and cutthroat to get ahead in life?

"No, I refuse to operate in that mode, and whatever success I have had
in life I have achieved without, as the saying goes, cutting any one else's
throat or cutting anyone else's legs off. Maybe it is because I am a
woman and was taught not to do those things or never felt the need to
be cutthroat."

Do you believe good guys finish last?

"Sometimes. But they are still good guys."

CHAPTER ELEVEN

TRUTH

JOHN NABER
Olympic Swimming Champion

"Rather than love, than money, than fame, give me truth."
—Henry David Thoreau

JOHN NABER'S STORY IS A TRUE SUCCESS STORY that is all about sports, life and character. John Naber has few peers when it comes to sports accomplishments. In Montreal at the 1976 Olympic Games, he distinguished himself by winning four gold medals and one silver medal and setting four records in the process. During these same Olympic Games, he also became the first swimmer in Olympic history to win two individual medals on the same day. He held ten NCAA individual titles at the University of Southern California, and he led his swimming team to four undefeated seasons. In 1977, his athletic feats were recognized when he won the Sullivan Award, which recognizes the nation's outstanding amateur athlete.

What does it take to become such an outstanding athlete? If you asked John Naber that question he would most likely tell you his "No Deposit, No Return" story. As the story goes, at age eleven, John learned a life-changing lesson from reading and internalizing the label "no deposit, no return" on a root beer bottle. He translated that label to mean "I have to invest in my dreams if I want to see those dreams come true. What am I depositing in order to see my dreams come true? What price am I willing to pay?" Consequently, he realized early on the importance of paying the price up front. He developed a willingness to invest in himself, and he came to understand that one must condition himself to work through the fatigue. Accordingly, for a good portion of his swimming career, he swam ten miles a day, six days a week, for eleven months of the year. At his daily practices he was usually the first swimmer in the pool; he usually sprinted his warm ups; he squeezed in thousands of yards during his "free" swim periods, and most of the time he was the last swimmer out of the pool. He viewed all of this practice time as an investment in his future. In John's words, "the hours of training now seemed like an investment in my future. You can't cram for the Olympics during the three weeks prior to the opening ceremony the way you study for a college midterm."

People do not spend all of this time practicing unless they believe in their ability to improve their performance. John Naber's faith in his ability to improve led to an increase in his willingness to set personal goals. John's primary swimming event was the backstroke, and as a senior in high school, he analyzed the performance and potential of the then-world record holder in the backstroke. He took the past Olympic results and extrapolated Roland Matthes' gold medal performances from 1968 and 1972 into 1976 and determined or estimated what his performance would most likely be in 1976. His estimate, based on past performances and improvement curve probability, was that the East German champion and Olympic gold medalist in 1968 and 1972, Roland Matthes, could possibly swim John's event in 55.5 seconds. This analysis allowed John Naber to concentrate on striving for a specific time rather than focus on a formidable competitor. In 1973, when John did his analysis, he was swimming the event in 59.5 seconds, which meant that John would have to drop his time by four seconds or one second a year or one-tenth of second per month, which, when viewed in that context looked manageable. This approach of aiming for small incremental improvements over a period of time enabled John to energetically take on the task of closing the gap between him and the then-world champion, Roland Matthes. Was it realistic for an eleven year old to imagine himself an Olympic champion or was it realistic for an eighteen year old to establish a series of incremental goals to lead him to a record breaking victory at the next Olympic games? Of course not, but Olympic champions do not deal in realism, they deal in the improbable if not the impossible. John Naber was an exceptional Olympic champion. He paid his dues, and earned his victories and he recalled and lived by the advice of Peter Daland, his head coach at USC: "The secret to swimming is not how far you swim, and it's not how hard you swim. The secret to swimming is how far you are willing to swim hard." John Naber believes that practice, steady conscientious practice, makes progress permanent — and permanent progress is the essence of achievement and victory.

For most people, the forgoing words and accolades would be sufficient. All of John Naber's achievements described above, however, do not fully define the man. What impressed me more than John Naber's Olympic gold is the depth of his character. In John's own words:

> *"The understanding that the price must be paid for in advance includes the realization that for the victory to mean anything, it must be earned fairly. To win a race, I must follow the rules and compete honorably against the competition. One of life's greatest lessons is one that should still be taught in the athletic arena: The lesson of character." John goes on to say: "If winning is all that matters, then cheating becomes an option. I've heard it said that if we're unwilling to lose, we had better be willing to do anything to win."*

It has been said that athletic competition doesn't build character it reveals character. That notion prompts me to describe a defining moment in John Naber's life — a defining moment that revealed his character. The moment occurred in 1973 when John Naber, as a recent high school graduate, competed in the U.S. National Championships. His goal was to win a position on the World Championship Team, which for an eighteen-year old high schooler would be quite an achievement. Despite his young age, John was favored to win the 100-meter backstroke event but his hand did not touch the wall as required. When the starter fired the gun, John got off to a quick start and at the end of the first lap he reached for the wall behind his head and initiated his flip turn. His feet swung around and he pushed off to proceed on his final leg of the event. As he surfaced he saw the official standing over his lane raising a hand to signal a rule violation. He swam a fast final lap and reached the finish line ahead of the rest of the swimmers. The applause from the spectators was deafening and the congratulations from the other swimmers was exciting, but John was more concerned by the conference taking place at the other end of the pool. Finally, the head referee walked up to John and said, "I'm afraid you've been disqualified. The turn judge says she didn't see you touch the wall." John's shoulders dropped and his chin hit his chest. The crowd seemed to be pulling for him, and John's teammates and his supporters hoped that the official had made a mistake. John's coach approached him and asked, "Do you want to fight this thing? Do you want to protest the call?" John's coach thought he could win if he protested strongly. There was a potential world title at stake and John's head was swirling. I suspect that John Naber didn't realize that this would be a turning point in his life, but he did know that how he handled this situation would follow him the rest of his life. "My decision whether to fight the judge's call or to accept her decision was made in the blink of an eye. I knew what I had to do. My parents didn't raise a cheater. With moist eyes, I looked at my coach, the man who was offering a way out of my disappointment, and I admitted, "Mike, I didn't touch the wall." John Naber would rather be disqualified than dishonor himself. And it was after this huge disappointment and after his courageous display of character that he went on to become one of the outstanding athletes of his time and subsequently, progressed even further to become a productive citizen and loving father and husband — and basically a good person. These are his thoughts on being a good person:

> *"Now, is being a person — what we call a person of character — just about obeying the rules? No, of course not. Character isn't about doing what you have a right to do (adherence to the rules) but about doing what is right. Rules and regulations exist for a reason, however. They may not necessarily make us better people, but they do provide some order to a given activity (say, competitive swimming or driving or paying taxes.) Rules offer a measure of predictability, and therefore fairness, to human interaction. Simply put, they make civilization possible. The rest is up to us."*

John Naber has offered his time and talent to help kids and athletes understand the importance of character by joining Character Counts — All Stars. These former and current champions are advocates for the values known as the six pillars of character: Trustworthiness, Respect, Responsibility, Fairness, Caring and Citizenship. It is his hope, along with all of Character Counts participants, to help build a stronger society that is built on a strong foundation. The preceding comments are my interpretation of John Naber and his character.

JOHN NABER Q & A

Do you think ethics are in decline in the U. S.?

"Yes, I do see a decline in ethics in the U.S. And, furthermore, I witness on a regular basis that unethical people are materially benefiting from their lack of ethics or character. In some cases, they are achieving "success" in spite of their unethical conduct, and in other cases it was self-ish or unethical behaviors or actions that got them their "success," or "power," or "money."

Is there some standard or guide for ethics?

"Yes, I think the Golden Rule and the Ten Commandments, especially the first two provide a standard. Most of the worlds religions have a version of the Golden Rule and similar Commandments. These have served as a guide or standard and could combine to do so — if parents, teachers and religious leaders would vigorously apply the standards and guide and model."

What is your feeling about groups like Promise Keepers and the Million Man March?

"My highest authority is not to do good, but my goal in life is to please the Creator. I have no problem with the Promise Keepers and/or the Million Man March. Their causes are good and well intentioned, but there must be follow up and continuing execution. It is important for all of us to keep our promises and mean what we say — but everyday and not just for one big event."

Do you feel that women ought to spend more time at home with their children?

"Yes, and fathers too! Children do have a harder time growing up and leading ethical lives in the absence of a mother or father. Parenting is the most important part of the process of successfully raising an ethical child."

Do you think that the growing number of single parent households has an adverse effect on the country?

"Marriage is an expression of love and commitment, and when couples split, they undermine the principal notion of love and commitment. We affect our children more by what we do than by what we say. So, divorce sends the wrong signals to children, and on top of that, they wind up feeling insecure and anxious. Children are affected by divorce in many ways, mostly negative."

Even conservatives are calling the war on drugs unwinnable. Do you agree?

"As far as I am concerned, the war on drugs is winnable in my house. It is incumbent on me as a parent and father to make sure that my wife and I win this war. I have the ability and responsibility to keep drugs away from my daughter, and it could be winnable in every household in America if parents take charge. Everything is possible if we pay the price. However, given the state of the family structure in America and the relative powerlessness of our schools and churches, we are fighting an uphill battle. There is so much "easy money" to be made with drugs that many people are tempted to the scene."

Who are your heroes?

"I like the "good guys," like the unheralded linemen on the football team — like my mother and father who were true role models who discouraged me from "show-boating" or personally calling too much attention to my exploits and successes. I like Eric Little from *Chariots of Fire*. I like Bjorn Borg, the former Scandinavian champion, who kept his pride under in victory and a stout heart in defeat."

How well do you think ethical values are being taught to children in school (or by their families?)

"Not well! Separation of church and state makes it more difficult. If you have difficulty in bringing stories of ethical behavior in front of students — and if you can't emphasize the moral in each story, then it is hard to teach ethics. Students are bombarded with unethical permissive behavior items but "pushing" the positive side has its constraints."

Several presidential candidates, including Al Gore and George W. Bush, talked more and more about their religious beliefs on the campaign trail. Is this an ephemeral phenomenon or, in your opinion, does this represent a true moral renewal in America?

"I don't think that it is too unusual to talk about character and religious beliefs right before an election — but is seems not to happen too much after the election. You don't have to be a Christian or any other religion to be ethical, but it seems to help. I use the principles and values of the Bible to guide my life; however, we have some politicians who carry around the Bible visibly and then conduct themselves in a hypocritical and immoral manner."

We have seen a number of depressing incidents in sports. Is this the result of the overcommercialization of sports? Has the emphasis on winning and on gaining lucrative TV contracts gotten out of hand?

"The commercialization of sports and the "big dollars" that are now available to sports franchises and athletes provide big temptations and big opportunities for exploitation and misbehavior. For example, to have your city selected as the site for conducting the Olympic games can affect the city's economy to the tune of nine or ten billion dollars. So when the rewards of misbehavior are so great we will encourage cheaters. When winning is the only objective, cheating then becomes an option — and in a society that overlooks this type of behavior, we have a sad situation."

We've heard a lot lately about the influence of TV, movies and video games on impressionable kids that may desensitize them to violence. Just how much influence do you think Hollywood has on children and adolescents of both sexes?

"The media is motivated by ratings and reviews. They sell papers and commercials, and they give the public what they think the public wants. For example, Dennis Rodman, the mischievous, professional basketball player, gets more "ink" than David Robinson, who is a better player and who appears to be a "straight arrow" in every sense of the word. Make no mistake about it, Hollywood and TV and video games have for the most part, a negative conditioning of our children's minds."

C H A P T E R   T W E L V E
MORAL COURAGE
DR. NANCY OLIVIERI
Professor of Pediatrics and Medicine
University of Toronto

AS I REVIEW THE NOTES FROM MY INTERVIEW with Dr. Nancy Olivieri and as I review the exhaustive array of studies, reports, symposia and news accounts on "the important case of Nancy Olivieri," I can only draw one conclusion. Nancy Olivieri has demonstrated an amazing degree of moral courage over the last eight years in taking a stand against a major Canadian drug company seeking to silence her concerns about a drug that was in clinical trials with sick children. Before I discuss the medical, legal and ethical issues of the incidents in question let me give you a little background information on Doctor Olivieri.

Nancy Olivieri was born in Hamilton Ontario Canada on June 1, 1954. She was raised in Hamilton and attended school at Loretto Academy through grade twelve. After a year at St. Mary's school she went to the University of Toronto and majored in biology. She received her Bacholor of Science Degree from the University of Toronto in 1975 and her Medical Doctorate at McMaster University in 1978. She also received postgraduate training at McMaster University of Toronto and Harvard University. Upon completion she returned to Canada in 1986 and served as a clinician and researcher in pediatric hematology at the University of Toronto. Dr. Nancy Olivieri also:

- is currently a Professor of Pediatrics and Medicine at the University of Toronto.

- has a long research career in thalassemia, sickle cell anemia, iron overload and transfusion medicine.

- is the author of numerous papers, book chapters and reviews. She is focusing her current research efforts on new therapies for patients with sickle cell disease and tha-lassemia with scientists in Canada, the United States, Europe and Asia. She is also working on the important issue of ethics of research.

- is the founding member of Doctors for Research Integrity, an organization dedicated to scientific integrity and the protection of patients in clinical trials. She was also elected to the American Society for Clinical Investigation in 1996 and is a member of many other societies, medical advisory boards, and scientific subcommittees.

- has received numerous awards including:

  - The First Annual Whistleblowers Award from the BC Freedom of Information and Privacy Association

  - The Shadeek Nader Foundation Callaway Award for Civic Courage

  - The Ordine Al Merito – awarded by the National Congress of Italian Canadians

  - Community Champion Award from the Civil Justice Foundation & American Trial Lawyers Association

– Milner Memorial Award — awarded by the Canadian Association of University Teachers.

With the above biographical background information about Dr. Olivieri in mind, let me try to explain the relevant issues in this important case. The Olivieri case revolves around the question of academic freedom in clinical research. Others might describe the issue as a classic conflict of interest between University/ Hospital Research or clinical trial versus the commercial entity that finances the research. On one hand you have an Academic Institution or a University Hospital seeking to conduct objective and safe clinical research and on the other hand you have a commercial entity seeking quick and positive clinical results so that the drug in question can be profitably marketed and sold. On the surface, the marriage between a University Hospital's financial needs and a major drug company's research needs seem workable if not compatible. But beneath the surface the rub comes when the dollars try to bias the research results or where the research entity squanders the money with inefficient, ineffective or nonconclusive clinical trials.

I will ultimately get to the ethical issue in this case but not until I lay out the medical, legal and organizational issues. Over the last seven years much has been written on the Olivieri case and I have reviewed most of it. The October 24, 2003 issue of *The New England Journal of Medicine* best summarized the case so what follows in the next few paragraphs is a simplified nontechnical version of the information from the medical journal.

The thrust from the *New England Journal of Medicine* was focused directly at the question of academic freedom in clinical research. The question that was asked again — "is the university — industrial complex out of control?" A 2001 article that appeared in *Nature* concluded that the connections between the academic world and the industrial world are sufficiently important to society at large that all concerned must review and revise their policies to assure public accountability and to assure that university academicians and hospital clinicians have the academic freedom to objectively report their findings.

The "Nancy Olivieri Case" provides a provocative case study on the question of conflicts of interest that can occur between commercial interests and university or clinicians objectively. The Olivieri case involved a long-standing dispute concerning Dr. Nancy Olivieri, a clinical researcher at the Hospital for Sick Children in Toronto and the University of Toronto and Apotex, a Canadian manufacturer of generic drugs.

Specifically, the Olivieri case involves the search for a safe and effective orally active iron chelator. The disease in question is thalassemia, a sickle sell anemia type disease, characterized by an iron overload in the blood. Although much research has been conducted on the cures for this disease only one compound with the generic name of deferiprone had entered clinical trial. Deferiprone is a bivalent iron chelator and its task is to remove excessive iron from a patient's blood. Unlike chelation therapy, which uses an intravenous process to extract extraneous minerals such as iron from the blood stream, deferirpone is an oral agent. According to *The New England Journal of Medicine* deferiprone was initially synthesized by Robert Hider and his colleagues and was briefly licensed to Ciba — Gigy but was abandoned by the company in 1993. Deferiprone was first investigated in an uncontrolled clinical trial at the Royal Free Hospital in London. Dr. Olivieri had read the results of the London trial and was sufficiently encouraged to produce enough of the drug to initiate clinical studies at the Hospital for Sick Children in Toronto. The preliminary results were encouraging so Dr. Oliveri entered into a collaboration with Apotex, a Canadian manufacturer of generic drugs. Apotex would produce the drug and Dr. Olivieri, the director of the largest hemoglobinopathy clinic in North America, would conduct a short term, uncontrolled clinical trial of deferiprone in patients with thalassemia who had iron overload. The trial was conducted under a grant from the drug company to the Hospital for Sick Children. To obtain the grant, Dr. Olivieri and the associate director for the Hospital of Sick Children Research Institute signed a confidentiality agreement and accordingly the hospital accepted the grant.

The initial results in 1995 were encouraging and it appeared that the drug deferiprone was reducing or maintaining liver iron levels in patients with thalassemia who had undergone multiple transfusions. Despite warnings that much more time would be required to determine the true efficacy of deferiprone expectations were high that the drug would prove useful in the management of the iron overload associated with long term transfusions. In the course of gathering data to answer this crucial question a nasty controversy developed among the principal participants which included Dr. Olivieri, the drug company Apotex, the Hospital for Sick Children and the University of Toronto.

A second prospective trial was initiated by Dr. Olivieri. In this trial she compared deferiprone treatment with the standard drug deferoxamine. It appears that patients who take deferoxamine regularly have a steady decline in hepatic iron levels. In Dr. Olivieri's second study deferiprone either failed to reduce hepatic iron levels or increased them to a value that was substantially above their starting points. Moreover, in some of the patient's who received deferiprone increased hepatic fibrosis occurred – and this condition was verified by four independent pathologists. In any event there appeared to be sufficient evidence to raise questions about the toxicity or efficacy of deferiprone as an iron — chelation therapy for thalassemia.

Here is how the *New England Journal of Medicine* describes Dr. Olivieri's actions after her second trial:

"When she became aware of the findings, Olivieri thought it was her responsibility to report these adverse events to her institutional review board, present them to a scientific meeting and submit them for publication. In response, Apotex stopped all clinical trials involving Olivieri and threatened to take legal action for her violations of

the confidentiality agreement that she had signed before the first trial if she released to the public the information gained in the second trail. Within a few years, two lawsuits totaling $20 million were formally lodged against her. Olivieri defied Apotex by submitting the material for publication and presenting it at a scientific meeting."

The New England Journal of Medicine went on further to describe the ethical struggle:

"The series of events that followed the disagreement between Olivieri and Apotex and the company's attempt to prevent the investigator from publishing her results are described in the CAUT report, an exhaustively researched and annotated 540 page document. The report describes years of harassment and the generation of misinformation about Olivieri, as well as providing even more worrisome accounts of a large donation that the University of Toronto was negotiating with Apotex. The report made clear that Olivieri's academic freedom to present her concerns to her peers was abridged. More important, although the Hospital for Sick Children and the University of Toronto knew that this freedom was under attack, Olivieri received harassment instead of support from the hospital and ineffectual support from the university in her legal stand against Apotex."

The Canadian Association of University Teachers' (CAUT), The Olivieri Report, The Journal of Medical Ethics, The New England Journal of Medicine, and numerous other publications have documented the legal, medical and ethical issues in considerable detail. I could write a complete chapter on the legal questions raised in the case but that is not the purpose of this book.

Suffice it to say that Dr. Nancy Oivieri, over a period of seven years faced threats, harassments, demotions, lawsuits, and public humiliation as she stood her ground in her efforts to raise concerns about the possible danger of drugs that were being clinically tested. Put yourself in the place of this medical professional whose job, career, reputation and mental health were gravely at risk because she had the moral courage to remain steadfast in their beliefs. How many of us could have withstood the pressure and the stress and remain relentless in the pursuit of what we believe is the correct thing to do?

Moral courage is the glue that helps us live our moral values in the face of pressure to rationalize or give in. Moral courage gives us the strength to do the harder right rather than the easier wrong. It is the foundation of trust and trust is the basis of trustworthiness, which facilitates all human relationships and friendships and marriages and organizational synergy and individual empowerment. Trust and truth are cornerstones of character and go a long way toward building a bridge of character, which helps us transcend from success to significance. Dr. Nancy Olivieri has talked the talk and walked the walk and has made a significant contribution to academic freedom and objective clinical trials and has proven herself to be a genuine moral exemplar.

DR. NANCY OLIVIERI Q & A

I. BACKGROUND

What is your date and place of birth?
I was born in Hamilton Ontario, Canada on June 1, 1954.

Where did you grow up?
I grew up in Hamilton Ontario, Canada.

3. Where did you go to school?
Loretto Academy, Hamilton — through the 12th grade
St. Mary's — One year of prep school

University of Toronto — Undergraduate degree in Biology
McMaster Medical School — 4 years

What were your scholastic or athletic achievements?
I was a very good student and was later an Ontario scholar.

What was your strongest subject?
Chemistry

Who were your heroes?
- Dr. Cecilioni — involved with Respiratory disease in Steel Town and protected Environmental medicine and championed the little guy.
- Ralph Nader — he in my mind is a god.
- Frances Kelsey — he wouldn't license the drug thalidomide, because of potential flipper limbs, for women who got nausea during pregnancy.

Tell me something about your parents.
- My dad was a Pediatrician. He was very outspoken, but at the same time a really great guy who retired 5 years ago.
- My mom was a Physical Therapist. She and my dad were married for 52 years. I would like to celebrate her by making a movie of their life and put it to song.

II. VALUES

Are there any values that you consistently try to uphold?
I try to uphold many values including:
- Honesty
- Not confusing accomplishments with fame

- Non-neutrality — being responsible/ accountable
- Research integrity/ Ethics
- Compassion
- Fairness

What values have played a major role in your life?

Responsibility and Integrity

Watching some drug companies experience a conflict of interest — they feel they exist only to serve their shareholders.

In your opinion, what are the three most important family values, in order importance?

1. Honesty
2. Compassion (for the underdog)
3. Sensitivity & generosity

Is it difficult to maintain your values and integrity while receiving so much adoration and attention?

No, I have tenacity and I would fight again for seven more years if I had to.

How can we improve upon the values and morals in our country?

We need to get to people early with teachable moments. Bring Civics back into school and teach people how to fight — for example in Civil Disobedience. We cannot soften the truth — the teacher of hurtful consequence.

Define your success for me and how did ethics, honor or integrity contribute to or detract from your success?

Whistle blowers face big pressure and harassment and I may have won the battle, but not I'm not sure about the war yet.

III. MORALS AND INTEGRITY

Who are the most ethical & moral people you know?

My Dad, "Gang of Four" and Ralph Nader. The gang of four are wonderful and loyal friends who supported me through most of my ordeal

Who was your best teacher? What did you learn from him/her?

I didn't really have a mentor. I admire people who deal with absolute oppression.

If you had the choice of becoming the Pope, the President or a famous entertainer, which would you choose to be?

I would choose the President so I could have an impact on the ethics of my profession and the nation at large.

Did you ever truly go "Beyond the Call of Duty?"

YES! My original action was not beyond the call of duty, but my subsequent actions were.

How do you define integrity? What does it mean to you?

Integrity is about doing the right thing in difficult or impossible circumstances.

IV. CHARACTER

Do you think a person's "character is formed at birth," or can it be changed?

It definitely can be changed!

What can you say about character and integrity as they relate to your life and your career?

If I had not stood for my beliefs, I would not have had a career or a meaningful life. The Hippocratic Oath states "Do no harm and serve your profession with uprightness and honor." I would add to that to always remember that fame is not accomplishment.

Define the word "Courage."

Courage is doing what is right when in the face of difficulty. Life is a series of 5 yard lines and we need to keep going. Ghandi said

> *"Curse the people of timid decency."*
> *"When going thru hell, keep on going."*

Real courage is when you are licked already, but you refuse to quit.

V. INNER STRENGTH AND INSPIRATION

1. What factors contributed to your success as a Doctor?

I am focused, hard working, tenacious — I won't give up, don't suffer fools easily. Toronto is the most culturally diverse city in the world and I have the opportunity to choose the people I want to work with.

2. What factors play a role in your decision making?

I am driven by my values. My life story is defined by heroism and betrayal. I look at life as who backs you and who doesn't.

3. From where have you drawn your inner strength?

I have always counted on my character. The keel was laid earlier by my Catholic faith.

VI. PERSONAL

How would you like to be remembered?

As a positive, uncompromising person.

What has given meaning to your life?

This whole story gives meaning to life. It is the story of loyalty and betrayal.

What are your strengths and weaknesses?

Strengths: Tenacity

       Sense of humor

       _____?

Weaknesses: Totally unforgiving

       Hold a grudge

       Impatient

Was there any particular or event in your life that influenced your management philosophy or style?

Seeing how people reacted to my cause and remained neutral.

What were the major turning points in your career and how do you feel about your choices now?

Let me just say that the truth prevailed in the end.

If you could express your gratitude for one thing in your life — what would it be and to whom?

My four colleagues who supported me throughout the entire endeavor.

Describe the time in your life when you experienced the most fear? How about the most courage?

- I experienced the greatest fear when I was getting fired and receiving dismissal letters from my hospital.

- I felt the most courageous when I decided I had to stay the course with my story because I knew it was the right thing to do. It was right but it was not easy.

Describe yourself, in one word, as a child.

I would describe myself as uncompromising and determined

Do you believe in fate?

I believe partially in fate.

What is your favorite novel? Magazine? Newspaper?

My favorite books are: *To Kill A Mockingbird* and *The Regeneration Trilogy*

If you had been President in 1945, would you have dropped the Atom Bomb?

I probably would have dropped the bomb.

What is the one personality trait you would change about yourself?

I would like to change the fact that I hold grudges.

Would you march on Washington for a "cause"?

I would march on Washington for a cause. When I truly believe in a cause I can give 110% to see it to fruition.

How do you fight prejudice?

I don't believe that I fight it very well.

Do you think America can still be the melting pot for all ethnic groups, races and religions?

Yes I do.

If you could have had any job in PAST HISTORY, what would it have been?

A Doctor

What job would you like to have now? Other than your own?

I would like to be a very high ranking politician so I could make a bigger difference in my world.

What major event (or events) inspire you to pursue the career you did?

My father was my inspiration. I learned that it is better to be idealistic than cynical or pragmatic. I also learned that merit will win out in the end.

Does religion play an important in your life? How?

Yes, in my past I have been aware of some kind of divinity.

If you had to choose one thing in your life you could go back and change, what would it be?

I realize that I am too trusting. I would rather be more cynical.

Was there a speech or presentation that you consider the VERY BEST you ever heard?

- Yes, March of 2001. Ralph Nader's speech.
- I also liked a speech by Stephen Lewis. He was the former ambassador to the United Nations and was fighting for a treatment of AIDS in Africa.

What was the biggest decision you had to make in your life?

The biggest decision in my life was to bring a legal challenge to the European Court concerning the approval and role of a drug that could do harm to children and their unsuspecting parents.

What is the name of the issue you think will be the most important in the next election?

Healthcare

What quote of yours would you want carved in granite or bronze? If none from your past, what thought would like to leave to posterity?

Dante's quote which states *"The hottest seat in hell is reserved for those people who in the middle of a crisis remain neutral."*

What is your best personality trait?

My best personality trait is my persistence.

CHAPTER THIRTEEN

RESPONSIBILITY

ROSE MARIE STRAUSE
Medical Secretary

This above all: to thine own self be true; and it must follow, as the night the day, thou canst not then be false to any man.
— William Shakespeare

L EST YOU THINK THAT ONLY famous people can be moral exemplars or moral role models, meet Rose Marie Strause. The fact that she is not famous has no bearing on her sense of ethics and depth of character.

Rose Marie Strause was born in Pottstown, Pennsylvania, on September 17, 1949 and grew up in Bechtelsville, a small farm town in eastern Pennsylvania. Most of her schooling was completed in the rural schools of Bechtelsville, Boyertown and Brandywine, wherein the values professed by her parents were reinforced by her teachers. Rose was raised in a Pennsylvania Dutch family who indoctrinated her with a strong work ethic and a personal sense of responsibility and respect. Her friends describe her as "a loving wife, a good mother, a good friend and a loyal employee." Those are simple pronouncements, but how great it would be if we were all viewed in a similar vein.

I met Rose Strause last year when my wife and I were having dinner with another couple at the Landis Store Hotel — a quaint, charming and remote restaurant in the farm country adjacent to Boyertown, Pennsylvania. We had a delightful meal that our waitress served in a most hospitable manner. When we finished our meal and before we got the door to depart, our waitress ran up to us and asked, "Did you mean to leave me a forty dollar tip for a ninety five dollar restaurant charge?" Apparently two twenty-dollar bills had stuck together, and I had inadvertently left a forty-dollar tip instead of twenty. As our waitress returned one of the bills, she simply commented, "I was good, but I wasn't that good." Yes, you guessed it. Our waitress was Rose Strause, who in addition to her medical secretary job, supplements her family income as a waitress. I was not surprised to discover that her full time employer, a successful plastic surgeon, and her part time employer, a successful restaurateur, both thought that she was indispensable to their business. As you might expect, Rose's husband and daughters, fellow employees and friends all have a special affection and respect for her.

As I preceded in search of her ethics and character, I discovered that Rose Strause was raised in a strict Pennsylvania Dutch home where hard work and honesty were emphasized. Rose's father was a warm, loving man who was very close to Rose. Her father unexpectedly died of a massive heart attack when Rose was ten years old, and his death had a major impact on her life. She was devastated, not only because they were very close, but also because she had never experienced the death of a loved one before. As children often do, she blamed herself for his death, because she was visiting with her grandparents when he died, and she was not with him. What she remembered about her father was his keen sense of the difference between what was right and wrong.

Rose's mother worked hard to support the family after Rose's father died. Her mother was a caring, loving mother and a great role model for her child. At the same time, however, she apparently was the strict disciplinarian of the family and left no doubts as to what was expected of her children. Four years after Rose's father died, her mother remarried. Rose was fortunate in that her stepfather was a good person who tried hard to be a good provider and role model for Rose.

ROSE MARIE STRAUSE Q & A

The following questions and answers should give you additional insight into Rose's values and character:

Are there any values that you consistently try to uphold?

"Yes. I do try to do the very best job possible in whatever I do at home or at work. I strive to be honest at all times, to be loyal to my husband and responsible to and for my children."

What values have played a major role in your life?

"Loyalty, responsibility and respect. These are the values inculcated in me by my father, mother and stepfather."

In your opinion, what are the three most important family values, in order of importance?

"Love, honesty, respect."

How can we improve upon the values and morals in our country?

"These concepts need to be taught to children at a young age by parents, grandparents and teachers. Also, I feel strongly that children must be taught the difference between right and wrong. That is why the family must play an important role in teaching children values and the difference between what is right and wrong."

Define your success for me and how did ethics, honor or integrity contribute to or detract from your success?

"My strict and value-oriented upbringing contributed immensely to my success as a mother and wife. I am very proud of my children because they are decent, honest, caring individuals. As far as my success as a medical secretary and waitress, I attribute that to the work ethic that was instilled in my by my mother. I was brought up in a Pennsylvania Dutch home where hard work and honesty were priorities."

Who was your best teacher? What did you learn from him/her?

"My parents and grandparents were my best teachers. They taught me much about the meaning of life. They encouraged me to live my values and not just talk about them."

How do you define integrity? What does it mean to you?

"Integrity means honesty and having a code of ethics and a value system and living your values."

Do you think a person's character is formed at birth, or can it be changed?

"If you are asking whether a person is born with character, I would say no. I believe character is formed by one's family, childhood experiences, teachers and other influential people."

What can you say about character and integrity as they relate to your life and career?

"I feel you need character and integrity to be truly successful in your life and in your career. We greatly underestimate the importance and power of character."

Define the word courage.

"Courage means bravery — having the guts to follow through with what you believe."

What factors most contribute to your success as a mother?

"The love I have for my children. Children are a gift from God. Patience and understanding are additional factors that are very important. Being consistent and following through with what you say are additional factors that facilitate good parenting. A little luck doesn't hurt!"

What factors play a role in your decision making?

"My gut feelings play a role in my decision making. I also try to be objective and look at all aspects of the situation before making a decision."

Can you give a specific example of a time you chose to act out a value or virtue, even though it seemed the more difficult path to follow? What was the outcome?

"Probably one of the hardest decisions my husband and I had to make was when our 16-year-old daughter became pregnant. This was devastating to our family, since she was still in high school and had plans of attending college and having a career. She wanted an abortion. We went to a gynecologist/obstetrician and had an ultrasound done to find out how far along her pregnancy had progressed. She was five months pregnant. It would have been illegal to have an abortion in the state of Pennsylvania. We would have had to travel to New York or Delaware to have the abortion. The father of her baby was dead set against the abortion. He wanted the baby and accepted full responsibility. We talked to many people in the next week including our minister and my daughter's pediatrician who said, "There has to be some sanctity of life." I knew then and there that my grandchild would be born. I knew this would be a difficult time for our family, most especially our daughter, Beth.

I knew also that together we would work through this and make our decision on what was good for the long term. My husband and I would stand by our daughter and support and love her and raise this child ourselves if we had to. We had to consider, or at least discuss, all options including abortion. I knew in our situation abortion was not the right choice. The pregnancy was not convenient, and it was not the right time but having the baby was the right decision for us.

Our daughter went back to school in September and graduated with her class. I think she earned great respect from her fellow students and teachers for her courage in carrying her pregnancy to term. Our beautiful granddaughter was born December 3, 1993. My daughter married the father of her baby three years ago, and they now have their own house a few miles away from us. She is attending college and hopes to become an elementary school teacher."

From where have you drawn your inner strength?

"I do not consider myself an extremely religious person, but I believe I would have to say that I draw my inner strength from God. It is during the critical crises in your life that your faith in God is tested and the commitment to your core values is tested."

How would you like to be remembered?

"I would like to be remembered as a loving wife, good mother, good friend and loyal employee."

What has given meaning to your life?

"My children."

What are your strengths and weaknesses?

"My strength is that I am a perfectionist. My weakness is that I am a perfectionist."

If you could express your gratitude for one thing in your life — what would it be and to whom?

"I am grateful that I am a decent person, and I thank my parents for that."

Describe the time in your life when you experienced the most fear? How about the most courage.

"Probably the most fearful time in my life was when our daughter was pregnant and we had to work out a lot of situations. A tremendous amount of courage was needed to follow through with the right decisions."

Do you believe in fate?

"Yes, I do."

What is the one personality trait you would change about yourself?

"My tendency to be jealous of people. I envy people who are confident and self-assured."

How do you fight prejudice?

"I don't believe it is possible because prejudice is something that is learned generation after generation. Prejudice is the result of a long conditioning process and it will take another strong conditioning and educational process to eliminate prejudice."

Do you think America can still be the melting pot for all ethnic groups, races and religions?

"Yes, but I think we will always have disagreements and problems because of all the differing beliefs. Diversity can be a strength, but it is not easy."

What job would you like to have now — other than your own?

"A registered nurse. I am a caring empathetic, sympathetic individual, and I believe I would be a great nurse."

Does religion play an important role in your life? How?

"Yes. I was brought up as a Lutheran going to Sunday school and church every Sunday. Even though I do not go to church every Sunday now, I try to be an honest, caring individual. I genuinely try to put into practice the beliefs of my church."

If you had to choose one thing in your life you could go back and change, what would it be?

"If it were possible, I would change the fact that my father died when I was ten years old."

What one thing in your life are you most proud of?

"My children, and especially my daughter Beth's accomplishments and her courage to accept responsibility for her high school pregnancy and for her determination to rise above her mistake and lead a good life."

If you could be in charge of one charity, what would it be? Why?

"Red Cross. I think they do wonderful things for people in need."

What was the biggest decision you had to make in your life?

"That's really hard to say, but I believe it would have to be the decision I made to not allow my daughter to have an abortion."

What is the name of the issue you think was the most important in the election?

"Character, morality and ethics."

If you had one wish granted, what would it be?

"World Peace."

Where in your life are you the least self-disciplined?
The most self-disciplined?

"Sticking to healthy diet is where I am least disciplined and being conscientious is where I am most disciplined."

If you had unlimited funds, what area of science research would you put it into?

"Cancer research."

What is your best personality trait?

"Friendliness."

What does it take to be a great leader?

"Ambition, wisdom, character and competence."

What is the nicest compliment ever given to you?

"I was told I was invaluable to my place of employment. I am the medical secretary to a successful and ethical plastic surgeon and I am gratified by any contributions I make."

What is more important to be a success in life, intelligence or social skills?

"Social skills — because human relation skills are the lubricant for a successful and happy life."

What makes you smile?

"My granddaughter."

Do you think there will truly ever be world peace?

"I am an optimist, so I would like to think so, but I don't believe there will be world peace in my lifetime."

If a book would be written about you in the future, who would you like to be the author?

"My husband."

Do you think we are put on earth to fulfill a purpose? What is yours?

"Yes. To raise my children to be decent human beings."

If a foreigner asked about your country, what would you say would be three things you are most proud of? Three things you are ashamed of?

"The things I am proud of would have to be freedom, free enterprise and freedom to practice any religion one chooses. The three things I would be ashamed of are our crime, drugs and slums."

What makes you the most angry?

"Lack of respect for one another."

What are the most important human traits?

"It is difficult to name the most important, but I would choose honesty and compassion."

Do you have to be aggressive and cutthroat to get ahead in life?

"I would say aggressive but not cutthroat."

Do you believe that good guys always finish last?

"No. I don't believe that is true."

What advice would you share with the young people of our country as they pursue their goals in life.

"Work hard and stay focused on your goals."

What is the duty of a parent?

"To raise a child to be a decent human being and a good way to start is by being a good role model."

If you could select a role model for your child, who would it be?

"I would unequivocally choose my husband, Fred, because he exemplifies all of the fine qualities I want my children to have."

From your past experiences, what are some guidelines you would like to pass onto your children?

"Stay busy and involved, work hard — no pain, no gain and aim high."

How can we help our youth bring pride and dignity back into their lives?

"By teaching them as young children to be proud of their accomplishments and to live by their values."

How can we rid our country of drug problems?

"My solution is basic. We must educate and communicate to young children over and over again about the dangers of drug use."

Are we as a nation guiding our children to be honorable, good citizens?

"As a nation, I feel we are not properly guiding our children because of the breakdown in the family and because children are left on their own too much."

How can we do better?

"People should take their marriage commitment more seriously and not choose divorce as an easy way out."

So my brief narrative and the answers to my interview questions simply define Rose Strause as a loving wife, good mother, loyal friend and conscientious employee. Those phrases that describe her may not make her famous but they surely do describe a successful person. She is a person who does her duty as she sees it; a person who connects with her values and who lives her values. I consider her a great success. Rose Strause is not a famous celebrity; she is more like the rest of us. In a way she reflects the thoughts and aspirations of the average individual and her straightforward example bids all of us to conduct our ordinary lives in an extraordinary way.

My discussion with Rose Strause reminds me that we should:

"Be ever mindful of strangers for we may be walking with angels, unaware.

CHAPTER FOURTEEN

HUMILITY

MONSIGNOR
JAMES ANDREW TRESTON
Pastor St. Ignatius Loyola Parish, Sinking Spring, PA

We make a living by what we get, we make a life by what we give.
—Winston Churchill

JAMES ANDREW TRESTON is a warm sincere human being and a compassionate friend. While he has attained status as a senior representative of the Roman Catholic Church, he remains, at heart, simply a parish priest. Ask his parishioners to describe him, and they will say he is sincere, attentive, humble, caring, honest, and dedicated. All would agree that Monsignor Treston *speaks with a straight tongue*, that he is easy to approach and communicate with, and that he has a marvelous sense of humor. My personal observation is that he wants to serve, he wants to minister to the needs of his parishioners — that he is a true shepherd to his flock.

Monsignor Treston demonstrates that earning trust is essential for successful leaders — only when leaders are trusted can they inspire others. By demonstrating humility, honesty and respect, he helps others to adopt ethical values that are essential for peaceful cooperation in human relationships. He inspires confidence and people go to extraordinary lengths to cooperate with him and support his programs. He knows his parish members by name and when he calls and asks them to serve in any church capacity they find it most difficult to refuse *the Monsignor* — this humble servant who gives so much of himself. He provides stewardship and he asks his parishioners to be involved. He asks them, according to their ability, to give their talent, time, or treasure to the church and its causes and its needs. There is nothing unusual in this — the clergy frequently makes these requests of their respective congregations. But when a sincere request comes from a respected religious leader of character and virtue it is almost impossible to refuse. From honest and ethical conduct comes trustworthiness; from trustworthiness comes respect; and when we respect each other we are fair and just. This is the key to peaceful and harmonious, productive, human relations. Put all of this together and you can see we have enormous capacity to cooperate in an effort to make significant and meaningful contributions to our society's quality of life. And this is what Monsignor Treston seeks to accomplish with the flock of parishioners at St. Ignatius Loyola Church, in the small community of Sinking Spring, Pennsylvania.

Unlike some of the other moral heroes in this book, Monsignor Treston does not employ and manage 200,00 employees or lead an entire Army Corps into battle or take his team to national championships. His is a small story, a quiet story, and a humble story; but it is a powerful story. It is also a success story about how a humble and ethical person can inspire others to live good and virtuous lives. Character does count and Monsignor Treston in his own unique way, in his own small way, is a living example of how it counts and why it counts. The point to be made here is that one person can make a difference in influencing the ethical behavior of others. One does not have to be nationally famous to make a positive contribution and to strive for the reality of a more ethical world. Monsignor Treston is an example of how his sincere efforts to do the right thing for the right reason can ultimately have a larger impact that anyone could have imagined. The moral of this story is that no one should ever underestimate the power of example or the power of character.

Let's take a close look at how one man, Monsignor James Andrew Treston, helped make a better world for many others.

James Andrew Treston was born in West Chester, Pennsylvania in the fall of 1934. All of his schooling occurred within 20 miles of his home. He went to parochial school at St. Agnes Grade School and St. Agnes High School and he attended St. Charles Borromeo Seminary in Philadelphia. In high school he was very interested in baseball and basketball but not at the expense of his studies. He applied himself diligently to his academic endeavors and graduated from his school as the valedictorian of his class. Now, let's see how he describes himself and his ideals.

JAMES ANDREW TRESTON Q & A

Are there any values that you consistently try to uphold?

"My answer to that question is quite simple and straightforward. The following values, in a way, define who I am or least what I am or what I want to be. The values that I deem most important are Trustworthiness, Compassion, Integrity, and Confidentiality.

It turns out that not only do these values define me but they also greatly facilitate my interaction with many, if not all, of my parishioners and allow me to serve their needs in an open and honest way."

What personal qualities have played a major role in your life?

"I don't know if I was born with it or whether it was developed, but my patience affords me an ability to listen. Coupled with patience and being a good listener I try to see the good in each person. I honestly believe there is innate goodness in everyone, and I try to build on the good values and good qualities in everyone. I believe in and have faith in the human condition and goodness that is part and parcel of most people. My experience has shown that if you appeal to a person's positive qualities and provide him or her the opportunity to demonstrate those qualities, most times they will not disappoint you."

In your opinion, what are the most important family values, in order of importance?

"In my opinion, Love, Faith, Hope, Trust, Confidence and Service are the most important family values. You asked a straightforward question, I hope the answer was also straightforward."

How do you remember to maintain your values when you receive so much attention and so much admiration?

"When I receive any praise I simply thank God for the opportunity to have contributed my God-given talent and temperament to someone who was in need. It is nice when someone takes the time to say thanks or to give a word of praise."

How can we improve the values and morals in our country?

"In my view, the best way is to convince parents that *their example* is the best way to teach their children anything, especially values. If values and morality are witnessed in the home our country would indeed witness an immense improvement in morality and values. If you look closely at those people who have a strong value system, you most likely will discover that somewhere an exemplary parent, teacher, coach or preacher was involved. I must reiterate that the power of example is profound."

Who was your best teacher and what did you learn from him or her?

"My mother taught me to have a loving concern for others — including all of the works of God's creation."

How do you define integrity? What does it mean to you?

"For me integrity means being true to yourself — the you that has been molded from practicing the virtues which keep one morally straight. I should also add that integrity doesn't unravel in times of pressure."

Do you think a person's character is formed at birth or can it be changed?

"I believe it can be developed through life's experiences and by the example of others."

What can you say about character and integrity as they relate to your life and career?

"As a priest, I try always to be what God wants me to be so that I can worthily serve His people. Just like all of us, I have my share of faults but I attempt, with God's grace, to rise above my faults."

What factor contributed to your success as a priest?

"The two factors that came off the top of my head are — the example of my parents and association with my home parish and school where I often met the priests and the sexton."

From where have you drawn your inner strength?

"Undoubtedly, my inner strength comes from my prayer life and from the bedside of many people I am privileged to minister to. I have heard the best and most inspiring sermons from their lips."

From where have you drawn your inspiration?

"From scripture readings and prayers offered at liturgy. Also, I have drawn strength from persons I have met over the years."

How would you like to be remembered?

"I would like to be remembered as someone who sought to alleviate the problem and needs of others — as one who was not too busy to hear and heed the cry of the poor."

What has given meaning to your life?

"My priesthood has given much meaning to my life."

What are your strengths?

"Patience and tolerance appear to be my strong suits. Perhaps I live up to the description of a Libra — *strong leader in a velvet glove.*"

Was there any particular experience or event in your life that influenced your management philosophy or style?

"I was privileged to serve as an associate pastor to Monsignor Francis J. Donnelly, Pastor at the Cathedral Parish in Allentown, Pennsylvania. He was a former Navy Chaplain and was very much respected by his peers and by his parishioners. No idea was too silly to mention to him. He listened and he allowed one the opportunity to fully explore a suggestion or topic. He taught me how to delegate, thus reaffirming in my adult life what I learned in scouting."

What were the major points in your career and how do you feel about your choices now?

"The following are what I consider to be the major points in my life:
- Attainment of Eagle Scout
- Graduation from high school
- Ordination to the priesthood
- First assignment — St. Peters, Reading, PA
- First Pastorate — St. Canicus, Mahanoy City, PA
- Conferral of Papal Honors

- Pastorate of St. Ignatius Loyola, Sinking Spring, PA
- Construction of new St. Ignatius Loyola Education Center
- Renovation of St. Ignatius Loyola Church

To become a priest was my choice. My assignments were made by my Bishop. I have never regretted any of these appointments. In fact each one has given me an opportunity to grow."

If you could express your gratitude for one thing in your life — for what would it be and to whom?

"To God for the gift of my priesthood."

Do you believe in fate?

"No, I believe God has a specific plan for all; we don't know every detail. *O felix culpa* (O happy fault) is a saying attributed to St. Andrew, the Apostle. This saying has become part of my life."

If you had been President in 1945, would you have dropped the Atom Bomb?

"This is a difficult question. I think it is not easy to project your mind back into the war time environment and certainly the 1945 situation was so much different than the 2000 situation. But if I were forced to give you an answer, I would say that in my 1945 mind set I agreed with President Truman's decision to drop the atom bomb. In my 2000 mind set I would probably say no — don't drop the atom bomb."

In general, what do you think molded you into the person you are today?

"The good example of my parents, my teachers, my scoutmaster, my coaches and my fellow priests."

Would you march on Washington for a cause?

"Yes, to uphold human rights in accord with God's Laws."

What is your opinion about present day music and film?

"Some music today is not good for impressionable minds. Often the lyrics express thoughts that undermine authority and sometimes express fatalistic notions. Present day films and TV demonstrate too much violence and sex. I don't think we fully understand the extent of the influence that music, films and TV have on young minds. Music, film and TV if used and programmed properly could have an immensely positive effect and influence on young people. However in 2000 I see more negatives than positives."

How important is a sense of humor?

"A sense of humor is very important. It helps one to see the silver lining in the cloud; it helps bring a smile to a face that needs it and it also allows one not to take oneself too seriously."

How do you fight prejudice?

"I try my hardest to instruct others that we are all God's children. I also will engage as much as possible in activities which are open to all. This is a very important issue and we all need to work hard and pray hard to solve this problem."

Tell me a little bit about your ethnic background. Who are you most like?

"My father was Irish. I have his sense of humor and his enjoyment of life. My mother was German. I have her sincerity, compassion and industry."

What one thing in your life are you most proud of?

"My patience and my ability to enjoy all of God's creations. Everyday is a new learning experience for me."

Did you ever have an adverse experience that taught you a great lesson?

"Yes, when I was about 24 years old my father, mother and I were involved in a serious head-on auto collision on Christmas Eve while we were on our way to the Cathedral in Philadelphia. Fortunately, no one died but all suffered severe injuries. After weeks of treatment we were approached by lawyers who were urging us to sue the young driver of the other vehicle who had been charged with seven technical violations of the law. However, my father asked only that our medical costs be covered. He said the young man erred and he was not going to exploit him on the situation. My father taught me a lesson for life."

What is your idea of a perfect day?

"My idea of a perfect day is to rise early, say an early Mass in the church, plan my day and then execute and complete my daily plan, engage in some moderate exercise and finally at least one meal with all present to engage in good conversation. For me the perfect finish of a good day is to watch a good baseball game — preferably one the Philadelphia Phillies win."

What is the issue you think was the most important in the 2000 election?

"Abortion vs. the right to life is the most important issue in my mind. Others might want to focus on balancing the budget and prioritizing what should be done with any budget surpluses if they materialize."

If you could be recognized for one thing in your life, what would it be?

"That I constantly reminded people that God loves them when they thought no one cared. Everyone needs hope and hope is available to all through God's love and mercy."

What makes your smile?

"Good jokes and children with their straightforward sincerity."

Do you think there will truly ever be world peace?

"Not in our lifetime."

Do you think we are put on earth to fulfill a purpose? What is yours?

"I won't speak for others, but I truly believe my purpose on Earth is to know, love and serve God in this world by serving the needs of His people — and in the end to be with God in heaven."

If a foreigner asked about your country what would you identify as the three things you are most proud of? The three things you are ashamed of?

"In our American way of life I am most proud of the freedom, opportunity and multi-culturism, and most ashamed and disappointed with the crime, with our inability to fully educate all of our citizens, and with the secularism I see in our society."

Do you have to be aggressive and cutthroat to get ahead in life?

"No, as St. Francis de Sales once said, *'More flies are caught with one drop of honey than with a barrel of vinegar'*."

What happened to family meals? Did your family eat dinner together? Is this important?

"We have allowed outside schedules to interfere with family meals. Yes, we did have family dinner together as I was growing up. I try to have at least one meal each day in the rectory with my fellow priests and I think it is very important. I also believe that families can benefit greatly by having meals together. Many teachable moments present themselves at the dinner table thus enabling parents to communicate their core values to their children and more importantly help children connect with their values."

What advice would you share with the young people of our country as they pursue their goals in life?

"I strongly advocate a sense of patriotism and I ask young people to try to understand why this country was founded, to be grateful for the freedom and opportunity this country offers, and to be more tolerant of its flaws."

What is the duty of a parent?

"To teach, to teach and to teach — to communicate, to illustrate, to exemplify and to provide roots and ultimately to provide wings."

How can we rid our country of drug problems?

"I wish I had the answer. But I do know that all of the education that is being offered on this subject will be to no avail, as long as the greed of non-users including those in upper levels of government, is not abated."

CHAPTER FIFTEEN

THE MORAL ORGANIZATION
Commitment to the Development of Character

WEST POINT — THE INSTITUTION

Duty —Honor —Country. The code which those words perpetuate embraces the highest moral law and will stand the test of any ethics or philosophies ever promulgated for the uplift of mankind.
— ***General Douglas MacArthur***

I N CHAPTER TWO I briefly described some representative codes of ethics. There are many institutions, organizations, and corporations that have effectively adopted codes of ethics and guides to behavior. Some of the better known include: the Boy Scouts and Girl Scouts of America, Rotary International, the

McDonnell-Douglas Corporation, the Smucker Company, the Minnesota Center for Corporate Responsibility, and the Institute for Global Ethics. Each of these have promulgated codes of ethics that have collectively influenced and guided thousands if not millions of people. In their own special way the Ten Commandments, as recorded in the Bible, and the Golden Rule also represent ethical principles. In Appendix A, I present in considerable detail another representative code of ethics.

In this section I want to focus on motivational commitment to an ethical standard and in this case the United States Military Academy at West Point is the standard I chose. The West Point Honor Code simply states: **A Cadet Will Not Lie, Cheat, Steal or Tolerate Those Who Do.** When compared to other honor codes or codes of ethics, the Cadet Honor Code is brief and to the point but, in a way, its brevity enhances its effectiveness. To get a complete understanding of the West Point Honor Code one needs to be aware of the mission of the U.S. Military Academy. The official mission of West Point:

> *To educate, train and inspire the corps of cadets so that each gradu-ate is a commissioned **leader of character** committed to the values of **Duty, Honor, Country;** professional growth throughout a career as an officer in the United States Army; and a lifetime of **selfless serv-ice** to the nation.*

The operative goal in this mission statement is *"leader of character."* Our nation has historically entrusted its sons and daughters to its com-missioned officers in matters of life and death and in military struggles that have involved the vital interests of our nation. I don't want to over-dramatize my case but, the welfare of our soldiers (our children) depends on the character and competence of the leaders who are mak-ing these crucial decisions. So, it is of paramount importance that our country's military leaders be men and women of character; leaders who are honest, fair, and who revere and safeguard the sanctity of life. The late Congresswoman Barbara Jordan may have said it best when she addressed the Corps of Cadets:

"If you do not develop honor, if you do not embrace the finest sense of justice that the human mind can frame, you will not be worthy of the confidence West Point and your country will place in you."

As a graduate of the Military Academy, I appreciate the fine education I received there. I am even more appreciative of the concepts of *Duty, Honor, and Country* that I initially embraced during my four years at West Point. The United States Military Academy has been described by many as the standard bearer for the American professional soldier and the values of the Armed Forces of the United States. This is so because leaders of character, committed to a lifetime of selfless service to the nation, must embrace values that inspire trust, respect, and courage. So, West Point as an institution represents the standard by which all Army officers are judged, regardless of the origin of their commissions. The military academy educates, trains, and inspires the corps of cadets to fully embrace the professional military ethic of the Army and values that are important to the society the Army defends. The seven values of *integrity, honor, duty, respect, loyalty, courage, and service* are the core values that the U. S. Army promulgates and considers of sufficient importance so as to highlight them in every officer efficiency report.

How can we define or describe these values?

ARMY VALUES ...
THE MORAL COMPASS

The values are the foundation of and the guideposts for character development.

Integrity: Making decisions and taking action based on our country's shared values.

Honor: Being honest, fair and just, and demonstrating due regard for the property of others.

Respect: Recognizing the infinite worth and dignity of human life — displaying compassion, consideration, and civility.

Duty: Accepting responsibility for one's actions and doing all that should be done as well as it can be done.

Loyalty: Being faithful, displaying fealty, devotion, and commitment (for the soldier loyalty means allegiance to the Constitution of the United State of America).

Service: Contribution on behalf of others; dedication to the goals of a group (unit, team, society, etc.), rendering assistance and support without regard for personal profit or gain.

Courage: Bravery, valor, fortitude in spite of risk, fear, doubt — acting in accordance with one's beliefs in the presence of adversity, danger and criticism.

What does all of this discussion about the mission of West Point and its commitment mean to the values of the U. S. Army? The answer to this question is a one word answer — *everything.* Values are the absolute cornerstones for developing leaders of character who serve the common defense of the Nation. Perhaps a better way to answer the question is to simply state the mission is the *what* the Academy must do and the Honor Code and its associated values are the *how.* To call on others to dedicate their lives to the defense of their country requires the ultimate in trust and confidence. Trust is derived from the Army values and it must be earned. Mutual trust between leaders and followers creates the conditions for mission accomplishment. This ultimate synergistic victory is extraordinarily important in the profession of arms because in war there is no substitute for victory.

This leads me to a discussion of the West Point Honor Code. The code represents the minimum standard of behavior that all cadets are expected to live by and in essence have contracted to live by. However, one must understand that cadets are appointed from all walks of life and every socio-economic background. There are high admissions standards, but an intelligent, healthy, high school graduate is not necessarily ethical. So, in many ways West Point faces its biggest challenge in developing ethical fitness concurrent with providing intellectual, military and physical development.

Within this challenging context, the Cadet Honor Code fosters a commitment to ethical behavior, essential to leaders of character for the nation. Specifically, by living according to the Honor Code as specified in USCC Pamphlet 632-1 it is intended that cadets:

1. *learn and practice the essential leader responsibility of establishing a healthy ethical climate within a unit.*

2. *develop an understanding of the importance of integrity as an essential aspect of leadership.*

3. *develop a strong desire to maintain an honorable lifestyle manifest in the spirit of the code.*

4. *achieve the level of commitment to honorable conduct necessary to prepare them for greater challenges to their integrity throughout a lifetime of service to the nation.*

The code is a simple standard to live by. It demands strict compliance. In order for the code, the minimum standard, to fulfill its role in the development of cadets, each cadet must be committed to living by this standard.

The Cadet Honor Code describes the minimum professional standard for ethical behavior, not an abstract ideal. Easy to understand, it is the expected baseline behavior for all who have joined the professional corps of cadets.

But, if the Honor Code is only a minimum standard, what is the ideal?

That ideal is the "Spirit of the Code," an affirmation of the way of life that marks true leaders of character. The Spirit of the Code goes beyond the mere external adherences to rules. Rather, it is an expression of integrity and virtue springing from deep within and manifested in the actions of the honorable man or woman. Persons who accept the Spirit of the Code think of the Honor Code as a set of broad and fundamental principles, not a list of prohibitions. In deciding to take any action, they ask if it is the right thing to do.

It is the Spirit of the Code that gives rise to specific positive tenets:

1. *The Spirit of the Code embraces truthfulness in all its aspects. The Honor Code prohibits lying.*

2. *The Spirit of the Code calls for complete fairness in human relations. The Honor Code prohibits cheating.*

3. *The Spirit of the Code requires respect for the property of others. The Honor Code prohibits stealing.*

4. *The Spirit of the Code demands a professional commitment to upholding the ethical standards which are the foundations of the profession of arms. The Honor Code prohibits toleration of violations.*

A cadet is truthful, fair, respectful of other's property and committed to maintaining ethical standards. This Spirit applies not only in the West Point environment but throughout the Army and the Armed Forces.

The development of each cadet, as a leader of character, is marked by strict adherence to the minimum standards of the Code, combined with continuous progress, maturation, and wisdom gained from education, training, and experience.

The non-toleration tenet in the Cadet Honor Code is perhaps its most difficult aspect for cadets to embrace. Perhaps it is difficult because in our society we are conditioned to believe that one who reports violators is a "stool pigeon," a "squealer," or a "whistle-blower." Also, some cadets are confused by misplaced loyalty to friends vs. loyalty to their professional ethics, duties, and responsibilities. It is crucial to understand that West Point is intent upon developing professional ethics and morals. Thus, when cadets join the profession of arms they must accept and live by the professional ethic. Anyone who cannot or will not, may not be a member of the profession. It is this strict adherence to the professional military ethic that has created the special bond of trust and confidence between the American society and the American armed forces. However, West Point has a unique set of conditions that facilitate the implementation of an enduring code of ethics. There is a mission statement that calls for leaders of character; there are nearly 200 years of tradition wherein an officer's word is his bond; there is a military organization with unity of purposes; there is stewardship of the Honor Code by cadets and for cadets; and there is a professional team of military and civilian staff and faculty who understand both the letter and spirit of the Honor Code. There is also an enormous system for external oversight that includes Congress, the Department of Defense, Department of the Army and the American people, all of whom see West Point as a national treasure and all of whom expect and demand that the institution reflect the highest standards and ideals of America, her ethos, and her laws.

Two very important functions in assuring the commitment to implementation, maintenance, and enforcement of an effective honor code or code of ethics are education and enforcement.

At West Point, the Cadet Honor Committee has the responsibility to supervise and administer the Honor System. The committee is comprised of one senior cadet and one junior class cadet from each company. Honor "Reps" are elected by their classmates. Additionally, there is a chairperson, an executive officer, four vice-chairpersons, a secretary and four regimental honor representatives. Some of the duties of the individual reps of the Cadet Honor Committee include:

1. *advising cadets in honor matters*

2. *educating their companies concerning the spirit as well as the letter of the Honor Code*

3. *conducting investigation of alleged honor violations*

4. *serving as liaison between the company tactical officer and the Cadet Honor Committee*

5. *serving on an Honor Board, when required*

We recognize West Point's institutional commitment to professional ethics by observing that for nearly 200 years West Point has been producing leaders of character.

That is not to suggest that the West Point System is perfect and that every graduate of West Point is a "perfect" example of moral fitness. However, I do mean to suggest that West Point is a very effective institution for developing officers who are leaders of character.

I singled out West Point because I lived there as a cadet and I know it well; and the concept of honor I learned there has served me well in all my endeavors. But, there are other schools, colleges, corporations, and organizations that have developed and promulgated effective codes of ethics and honor systems.

It is encouraging to note that the number of institutions committed to codes of ethics is increasing — this is good news.

S E C T I O N   I I I

THE ETHICS SOLUTION

SHOW ME THE WAY
The Development of Character

"The shortest and surest way to live with honor in the world is to be in reality what we would appear to be. All human virtues increase and strengthen themselves by the practice and experience of them."

—Socrates

I LIKE TO PARAPHRASE SOCRATES with the following — if we only could be what we pretend to be, what a great world it would be. Generally, we agree on what is right and what is wrong; and we widely accept the values and qualities, which define a person of character. We understand that moral qualities such as honesty, respect, responsibility, justice, and compassion are among the bedrock values that define a person of character. Yet, there is a major disconnect between the values we profess and the behavior we exhibit — that is, we tend to "talk the talk" but not "walk the walk".

In many ways, our lives are "blessed" with the opportunities and things that are plentiful in our society. However, these same material attractions can also be a "curse". We are faced each day with temptations for power, wealth, prestige, and promiscuity (to name only a few of the prevalent vices). Our media expose us to an unbelievable amount of violence and perfidy. If we are not careful, the messages will influence us in a direction not in our best interests.

Clearly, being a truly ethical person is no simple task. This worthy and essential goal requires serious concentration and day-to-day commitment. The challenge is compounded when children experience little supervision at home. It is complicated by diminished ethical education in our schools. It is compounded by the toleration of dishonest practices at our places of work. Most unfortunately, we seem to be embracing the misperception that "tolerance of human differences" in race, culture, ethnicity, religion, or political persuasion suggests that we should be tolerant of unethical practices, as well. In light of these observations, it is an extremely difficult challenge to be a person of character.

So what do we do about the challenge? We have to address it – and the purpose of this chapter is to suggest a way. I am offering you three approaches, none of which are original with me. These are concepts I have adopted over the years. I will start with the simplest methodology and progress to the most complete approach. I call these methods: ***The Psychologist's Approach, The Ben Franklin Method, and The West Point Model.***

THE PSYCHOLOGIST'S APPROACH

Psychologists tell us that we tend to become the kind of person who occupies our thoughts and aspirations. Accordingly, athletic coaches encourage their athletes to visualize performance at optimum levels and to embrace images of the way they want to compete. This concept applies to character development just as it effects athletic performance. That does not mean it is "easy". Nonetheless, we must have "vision" of the kind of person we want to be. To get there, we may have to break old habits and make some important changes in our life-style. Such change requires commitment and courage. This approach is best explained by the following:

WATCH YOUR THOUGHTS
THEY BECOME YOUR WORDS

WATCH YOU WORDS
THEY BECOME YOUR ACTIONS

WATCH YOUR ACTIONS
THEY BECOME YOUR HABITS

WATCH YOUR HABITS
BECAUSE THEY BECOME YOUR CHARACTER

WATCH YOUR CHARACTER
BECAUSE IT BECOMES YOUR DESTINY

THE BEN FRANKLIN APPROACH

In his autobiography, Ben Franklin described his program for self-improvement. From his readings and experience, he developed a list of virtues that would help him achieve "moral perfection." Benjamin Franklin understood the need for a methodology that would assist him to focus, to be committed, and to be consistent. Rather than try to paraphrase Ben Franklin's thoughts, let me extract from his autobiography:

> *"It was about this time I conceived the bold and arduous project of arriving at moral perfection. I wished to live without committing any fault at any time; I would conquer all that either natural inclination, custom, or company might lead me into. As I knew, or thought I knew, what was right and wrong, I did not see why I might not always do the one and avoid the other. But I soon found I had undertaken a task of more difficulty than I had imagined. While my care was employed in guarding against one fault, I was often surprised by another; habit took the advantage of inattention; incli-*

nation was sometimes too strong for reason. I concluded, at length, that the mere speculative conviction that it was our interest to be completely virtuous, was not sufficient to prevent our slipping; and that the contrary habits must be broken, and good ones acquired and established, before we can have any dependence on a steady, uniform rectitude of conduct. For this purpose I therefore contrived the following method.

In the various enumerations of the moral virtues I had met with in my reading, I found the catalogue more or less numerous, as different writers included more or fewer ideas under the same name. Temperance, for example, was by some confined to eating and drinking, while by others it was extended to mean the moderating every other pleasure, appetite, inclination, or passion, bodily or mental, even to our avarice and ambition. I proposed to myself, for the sake of clearness, to use rather more names, with fewer ideas annexed to each, than a few names with more ideas; and I included under thirteen names of virtues all that at that time occurred to me as necessary or desirable, and annexed to each a short precept, which fully expressed the extent I gave to its meaning.

These names of virtues, with their precepts, were:

1. ***Temperance.*** *Eat not to dullness; drink not to elevation.*

2. ***Silence.*** *Speak not but what may benefit others or yourself; avoid trifling conversation.*

3. ***Order.*** *Let all your things have their places; let each part of your business have its time.*

4. ***Resolution.*** *Resolve to perform what you ought; perform without fail what you resolve.*

5. ***Frugality.*** *Make no expense but to do good to others or yourself; i.e., waste nothing.*

6. **Industry.** *Lose no time; be always employed in something useful; cut off all unnecessary actions.*

7. **Sincerity.** *Use no hurtful deceit; think innocently and justly, and, if you speak, speak accordingly.*

8. **Justice.** *Wrong none by doing injuries, or omitting the benefits that are your duty.*

9. **Moderation.** *Avoid extremes; forbear resenting injuries so much as you think they deserve.*

10. **Cleanliness.** *Tolerate no uncleanliness in body, clothes, or habitation.*

11. **Tranquility.** *Be not disturbed at trifles, or at accidents common or unavoidable.*

12. **Chastity.** *Rarely use venery but for health or offspring, never to dullness, weakness, or the injury of your own or another's peace or reputation.*

13. **Humility.** *Imitate Jesus and Socrates.*

My intention being to acquire the habitude of all these virtues, I judged it would be well not to distract my attention by attempting the whole at once, but to fix it on one of them at a time; and, when I should be master of that, then to proceed to another, and so on, till I should have gone thro' the thirteen; and, as the previous acquisition of some might facilitate the acquisition of certain others, I arranged them with that view, as they stand above. Temperance first, as it tends to procure that coolness and clearness of head, which is so necessary where constant vigilance was to be kept up, and guard maintained against the unremitting attraction of ancient habits, and the force of perpetual temptations. This being acquired and established, Silence would be more easy; and my desire being to gain knowledge at the same time that I improved in virtue, and considering that in conversation it was obtained rather by the use of the ears than of the tongue, and therefore wishing to break a habit I was getting into of prattling, punning, and joking, which only made me acceptable to trifling company, I gave Silence the second place. This and the next, Order, I expected would allow me more time for attending to my project and my studies. Resolution, once become habitual, would keep me firm in my endeavors to obtain all the subsequent virtues; Frugality and Industry freeing me from my remaining debt, and producing affluence and independence, would make more easy the practice of Sincerity and Justice, etc., etc. Conceiving then, that, agreeably to the advice of Pythagoras in his Golden Verses, daily examination would be necessary, I contrived the following method for conducting that examination.

I made a little book [see figure 1], in which I allotted a page for each of the virtues. I ruled each page with red ink, so as to have seven columns, one for each day of the week, marking each column with a letter for the day. I crossed these columns with thirteen red lines, marking the beginning of each line with the first letter of one of the virtues, on which line, and in its proper column, I might mark, by a little black spot, every fault I found upon examination to have been committed respecting that virtue upon that day.

I determined to give a week's strict attention to each of the virtues successively. Thus, in the first week, my great guard was to avoid even the least offence against Temperance, leaving the other virtues to their ordinary chance, only marking every evening the faults of the day. Thus, if in the first week I could keep my first line, marked T, clear of spots, I supposed the habit of that virtue so much strengthened and its opposite weakened, that I might venture extending my attention to include the next, and for the following week keep both lines clear of spots. Proceeding thus to the last, I could go through a

FIGURE 1.

TEMPERANCE

EAT NOT TO DULLNESS
DRINK NOT TO ELEVATION.

	Su	M	T	W	Th	F	Sa
T.							
S.	*	*		*		*	
O.	**	*	*		*	*	
R.			*			*	
F.	*				*		
I.			*				
S.							
J.							
M.							
C.							
T.							
C.							
H.							

course complete in thirteen weeks, and four courses in a year. And like him who, having a garden to weed, does not attempt to eradicate all the bad herbs at once, which would exceed his reach and his strength, but works on one of the beds at a time, and, having accomplished the first, proceeds to a second, so I should have, I hoped, the encouraging pleasure of seeing on my pages the progress I made in virtue, by clearing successively my lines of their spots, till in the end, by a number of courses, I should be happy in viewing a clean book, after a thirteen weeks' daily examination."

This is an interesting and workable approach that will help us adopt our personal vision of the kind of person we want to be. Each of us must to tailor the list of virtues or values in order to reflect those that are most important. If we will practice being who we want to be, we enhance our probability of success. By assessing our progress, using a table like Ben Franklin's we will be pleased to see the progress we are making.

THE WEST POINT MODEL

In Chapter 15, I presented the United States Military Academy, at West Point, as an institutional exemplar. In this chapter, I want to carry that example a step further by describing the West Point concept for developing competence and character. I am sure that there are other good institutional examples. However, my personal experience with West Point encourages me to describe and share its approach. My colleague and friend Colonel (Retired) Patrick Toffler spent a number of years at West Point as the Director of Policy, Planning, and Analysis. He was closely involved with the design, description, and assessment of the **Cadet Leader Development System**, whose sole purpose is to develop Commissioned Leaders of Character for our Army and the nation. I sincerely thank Colonel Toffler for his meaningful contribution to this chapter.

THE DEVELOPMENT OF CHARACTER
"Show Me the Way"

The objective evidence is very compelling; ethics are essential for successful, enduring relationships on every level (personal and professional). Commerce, industry, government, friendships, and families thrive and prosper on the basis of *Trust*. Everyone in every organization, group, or family wants the people around them to be trustworthy. We all want to be lead by people of character; and all leaders want their subordinates to be trustworthy, as well. This is not to gainsay competence. Clearly, character without competence is not acceptable. No one will retain an ethical lawyer who cannot make a proper argument. However, competence without character is very dangerous. At every level of human development (young children through senior citizens) and at every level of organization (schools, loading docks, and boardrooms — not to mention all aspects of government, both national and international), we see very competent people behaving badly. History and today's news are replete with accounts of able people wrecking enormous harm through perfidy; their actions threaten our well being, indeed our very lives.

Character, like competence, is not bestowed. Character and competence must be developed — continuously. Yet, institutions, organizations, groups, and families sometimes neglect character development, perhaps taking it for granted. Even when character is explicitly addressed, the focus is not on *development*, but on *motivation*. Over the years, we have all listened to many speeches, lectures, and sermons discussing ethics, morals, and character. The intent is usually to inspire or motivate us to want to be people of integrity — people who can be trusted. In sharp contrast, if a speaker is talking about a competency (investing, marketing, advertising, etc) the focus is on *"How"* to do it — not on *"Why"* it should be done.

Initially, *"To be or not to be?"* is the apt question. However, even when we agree "to be", we have only answered the question: "What?"

This is an essential first step. Motivation is imperative to the development of both **Character & Competence**. If we do not care about something, we will not invest much time and energy into getting it done. However, motivation alone is insufficient. For example, one can desire to be in good physical condition or to be a successful professional in any endeavor, but without knowledge and proper effort, the goal will never be realized. Similarly, character, no matter how much we may want it, will not accrue unless we know how to achieve it — and then we must work on it, always. This is a most important commitment. *Our character is our destiny*, it is our true nature (including our values, virtues, morals, & dreams), and it is manifest in our decision-making and actions. We must learn how to develop character in others and ourselves.

A CASE-STUDY

As the United States Military Academy was preparing for it middecennial accreditation, scheduled for 1994-1995, it was challenged by the General Accounting Office (GAO) to demonstrate how it was accomplishing the Mission to develop *Leaders of Character*. This question was posed as part of a GAO Review of Academy activities commissioned by then Senator Sam Nunn (D-Georgia, Chairman of the Senate Armed Service Committee). In testimony before his committee, the Superintendent, Lieutenant General Howard D. Graves had stated that *Character Development* was the Academy's number one priority. While such a commitment was well received by the members of the Committee, it was logical for them to ask what the Academy was doing to develop character in Cadets.

In order to answer the question specifically and objectively, the Academy provided the GAO with a full description of its *Cadet Leader Development System (CLDS)*. This system provided for coordinated, integrated, sequential, and progressive activities within the academic, military, and physical programs. Each Program was designed to support intellectual, military, physical, social, and moral-ethical development for each Cadet. In effect, the entire four-year *West Point Experience* was created to provide the Army with Commissioned Officers who would demonstrate both competence and character, throughout a lifetime of service to the Nation.

Several important points were emphasized during the GAO Review. *First, competence and character are and must be developed simultaneously — in concert and in harmony. Second, the process by which one develops competence is essentially the same process by which one develops character. Finally, simultaneous pursuit of character and competence is a life-long process, it requires our continuous attention, or we risk losing both.*

THE PROCESS

The development of both competence and character requires four essential elements: **knowledge, adherence, belief, and leadership.** They are not "ordered" (they do not occur in predetermined sequence). They are not "structured" (they do not hold a predetermined priority). Each can occur at the same time, in varying degrees. Most importantly, they are all necessary for both competence and character to develop. The method can be well illustrated with a simple example.

On the day that New Cadets report to USMA (R-day) they are introduced to the Cadet Honor Code (Cadets will not lie, cheat, steal, or tolerate those who do.). They are expected to adhere to the tenants of the Code from the moment they take the Oath to "...support the Constitution of the United States...." By habitually practicing the art of being honest, respecting the rules of fair play, demonstrating due regard for the property of others, and expecting that others act in the same manner, it is hoped that Cadets will come to believe that such habits are truly proper and in everyone's best interests. Given such belief, Cadets should be willing and able to profess their Code and to lead others in adopting and incorporating its tenants within their own lives. Thus, knowledge, adherence, belief, and leadership develop character (and competence).

Knowledge derives from instruction and study. The teacher and the student work together (as teammates) to help each realize their potential. **Adherence** means putting what has been studied and taught into practice. It is through practice that the degree of understanding and competence is revealed. The student must receive feedback and assessment in order to grow and improve. The teacher must assess in order to understand the degree to which the instruction and practice have been effective. Firm **belief** in and the confidence to **profess** the value of the instruction and practice will accrue as the student and teacher see positive results from their efforts. Ultimately, the student becomes a teacher and exercises **leadership**, helping others to develop character.

Thus, just as one learns and develops competence, one develops character.

Knowledge	<-------->	**Instruction/Study**
Adherence	<-------->	**Practice**
Belief	<-------->	**Feedback/Assessment**
Leadership	<-------->	**Experience**

The mission of the United States Military Academy is to educate, train, and inspire the Corps of Cadets so that each graduate is a commissioned *leader of character* committed to the values of Duty, Honor, Country; professional growth throughout a career as an officer in the United States Army; and a lifetime of selfless service to the Nation.

KNOWLEDGE

How do we come to **Know** anything? Well, there are two ways. One is by *discovery* the other is by *revelation*. The former is a complex endeavor (e.g., Scientific Method). Things that we come to know by discovery should be verifiable. We come to believe that discovered facts are true because we see evidence supporting our hypothesis, method, or opinion. Experience supports our view and we tend to follow certain procedures or practices because we see that "they work!"

In the case of things that are known by revelation, the issue of *Faith* comes into play. That is, what we believe (or know) cannot be verified by objective methods. We believe something to be true even though we cannot prove it. Again, however, we believe it to be true because we see that it is works for us and helps us achieve.

Regardless of how we get our knowledge, where does it come from? Knowledge comes from study (reading, watching, listening), experimentation (giving it a try, assessing results, making adjustments), and instruction (taking advice, following example, accepting honest critique).

The key to growing in wisdom is to recognize that what may be known is infinite, while what we can know is finite. To make matters even more daunting, as one sage noted wisely: "It ain't so much that there are things we don't know, it's that so much of what we know ain't so." This acceptance of our limitations and the possibility that our opinions may be in error is the essence of humility (a cardinal virtue) and the beginning of wisdom (the prayer of Solomon).

ADHERENCE

Simply put, we must practice what we know or believe to be right, true, proper, etc. Being true to ourselves and our understanding of truth is the essence of integrity (a cardinal value). To know or believe something to be true or correct while behaving in a contrary manner is hypocrisy (a cardinal vice). Sometimes, we adhere out of fear of adverse consequences. Such fear may promote a behavior that is consistent with desired societal norms, standards, rules, or law — but, not for the essentially right reason. Inevitably, behavior that is motivated by fear may change completely when or if the fear factor is removed. Rather, behavior that is self-motivated, based on the principle of "doing what is right for its own sake" is enduring and meaningful. Such principle-based behavior is often difficult to achieve and to sustain. It takes courage (a cardinal value) and it often needs help. This suggests the importance of community and service.

BELIEF

Beliefs are strongly held opinions. They are often controversial and contentious. Political, religious, scientific, and economic beliefs are the source of many arguments, even wars. If we want someone, including ourselves, to believe that something is true then we have to do something to influence the action. If it is important, we cannot just hope for the desired outcome. For example:

> *"I have come to believe in the truth of the Golden Rule. I would like my children to believe in it, as well. So, I have to let them know what the rule says and model it in my actions. I have to foster their adherence to the rule, encouraging and rewarding rule-consistent behavior and discouraging deviations."*

Hopefully, they will come to believe in the value of the rule, too. They will, if they see that it works in their lives.

LEADERSHIP

It is often noted that we really learn something when we have to teach someone else. So, if we want to learn, we have to lead. This is not just a matter of winning a leadership position. It is in fact simply taking advantage of daily opportunity. All of us are leaders — those who influence others. Similarly, we are always followers — those who are influenced by others. We are both leaders and followers at the same time. In the process of helping others to develop competence and character, we must give them leadership opportunity and encourage them to take advance of the opportunity. In the process of continuously developing ourselves, we must exercise leadership, growing and learning from our experiences.

GOOD VS. EVIL

The aphorism: "Beauty is in the eye of the beholder", is open to debate. Research suggests that we humans are in general agreement on what is beautiful and what is not. That does not mean that we all like the same things. It does mean that what is beautiful is not completely arbitrary; something within us draws us to appreciate a colorful sunset while we recoil from the image of a malodorous landfill.

In matters of what is "Good" there is a similar commonality among humans. We tend to believe in a "natural moral law"; and it has been discovered. The Greek philosophers (Socrates, Aristotle, Plato), the Talmud, the New Testament, the Koran, and the doctrinal guidance of essentially all religions and cultures teach the Golden Rule and extol justice, mercy, respect, and similar values. Unfortunately, we do not always practice what we believe to be ethical and moral.

It is interesting to note that the process by which we develop character and strive to improve (i.e., to be better at being good) is the same regardless of how one defines "good." It is disturbing and puzzling to read about an 18-year-old girl, who dresses in religious, ethic clothes in order to conceal explosives so that she can board a bus and kill or maim dozens while committing suicide. Did she think she was doing evil? If so, why did she do it? Did she think she was doing good? If so, why did she think so? Unless, we classify her as insane, we have to discount the possibility that she thought she was doing wrong. That leaves us with trying to understand how she came to believe that an act that is so clearly evil (in our eyes) could make her a hero and a martyr in the eyes of her God. Interestingly, the vast majority of humanity is monotheistic, so regardless of what name we use, we must believe in the same God.

The people who need and want others to be willing to sacrifice their lives for an "evil" cause know that such motivation must be instilled. They do not take it for granted, they work at it. On June 25, 2000, long before the World Trade Center was attacked and destroyed (September 11, 2001) Jeffrey Goldberg published: "Inside Jihad University, The Education of a Holy Warrior" (*New York Times Magazine*). The story chronicled his experience in Pakistan, primarily at a school for boys. The curriculum, other activities, and events subsequent to "graduation" are a case study in how to develop the *character* of a "perfect jihad machine." The developmental elements are all there: knowledge (deriving from education), adherence (habits formed from relentless practice), belief (instilled by perceived efficacy of the teachings and practices), leadership (experience gained by giving the older students responsibility for the guidance and instruction of the younger ones). What distinguishes the **Haqqania Madrasa** from the convent that produced Mother Teresa is not the process of development, it is the content. Most importantly, the 10 to 12 year experience of the students at the **Haqqania** is not focused on the development of competence. It is almost totally on the development of the character of the students. It is not until after graduation that they begin training in the competencies that enable them to kill.

The moral is that we cannot take the development of character for granted. When we come into the world, disregarding genetic predispositions or ingrained personality traits, our character is a "blank slate." By the time we enter the 1st grade, it has developed a great deal. We have a sense of right and wrong (conscience), we have a set of values (those things that are always important to us), and we demonstrate certain virtues (moral qualities). Hopefully, we have been well grounded. Even so, we have only just begun. The process of character development is life-long, and people can learn to be good, and they can get better at it — but, not by accident.

STARTING NOW

In order to develop character in ourselves and in others we must understand what we want (goals, hopes, dreams, aspirations, etc.). We must know what we value (that which is always important). We must know whom we admire and want to emulate. We must know and understand our fundamental beliefs. We must know why we hold these to be true. In essence, **we must examine our life**.

It is useful to embrace a Code*, one that simply and clearly captures the foundation of our personal philosophy (an example is below). It is essential to read, to listen, and to watch others in order to learn what they believe. We must be willing to challenging our own opinions in light of facts or views to the contrary.

OUR DECISION, OUR COMMITMENT

Character is manifest in decision-making and action. The process of making decisions begins with understanding the situation or circumstances in which we find ourselves. We must determine the difference between where we are and where we want to be. Then, in light of our goals, aspirations, values, and means we must determine or define our options. That is, we must ascertain what we can do to make things better or to make progress. We must next decide which among our choices seems best. Having selected an alternative, we must plan for implementation. We must know what resources we require (money, time, materials, assistance, etc). With a fully resourced plan, we can begin to put our decision into action. As we implement our plan, we must assess progress and make adjustments as results reveal the efficiency and effectiveness of our efforts. From all this, we gain experience, contributing to our wisdom (our ability to make better decisions in the future). As we grow in wisdom and understanding, we are better able to help others (through mentoring and setting the example). Thus, we develop in character by helping others and ourselves. In effect, we serve others and ourselves at the same time.

The entire process of character development, including all four elements, is a continuum. We gain knowledge and we share knowledge. We practice virtue and help others to be virtuous. We receive honest feedback and critique and we share it, as well. We lead (by influencing others) and we are led (as others influence us). Always, we are striving to live up to our ideals while helping and encouraging others to do so, too. When we err, as inevitably we will, we learn from our mistakes (admit them honestly) and move on.

A CODE OF ETHICS*

Purpose: In order to foster **trust** in all our endeavors, personal & professional, we adopt this *Code of Ethics* to guide our decisions & actions, in pursuit of excellence.

Premise: *Trust* is belief in and reliance on the **integrity** & **competence** of another person, organization, or institution. Trust is the foundation for successful relationships & endeavors.

Goal: In order to be trustworthy, we aspire to be people of **character**. As such, we seek to discover the *truth*, decide what is *right*, & demon-

---

*Originally Prepared 25 Nov '02, by Group 7, USMA Conference on Ethics in America: Patrick A. Toffler (Group Facilitator); Gisele Le Bleu, Cal St, Monterey; Beth Thompson, Patrick Henry College; Tony Donis, USCGA; Garrick Throckmorton, Bradley Univ.; Brian Housman, Haverford School; Sean Bell, Texas A&M; Alexander Martin, USNA; David Nylen, VPI; Kristy Laudick; USMA -- revision: 17 May '04.

strate the *courage*, & *commitment* to act accordingly.

We pledge commitment & allegiance to our *values*, including:

- **Integrity** — Decision-making & action based on principles.

- **Honesty** — Being truthful.

- **Responsibility & Duty** — Fulfilling obligations & accepting consequences.

- **Respect** — Recognizing the infinite dignity & worth of people & the sanctity of their property.

- **Service** — Contribution to the welfare of others.

- **Community** — Teamwork & Consideration-for-others.

- **Justice & Mercy** — Adherence to moral law: fairness & compassion.

- **Competence** — Proficiency, expertise, professionalism, intellect, & wisdom.

- **Moral Courage** — Willingness & Commitment to do what is right despite uncertainty, risk, & fear.

In the conduct of our activities we will strive to continuously develop our *Character & Competence*, seeking to improve these attributes in order to be worthy of trust & to contribute to the common good.

That which is **good** is consistent with our sense of aesthetics, virtue, righteousness, & morality.

That which is **moral** is known to our conscience — to which we pledge to be true.

HOW WE LEARN

The Learning Model
Instruction & Study
Coaching & Practice
Performance to Standards?
Progress or Remediation

Instruction & Study:

This element of the Learning Model may be formal or informal. An example of formal "instruction & study" is classically represented by a course in school. This may be in the form of education (requiring intellectual inquiry, interpretation, and reasoning) or training (focused on procedure, algorithm, or process). Formal learning activities have specific goals, objectives, required elements, grades, and are often recognized by a certificate, transcript credit, or graduation diploma.

However, the logic of how we learn applies just as well informally when, for example, a parent works with a child on a project at home, let's say, waxing the car, demonstrating the technique and encouraging the child to read the directions for application of the wax that is printed on the container.

In both the formal and informal case the instructor and the student are working together, as teammates, in pursuit of the common goal — to learn.

Coaching & Practice:

In order to gain better understanding and familiarity with anything introduced by instruction, complemented by study, it is important to practice the application of the new material. This can be through writing, as in a course in journalism; hitting a back-hand, as part of learning to play tennis; or engaging in conversation, as part of learning social discourse (and civility). However, the old maxim: "practice makes perfect" is not quite right. Practice must be proper or the practice can actually lead to, reinforce, or develop bad habits. Thus, the role of an experienced coach within the practicum is very useful and important. The coach should observe, offer constructive critique, demonstrate proper technique or behavior, and generally help the student apply the theory of what is to be learned in the correct manner.

Standards & Evaluation:

The learning process is enabled when we continue to challenge ourselves and others to address new issues. However, in order to measure the degree of learning that has taken place and to determine if an appropriate level of understanding and competency has been attained, it is important to establish standards (sometimes these are equivalent to goals or objectives). Learning to a particular standard and demonstrating a specific level of competence is important to the student, the instructor, and others who may need to rely on the competency. This is why students are tested before being issued a "driver's license", it is why financial advisors must be "certified", and doctors must pass "boards" in order to practice.

Applying standards and conducting evaluation is a critical element of the learning process (whether formal or informal). For example, a coach designs a new play (something to be learned):

- He presents the elements of the play to his team in a "chalk-talk";

- The players review diagrams in order to understand their roles and responsibilities;

- The team takes the practice field and runs through the play several times, first at slow speed, eventually at full speed with contact;

- Finally, the coach runs the play under scrimmage conditions — to assure himself and the players that they have attained an appropriate level of competence and are ready to run the play during a game.

Progress or Remediation:

There is an important decision, both within the formal and informal learning paradigms: when is it appropriate and necessary to move-on to new learning (progress) vs. continuing the effort to attain a specific level of competency (remediation)? Sometimes, circumstances dictate the answer. For example, an academic term ends and a student has failed a course, normally the failure must be redressed. In the case of informal learning, the instructor (e.g., a parent) must determine what action to take when the student (in this case their child) must "remediate". For example, if the child is frequently untruthful or unreliable, do they just ignore the problems, hoping the character flaws will repair with time; or do they continue to work on repairing the manifest vices? While the preponderance of parents might agree to continue addressing the problem, what to do is another matter. This is why the process of character development is both continuous and co-incident with the development of competence. The parents must read, consult with others, try different approaches, etc. All of which will better themselves (as parents) while helping them develop of character within their children. This, in turn, not only helps the children be better adolescents, it will also help them be better parents, one day.

THE LEARNING MODEL FOR COMPETENCE & CHARACTER

ESSENTIAL ELEMENTS

- Instruction & Study
- Coaching & Practice
- Standards & Evaluation
- Progress or Remediation

APPLICABILITY

- The approach will develop both competence and character, in all endeavors.
- To be truly effective the competency goal and the character goal are pursued (using the model) at the same time.

CHAPTER SEVETEEN

LEADERSHIP AND ETHICS

Character is the bedrock on which the whole edifice of leadership rests. It is the prime element for which every profession, every corporation, every industry searches in evaluating a member of its organization. With it, the full worth of an individual can be developed. Without it — particularly in the military profession — failure in peace, disaster in war, or at best, mediocrity in both will result.

— General Matthew B. Ridgeway

I S IT APPROPRIATE TO SPEAK of leadership and ethics in the same phrase? Not only is it appropriate, it is absolutely essential, because without ethics a leader cannot be trusted. The ethics of a leader enable followers to align and commit their efforts in the pursuit of common goals.

It is my belief that people will go to extraordinary lengths and will provide extraordinary performance for a leader that they can trust. Before people will align their efforts and devote their time to a leader or an organization, they must believe in and trust the leader's visions, goals, and ethics. Of course, the leader must be competent, but most important, the leader must be trustworthy.

Ethics that guide action and decision-making are essential for trust, that's why we need leaders of character. Character is that which constitutes a person's true nature and being. A person of character seeks to discover and know the truth, decides what is right, and demonstrates the courage and commitment to act accordingly. Leaders of character can be trusted and this trust is the basis for effective cooperation. Effective professional relationships and successful effort to achieve organizational goals occur when there is trust. All of us who have followed a winning athletic team or a profitable business organization wherein everyone is contributing his or her best understands the powerful synergy that comes from teamwork built on trust and mutual respect. Trust is the essential element which enables leaders and followers to work together in pursuit of common goals. Consider, for example, a leader who is motivated by power, greed, fame, or profit. He knows that others will hardly sacrifice themselves for his own glory. So, the leader must feign loftier purposes. This deception is clearly unethical. Eventually, it will be discovered and that leader will have lost the trust and confidence of all those selfishly used for personal gain. In all future endeavors, this leader's motives will be questioned. Potential followers will be skeptical, at best, more likely they will be cynical, and this leader will not be effective. Once trust is destroyed, no meaningful relationship is possible.

Ethics enables the leader to succeed. With ethics and values-based behavior, the effect of leadership is powerful — without it a leader must compel obedience — history is replete with stories of such tyrants, despotic kings, dictators, and conquerors. These are not the leaders of character we seek and need. Take, for example, a U. S. military operation where a platoon leader sends one squad forward on the left side of an enemy position. Another squad is sent on the right side. The "weapons squad" sets up in the middle in order to "pin down" the enemy with fire, while the others move into position. The third squad is in "reserve" to assist at the precise moment of decision. As the platoon maneuvers for the attack each soldier is now risking his life. For this tactic to succeed, everyone must be trained and competent. The lieutenant must know tactics and select an option that has high probability of success with low probability of friendly casualties. The squad leaders must know how to employ their "fire teams" and how to move with stealth in order to mask their movements until the moment of attack. Everyone must rely on and trust the others to do the right thing with courage and commitment. Otherwise, the mission will fail, and friendly soldiers will die. While trust does not guarantee success, success is impossible without it. In effect, ethics and values help provide direction, enthusiasm and impetus to the leader's vision and goals.

Yes, there are some leaders who manipulate, who operate without ethics or morals and somehow seem to get the job done. But, the leaders without character will find their ultimate results diluted and, in the long run, will fail. The organization that is run by leaders of character will produce a higher quality product, treat its customers and employees right, provide a higher profit for its shareholders, and endure for a long, long time. Yes, all of that can come from leaders of character who are competent.

To fully understand the context in which leaders operate, one needs to understand the derivation of a leader's authority. There is constitutional authority for government leaders, and authority is often further legitimized by democratic elections. There is positional authority in corporate and private organizations, and these positions are authenticated by corporate or organizational bylaws, and there are boards of directors or boards of governors to provide oversight over these positions. Often a leader's effectiveness is enhanced by virtue of personality, people skills, or charisma. A persuasive, charismatic, leader with legitimate positional authority can usually motivate or create a loyal following. However, if this charisma is a veneer, masking a corrupt core, the leader's effectiveness will be short-lived.

In my view, the most powerful and enduring force for any leader is "moral authority." One may have constitutional authority or positional authority and charisma, but these without moral authority are vacuous. Moral authority comes from trust and with trust there can be great synergy. **DO NOT UNDERESTIMATE THE POWER AND VALUE OF MORAL AUTHORITY.** It is essential; and it depends on trust. Leaders earn that moral authority by their behavior, by straight forward communication of vision and objectives, by adherence to the shared values of the group, by fair and equitable treatment of all the organization's stakeholders, and by setting an example of genuine ethical decision-making.

I know that some skeptics or cynics might disagree: "*Get real, the real world doesn't operate like that*". The real world, some assert, is led by people who are driven by insatiable pursuit of power and money. These real world leaders will run over their mothers and brothers to climb another rung in the corporate or political ladder or earn a few more dollars. They will manipulate people and events, then will lie, cheat or steal at the same time as they put on their halos. I do not deny that there are many leaders who fit this description. Some people in positions of authority and influence and those who aspire to such power, fame and wealth, may believe that their motivational goals are paramount and that the means they use are justified by the "ends." But all of us, in our hearts, know that this logic is fatally flawed. It breeds hostility, resentment, cutthroat competition, and even war.

This observation is not new. Niccolo Machiavelli, in his famous work *The Prince*, wrote the following pronouncement nearly five hundred years ago:

> *Everyone understands how praiseworthy it is in a prince to keep faith and to live uprightly and not craftily. Nevertheless, we see, from what has taken place in our own days, that princes who have set little store by their word but have known how to overreach men by their cunning, have accomplished great things and in the end got the better of those who trusted to honest dealing.*

Be it known, then, there are two ways of contending, one in accordance with the laws, the other by force; the first of which is proper to men, the second to beasts. But since the first method is often ineffectual, it becomes necessary to resort to the second. A prince should, therefore, understand how to use well both the man and the beast...a prudent prince neither can nor ought to keep his word when to keep it is hurtful to him and the causes which led him to pledge it are removed. If all men were good, this would not be good advice, but since they are dishonest and do not keep faith with you, you, in return need not keep faith with them; and no prince was ever at a loss for plausible reasons to cloak a breach of faith.

It is necessary indeed to put a good color on this nature and be skillful in simulating and dissembling. But men are so simple and governed so absolutely by their present needs that he who wishes to deceive will never fail in finding willing dupes.

A prince should therefore be very careful that nothing ever escapes his lips which is not...the embodiment of mercy, good faith, integrity, humanity and religion...

It is not essential, then, that a prince should have all the good qualities which I have enumerated above, but it is most essential that he should seem to have them; I will even venture to affirm that if he has and invariably practices them all, they are hurtful, whereas the appearance of having them is useful. Thus, it is well to be merciful, faithful, humane, religious and upright, and also seem so; but the mind should remain so balanced that were it needful not to be so , you should be able and know how to change to the contrary.

And you are to understand that a prince, and most of all a new prince cannot observe all those rules of conduct in respect whereof men are accounted good, being often forced in order to preserve his Princedom, to act in opposition to good faith, charity, humanity and religion. He must therefore, keep his mind ready to shift as the winds and tides of Fortune turn, and, as I have already said he ought not to quit good courses if he can help it but should know how to follow evil courses if he must...

Moreover, in the actions of all men and most of all of princes, where there is no tribunal to which he can appeal, we look to results. Wherefore, if a prince succeeds in establishing and maintaining his authority, the means will always be judged honorable and be approved by everyone. For the vulgar are always taken by appearance and by results, and the world is made up of his vulgar, the few only finding room when the many have no longer ground to stand on.

In other words, Machiavelli is supporting the view that unethical means are justified by the "ends" (which are for the powerful to remain powerful). Therefore, by this logic, deceit, hypocrisy, cheating, and even force are necessary to achieve one's goals. I cannot know how many of today's leaders or aspiring leaders agree with Machiavelli, but I do see numerous examples of Machiavellian behavior in our personal, political and professional lives. I agree that such practices appear to provide temporary successes and gains. And although it may appear that some people always *get away with it and never seem to get caught*, this just is not so. More important, the "gains" of unethical conduct are fleeting and there is a "huge opportunity cost." Trust is compromised or destroyed and what could have been achieved through ethical practice is lost, perhaps irretrievably.

There are better ways to lead and the moral exemplars of Section II serve as illustrative examples of what enduring benefit derives from positive, moral leadership. Let's take a look at various thoughts on this subject from some of the great modern students of leadership.

Warren Bennis is a prolific writer and a perceptive thinker on the subject of leadership. In his classic book ***Leaders*** which he co-authored with Burt Nanus he writes:

The leader is responsible for the set of ethics or norms that govern the behavior of people in the organization. Leaders can establish a set of ethics in several ways. One is to demonstrate by their own behavior their commitment to the set of ethics that they are trying to institutionalize. Consider the J.M. Smucker Company of Orrville, Ohio, which dominates the nation's markets for jams and jellies with nearly three times the market share of its closet competitors. Ever since the first Mr. Smucker actually signed every label to show he personally stood behind each product, all company leaders in successive generations of Smuckers have served as personal models of integrity, social responsibility and high ethical standards. For example, company policy is to fill every jar with a bit more than the customer pays for. The company refuses to advertise on television shows that exploit sex or violence. It was the first in its industry to put nutritional information on every label, and it pays for a full time federal inspector at every plant, though not required to do so. No one in the company dares to cut any corners.

Leaders set the moral tone by choosing carefully the people with whom they surround themselves, by communicating a sense of purpose for the organization, be reinforcing appropriate behaviors and by articulating these moral positions to external and internal constituencies.

In the end trust, integrity and positioning are all different faces of a common property of leadership — the ability to integrate those who must act with that which must be done so that it all comes together as a single organism in harmony with itself and its niche in the environment.

In another section of this same book Bennis and Nanus attack several myths, one of which is that:

The leader controls, directs, prods, manipulates. This is the most dangerous myth of all. As we have stressed with monotonous regu-

larity, leadership is not so much the exercise of power itself as the empowerment of others. Leaders are able to translate intentions into reality by aligning the energies of the organization behind an attractive goal. It is Carlo Maria Giulini, formerly the conductor of the Los Angeles Philharmonic, who claims that "what matters most is human contact, that the great mystery of music making requires real friendship among those who work together." It is Irwin Federman, past president of Monolithic Memories, who believes that "the essence of leadership is the capacity to build and develop the self-esteem of the workers." It is William Hewitt, who took over John Deere & Company in the mid-fifties when it was a sleepy, old-line farm implements firm and made it into a world leader because, as one employee put it, "Hewitt made us learn how good we were."

These leaders lead by pulling rather than by pushing; by inspiring rather than by ordering; by creating the achievable, though challenging expectations and rewarding progress toward them rather than by manipulating; by enabling people to use their own initiative and experiences rather than by denying or constraining their experiences and actions.

The leadership of Bennis and Nanus is not "Machiavellian" or "power politics" or the "politics of greed." It is defined by trust, shared values, and "empowerment." Let me say again, trust is the glue that binds and bonds the leader to his followers and the followers to their leader; and trust must be earned.

Max DePree in his book ***Leadership Jazz*** makes the very succinct observation when he states:

Integrity in all things precedes all else. The open demonstration of integrity is essential; followers must be wholeheartedly convinced of their leaders' integrity. For leaders who live a public life, perceptions become a fact of life. Leaders understand the profound difference between gestures and commitment. It's just impossible to be a closet leader.

DePree goes on to say:

One of the most sacred relationships among teams of people is that between leaders and followers. This relationship, so central and crucial, depends to an extraordinary degree on the clearly expressed and consistently demonstrated values of the leader as seen through the special lens of the followers. This is why leadership and ethics are inextricably woven together.

Colonel Larry R. Donnithorne (Ret.) in **The West Point Way of Leadership** describes how the United State Military Academy strives to develop leaders of character. Two cardinal chapters are entitled, *Honor Is The Language We Speak* and *The Harder Right.*

Honor is the Language We Speak. *The cadet's moral education, as with many other aspects of the Academy's program of leadership begins with rules — with the Honor Code. When they enter, these budding leaders receive as their first and most important matter of business, this law, which is short, sweet and to the point: "A cadet will not lie, cheat or steal or tolerate those who do." The language of honor is spoken in this code. This honor code may seem simple but it is the linchpin of a value system shared by all Army officers. West Point believes that an organization, like an individual, can fulfill its highest function only when guided by moral principles. Creating this particular sort of high-performance organization, in which every member is guided by the same bedrock principles is not easy.*

Concerning the chapter in Colonel Donnithorne's book entitled **The Harder Right**, perhaps an excerpt from the *Cadet Prayer* is appropriate:

"Make us to choose the harder right instead of the easier wrong and never be content with a half truth when the whole can be won."

Larry makes several strong pronouncements in his book, one of the more important of which is: "**Character is a prerequisite for greatness**", and the second of which is: "***Leaders of character create organizations of character***."

Concerning the first precept that "character is a prerequisite for greatness", let us go all the way back to our first president, George Washington. Here are his thoughts on the subject:

I hope I shall always possess firmness and virtue enough to maintain what I consider the most enviable of all titles, the character of an Honest Man.

In 1904 at a speech in Groton Massachusetts, President Theodore Roosevelt made this claim — "A sound body is good, a sound mind is better but a strong and clean character is better than either."

Thomas Jefferson is quoted as saying:

"God grant that men of principle be our principal men." He is also credited with saying: "In matters of principle, stand like a rock; in matters of taste, swim with the current."

Melvin R. Laird, a former Secretary of Defense makes the point in another way:

"No intellectual brilliance and no technical capacity will be enough to qualify one for military leadership unless it is combined with qualities of character that inspire other men to give forth their best effort in a common cause."

Nearly five hundred years before the birth of Christ, Hereclitus stated:

"A man's character is his fate."

Ralph Waldo Emerson among his many profound thoughts has left us with the following two quotes that I find quite relevant to the subject at hand:

"The force of character is cumulative." And… "Don't say things. What you are stands over you, the while, and thunders so that I cannot hear what you say to the contrary."

The conclusion that character is a prerequisite for greatness is captured so well by General S.L.A. Marshall, writing in 1950:

"The traditional esteem of the average citizen for military officers is a major ingredient, indeed a prerequisite, of the national security. The Armed Services have recognized this since the time of Valley Forge. That is why there is such extreme emphasis on the imperative of personal honor in the military officer; not only the future of our arms but the well-being of our people depend upon a constant reaffirmation and strengthening of public faith in the virtue and trustworthiness of the officer body. Should that faith flag and finally fail, the citizenry would be reluctant to commit its young people to any military endeavor however grave the emergency. The works of goodwill by which leaders of our military seek to win the trust and approval of the people are in a direct sense a preservative of our American freedoms. By the same reasoning, high character in the military office is a safeguard of the character of the Nation. Anything less than exemplary conduct is therefore unworthy of the commission."

With regard to the second concept quoted earlier *"that leaders of character create organizations of character,"* I want to cite an example that many of you already know.

Not long ago, Johnson & Johnson's organizational character was tested in an extreme manner when one of its most popular products, Tylenol, was found to have been tainted by tampering. Like some other successful companies, Johnson & Johnson has a credo that defines its essential values. Simple statements specify its responsibilities to customers, communities, employees and stockholders — in that order.

Adherence to its credo first, priority to the health of its customers, enabled the company to react decisively to the crisis without hesitation by immediately recalling the entire nationwide inventory of the product. This was carried out despite the loss of $240 million, (i.e., at the risk of corporate survival).

Johnson & Johnson was an example of an organization of character living by its espoused values, even at time when it was not only difficult, but potentially disastrous.

Donald T. Phillips presents President Lincoln's leadership qualities in his book, ***Lincoln On Leadership***. Phillips devotes a whole section of his book to character and a special chapter to honesty and integrity. Here is just a little bit of what he had to say:

"The architecture of leadership, all of the theories and guidelines, fall apart without honesty and integrity. It's the keystone that holds an organization together. Tom Peters reported in his research that the best, most aggressive, and successful organizations were the ones that stressed integrity and trust. "Without doubt," Peters stated, "Honesty has always been the best policy." Managers do things right. "Leaders do the right thing," wrote Bennis and Nanus.

Integrity must be sincere. That's one reason that Lincoln was so admired in his lifetime. Through an individual's words, deeds and actions, integrity can be judged to be genuine. And integrity is tied closely to the values espoused by an effective leader. As a rule, leaders must set and respond to fundamental goals and values that move their followers. In addition to being much-needed moral standards, values tend to be motives by which subordinates act and react. The possession and preaching of wide-ranging, appealing goals and values will result in broad support from the masses. People will be involved participants in a shared group effort. Put more simply, values motivate.

Any successful organization, whether a business or a country, must possess strong shared values. These values must be "owned" by not only the vast majority of the organization but in some cases by all its members."

James MacGregor Burns discusses moral leadership in the following way:

"Moral leadership emerges from and always returns to the fundamental wants, needs, aspirations and values of the followers. I mean the kind of leadership that can produce social change that will satisfy followers' authentic needs."

John W. Gardner, who is the founder of *Common Cause*, and who has served six presidents, makes the following point:

Shared values are the bedrock on which leaders build the edifice of group achievements. No examination of leadership would be complete without attention to the decay and possible regeneration of the value framework.

Short excerpts from two of Warren Bennis' other books on leadership, **On Becoming a Leader** and **Why Leaders Can't Lead** shed some additional light on the subject.

In the first work Warren Bennis discusses trust in the following way:

Leaders who trust their co-workers are in turn trusted by them. Trust, of course, cannot be acquired but can only be given. Leadership without mutual trust is a contradiction in terms. Trust resides squarely between faith and doubt. The leader always has faith in himself, his abilities, his co-workers and their mutual possibilities. But he also has sufficient doubt to question, challenge, probe and thereby progress. In the same way, his co-workers must believe in him, themselves and their combined strength, but they must feel sufficiently confident to question, challenge, probe, and test, too.

Maintaining that vital balance between faith and doubt, preserving that mutual trust is a primary task for any leader.

Vision, inspiration, empathy, trustworthiness are manifestations of a leader's judgment and character. University President, Alfred Gollschalk said, "Character is vital in a leader, the basis for everything else. Other qualities would include the ability to inspire trust, some entrepreneurial talent, imagination, perseverance, steadfastness of purpose…Character, perseverance and imagination are the sine qua non of leadership."

One final point from Bennis' **Why Leaders Can't Lead**, has to do with integrity:

By integrity I mean standards of moral and intellectual honesty on which our conduct is based. Without integrity, we betray ourselves and others and cheapen every endeavor. It is the single quality whose absence we feel most sharply on every level of our national life. But the nation's integrity will be restored only when each of us asserts his or her own integrity. By their very existence, people of integrity lend hope to our innate conviction that we, as a people, can rise above the current moral cynicism and squalor. As Aristotle wrote, "If you would understand virtue, observe the conduct of virtuous men."

Much of this chapter consists of quotations because I wanted you to understand that there is widespread belief among the most experienced and intellectual thinkers, writers and practitioners concerning the central and pivotal roles that ethics and character play with regard to leadership. Our character is our destiny, and we are the architects of our own character, which, along with competence, establishes the cornerstones of leadership.

C H A P T E R   E I G H T E E N

VALUES IN THE WORKPLACE

When work is a pleasure, life is a joy! When work is a duty, life is slavery.

—Maxim Gorky

I F YOU LOOK CAREFULLY AT THE VALUE SETS presented in Chapter Two, you can readily conclude that there is a common moral baseline of shared values. So, it is not a matter of imposing values on others or expecting others to share our values, rather, we can be heartened by the knowledge that there appears to be a universal common set of shared values.

If most human beings share in these values, then it is easy to understand that customers, employees, shareholders, vendors, neighbors, students, children, all of us want to be treated fairly. Customers want a quality product or service at a fair price. They also expect truth in advertising and in sales presentations and they expect merchants to stand by their products. Employees want a fair wage for an honest day's work and they want to work in a safe and healthy environment. Employees expect straight talk and honest dealings with their employers.

Employers expect a full day's work for a full day's pay and they would also like a continuing improvement in productivity. Employers want employees to align their individual goals with the goals of the organization in order to achieve a genuine synergy.

Shareholders want managers to remember that they own the company and they want managers to enhance shareholder value. Shareholders would prefer that managers create real value through quality products at fair prices.

Vendors also want to be treated fairly, receiving a fair price for their products. They also would prefer to be informed in a timely manner concerning the specifications and schedules that are expected of them.

Regardless of one's perspective, and regardless of how we orient our thinking, it all comes back to values — shared core values like integrity, honesty, justice, respect, responsibility, and loyalty don't have to be imposed — they are almost universally embraced.

In Chapter Seven, we looked at Dr. Earl Hess who had been the Chairman and CEO of Lancaster Laboratories, Inc. Dr. Hess started his company with just three people and led it to become a successful enterprise with annual revenues of over $30 million. His success is apparent in the quantitative results. The qualitative way he did this is the real story. Earl was trustworthy. He was honest, fair respectful, loyal, caring, and selfless. In the early 1980s, Dr. Hess knew that his technical expertise and efficient management were not enough for enduring growth and prosperity. He understood the importance of technical competence. However, his values and his ethics demanded a corporate ethos that fostered and recognized character. He understood that trust and teamwork are necessary to develop quality products. He knew his vision, and he knew he could achieve it only by being a leader of character. In a rational participative process, Earl and his team conducted a comprehensive evaluation of their managerial approach to the business. That review resulted in the following mission statement and principles:

Lancaster Laboratories Mission Statement and Principles
We will provide quality, independent laboratory services in the chemical and biological sciences by:

- fully understanding and always meeting the requirements of those we serve,

- relating to our clients, coworkers, suppliers and community in a fair and ethical manner, and

- managing our growth and financial resources so we can serve our clients well, preserve our independence and maintain our meaningful and enriching workplace.

Dr. Hess initiated an Ethics Committee at one of his leadership retreats and then had the foresight to broaden the composition of the committee to include a cross-section of all employees. The purpose of the Ethics Committee of Lancaster Labs is as follows:

STATEMENT OF PURPOSE

It shall be the responsibility of the Ethics Committee to:

- encourage and maintain commitment among employees to our core ethical values.

- act as a think tank in developing a total ethics process for orienting new employees

- and maintaining a high level of awareness and commitment of all within our organization.

- serve as a monitoring/oversight group for that process.

Dr. Hess also knew, early on, that the Lancaster Laboratories Ethics Committee must provide education for all of his employees on ethical fitness.

The instruction program chosen was modeled after the ethical fitness training materials developed by the Institute for Global Ethics. The IGE approach is organized in four modules:

Development of Moral Awareness — It is important to discuss and assess the state of moral conduct in society in general as well as in the workplace. Understanding the moral mood and corporate culture are necessary elements in progressing to the next module or next phase.

Defining Corporate Core Values — Although each corporation may develop a slightly different value set, the results usually reflect society's core values. The Lancaster Laboratories' Statement of Values was guided by the following principles:

- Fairness and honesty in all our relationships.

- Mutual trust.

- A respect for ourselves and others.

- A sense of caring that leads us to act responsibly toward each other in society, now and in the future.

- Loyalty to our clients and one another.

- A spirit of open-mindedness as we deal with all.

- Dedication to service.

- Good stewardship of our resources.

- A commitment to flexibility and continuous improvement.

- *We each take personal responsibility to live these values in all of our dealings, knowing full well our pledge may involve difficult choices, hard work, and courage.*

One must observe that this statement of values has a measure of depth to it. It goes beyond the normal "we will tell the truth and not steal company property." The loyalty, the caring, the mutual respect, inherent responsibility, and the tolerance of diversity are added dimensions.

Defining and Analyzing Ethical Dilemmas — One of my basic theses is that there is a disconnect between our stated, shared, core values and our behavior. That disconnect reflects a lack of commitment, a lack of discipline, and perhaps a lack of moral courage. This disconnect is serious because its manifestation destroys trust.

It is for this reason that the approach used by Dr. Rush Kidder and the Institute of Global Ethics makes sense. The approach deals with the notions of right vs. wrong and right vs. right. Given the establishment of, or the recognition of, core values, it is a relatively simple task to distinguish between right and wrong. In this case, one then needs the self-discipline, courage and commitment to do what he or she knows is right.

A more challenging difficulty arises in the face of a dilemma — a right vs. right dilemma. The Institute for Global Ethics has developed and Lancaster Laboratories, Inc, along with many other groups, has embraced the following four right versus right dilemma paradigms:

- Truth versus Loyalty
- Short Term versus Long Term
- Justice versus Mercy
- Self versus Community

These four paradigms provide an explicit framework for analysis. This process helps to define the dilemma and facilitates making the best values-based decision.

Understanding and Applying Decision Making Rules — The moral philosophers have discussed several esoteric approaches to make ethical decisions. By way of review, the following three decision rules are practical derivations taken from moral philosophy:

1. **Ends-Based Decisions** — decisions that benefit the greatest number provide the greatest good. This rule is otherwise known as utilitarianism or consequentialism.

2. **Rule-Based Decisions** — decisions based on a suitable rule that everyone should follow in similar situations. This is often referred to as Immanuel Kant's *categorical imperative.*

3. **Care-Based Decisions** — decisions that are consistent with the Golden Rule: *"Do unto others as you would have them do unto you."*

The three decision-making concepts can be applied, as appropriate, with the following foundations:

- Understand the moral environment.
- Define the core values.
- Determine which values appear to be in competition.
- Apply one or more of the decision rules to make a choice.

So what did Lancaster Laboratories achieve by managing in this manner? Here are some of the results:

- Quality Services
- Satisfied Clients
- High Employee Morale
- Excellent Financial Performances
- Responsive Support from Vendors
- Ultimate Sale of the Company with a significant, fair capital gain
- Enthusiastic Community Support

And, in addition to all of the above, the Lancaster Laboratories, Inc. built for its employees:

- A day care center for children of employees
- An adult care center for parents of employees
- A gymnasium and fitness center for employees and their families

And when any of these centers had unused capacity, Dr. Earl Hess opened his facilities to the local community.

So managing by values had a payoff for all. And, thus we have a personal success story in Earl Hess and a corporate success story for the Lancaster Laboratories — all of it built on an ethical foundation of shared values.

This is hardly an isolated example. There are many who affirm this approach:

The most effective organizations are based on communities of shared ethical values. If people who have to work together in an enterprise trust one another because they are all operating according to a common set of ethical norms, doing business costs less.
— ***Trust,*** *Franics Fukuyama*

In a company that truly manages by its values, there is only one boss — the company's values.
— ***Managing By Values,*** *Ken Blachard, Michael O'Connor*

They (CEO's) know for example that a strong customer franchise is critical to business success, and that doing business with people you trust and understand is more predictable and efficient, and thus more profitable, than doing business with uninvested strangers.
— ***The Loyalty Effect,*** *Frederick E. Reichhold*

When you introduce shared core values into the workplace and when those values are truly embraced by workers and managers at all levels, you have created tremendous potential for synergy and extraordinary performance. But this focus on values cannot be artificial or superficial. The inspiration and the commitment must come from within the hearts and souls of all employees and managers. That is, it must be a people thing — real changes must come from and occur within the people as they relate to the shared values. Communication must be open and two-way. The shared values establish a foundation for trust, respect, responsibility, and personal accountability. A superior military organization, a superior athletic team, and a superior business organization have in common the imperative of shared values, with trust as the unifying force. Witness the results of the 1998 World Cup finals, wherein a French soccer team defeated an admittedly superior Brazilian soccer team with a tenacious defense that appeared to be tightly knit based on the mutual trust and respect among the French players. I could cite similar military examples and business examples. Walter Wriston may have said it best when he stated that:

The person who figures out how to harness the collective genius of the people in his or her organization is going to blow the competition away.

The surest way to harness the collective genius of all of the people in any organization is to create and communicate a vision based on shared values, promoting trust, and fairness. Integrity and honesty foster trust; and trust enables commitment, and commitment produces synergy; and synergy produces superior performance.

CHAPTER NINETEEN

ETHICS AND CHILDREN

RABBI STEVEN CARR REUBEN

Character building begins in our infancy and continues until death.
—Eleanor Roosevelt

I N MANY WAYS THIS IS THE MOST important chapter. If the thesis that I pronounced earlier — a thesis that is a hallmark quote from the Institute of Global Ethics — that *"we will not survive the twenty first century with the ethics of the twentieth century,"* then we need to pay special attention to our children.

The finest gift we can give our children is a meaningful set of values, a sense of morality, a code of ethics, and a framework of social responsibility. Moral, ethical people generally live happier, less stressful lives, and at the same time they contribute fundamental decency to our society. However, the big question is: how can we raise ethical children in the face of the temptations of drugs, alcohol, theft, violence, cheating, promiscuity, permissiveness, and deceit?

Much of what is presented in this chapter was derived from my interview with Rabbi Steven Carr Reuben and from his two books on children and ethics.

Dr. Steven Carr Reuben in his book, **Raising Ethical Children** makes some important points when he states:

> *"This process of raising ethical children requires the constant reminder that ethical insights come to children in stages, slowly over many years. Parents must realize that they have to talk about ethics and teach their children both by word and action at age-appropriate levels, or they simply will not understand the point you are trying to make. Until they are emotionally, intellectually, and even spiritually ready to experience the greater connection to humanity as a whole, all the preaching in the world will be meaningless.*
>
> *Ethical child raising can be the result of a natural progression of shared experiences, conscious parenting role model moments and thoughtful talks with your children about how to make the right ethical decisions in the different situations that arise in the course of daily living. When you allow the ethical reasoning of your children to progress in a natural but guided fashion from one stage to the next, with your help and your love, they will eventually arrive at the appropriate higher stages of ethical development."*

Dr. Reuben's eloquent explanation describes the process as straightforward and uncomplicated. But, make no mistake about it, the art of raising ethical children is often frustrating, demanding and complex; it requires dedication, persistence, creativity, and unqualified love. It will be a "labor of love" and hope, but a labor nevertheless. There are important concepts that surround the notion of an ethical child in much the same way as they surround the notion of an ethical adult. The values that children learn to embrace and exemplify, the derivation of those values, the framework of discipline within which they operate, the friendships they develop and nurture, the self-worth and self-esteem they gain, the role models that influence their behavior, and ultimately the meaning that they attach to life are all part of the effort. These are all important concepts and ideally, family plays the most meaningful and positive role in helping children develop to become more and caring adults.

In the June 15, 1998 issue of *Sports Illustrated Magazine* CIGNA presented a special advertising feature entitled, "*The Power of Caring — On and Off the Screen Character Counts to Selleck.*" In the accompanying article, Tom Selleck, the movie actor, is quoted as saying,

> *"We need future citizens and present ones who will make the right choices. A person of character does the right thing for the right reasons. But it is difficult for kids to do the right thing when they don't know what the right thing is."*

Selleck goes on to say that when people ask him whose values or whose principles should be taught to children he responds,

> *"It's all of our values. When I get that question I mention what we call the Six Pillars of Character:*

TRUSTWORTHINESS

RESPECT

RESPONSIBILITY

FAIRNESS

CARING

CITIZENSHIP"

Notice how similar the six pillars of character are to the value sets presented earlier. Even each of the value sets comes from a different source, representing several geographical and cultural venues. One can see that it is not difficult to identify and enumerate the values that we hold precious. The difficulty comes in truly understanding, embracing, and exemplifying these values. The challenge for parents is to eliminate the dis from the disconnect and to help their children make the connection. As Dr. Steven Carr Reuben says,

> *"I believe that it is our responsibility as parents to pass on the best of that ethical tradition to our children. Giving them clear message regarding the ethical implications of the choices that they make each day and helping them to understand that every decision they make becomes part and parcel of forming the very essence of their moral character are the most challenging and important jobs we will every have."*

In the industrial world, managers and leaders strive to create climates or environments where employees can do their best work. Similarly, in our families we, as parents, must create environments in our homes that facilitate ethical behavior. Parents set the standards and enforce the limits and promote discipline in the home. Discipline, in some quarters, takes on a negative tone. However, to be effective, discipline and standards need to be structured in a positive way. Discipline, as we define it, means adherence to a code of conduct, and it entails all of the things you have to do, as a parent, to help your children become the ethical, moral, and socially responsible adults you want them to be. Put another way, discipline is instructing a child on the way he or she should behave or act and helping the child come to believe that such is the way he or she wants to act.

How do you do this? The most powerful and yet subtle way to teach your child to do the right thing is by example. Children in their own way watch your actions more than they hear your words. The power of example is magnified when what you do is the same as what you tell your children to do.

"You are constantly demonstrating to your children your values, your goals, and your ethical standards by your own daily behavior — whether you want to or not.

Whether you take a positive nurturing approach to discipline, or a negative and emotionally damaging approach, you will be teaching a whole series of lessons about self-esteem, parent–child relationships, and acceptable ethical behavior that your child will internalize."

So, the power of parental example and guidance along with the power of the role models, friends and heroes your children choose go a long, long way toward determining their values. Consequently, in subtle and, sometimes, not so subtle ways parents must help their children select their friends and their heroes.

Parents must take every opportunity in the course of daily living to acknowledge positive ethical behavior in their children. Parents must positively reinforce the *"good examples of behavior and when possible relate their behavior and experience in a given situation with similar examples they may have had when they were children."* Parents must take every opportunity to teach responsible behavior. For example, they must teach children to cultivate friendships and to cherish their friendships. One way to do this is to demonstrate to the children how to be a friend. In fact, friendship within the family and with children goes a long way toward influencing respectful behavior in children. Remember, everything we do or say as parents influences the behavior of our children. For years psychologists have been extolling the virtues of positive self-esteem. To be sure, there are those people who contend that if you had only one gift to give your children the single most important gift might be the gift of self-esteem. Self-esteem and self-confidence, accompanied by a positive attitude and outlook on life, fortified by the moral example of parents or heroes, helps create the ethical child we all hope to raise.

The best way to drive home the points I want to make is to refer once again to Steven Carr Reuben's book, ***Raising Ethical Children***. Dr.

Reuben enumerates ten keys to helping children become moral and caring:

1. BE A MORAL MODEL

In all of the interviews I conducted with the moral exemplars, each cited the importance they attached to one or both parents' guidance and example. The power of example is of paramount importance and although parents' moral example is primary because of the day-to-day exposure, the moral example provided by the child's heroes or role models or peers also has extraordinary importance. Since children often emulate parents, they may also favor the heroes you admire, so choose your heroes carefully and help your children select the right heroes who do the right things for the right reasons. I have often heard it said that children "watch you feet not your mouth." Of course that is another way of saying actions speak louder than words. So, in dealing with your children say what you mean and mean what you say and make sure that the example you set establishes the moral baseline you want your children to follow.

2. USE THE POWER OF POSITIVE REINFORCEMENT

In much of today's management and leadership parlance, people speak of employee alignment with corporate goals as important because it creates positive synergy and increased productivity. However, no amount of philosophical alignment of vision and goals will suffice without mutual trust and respect between the corporation and its employees.

In much the same way the interaction between parent and child must be based on a foundation of trust. Children must know that their parents are honest and fair. Parents must believe in their children and offer them uncompromising and unconditional love. This relationship based on trust takes years of commitment and dedication to nurture and develop. It can be undermined by even a trivial instance of unethical behavior on the part of either the parents or the children. Here is where forgiveness and unconditional love must be manifest.

> *"The key here is that once you realize how important attention is to a child, you will reward that child with positive attention for the behaviors that you desire, realizing that this is the single best way to reinforce that child's inner psyche with the importance of experiencing that behavior as an integral part of his or her being and self image.*
>
> *When you think of the phrase, **catch them** doing something right, let it remind you from time to time that your children are already acting in caring, sensitive, appropriate ways, but your tendency (if you are like most) is to ignore them unless they act our negatively. The challenge is to catch them acting in the positive ways that you approve, and then be sure to give them as many rewards and as much reinforcement and support as you can. In this way when they need attention they will more likely seek it by acting in a way that will make your proud so that you will reward their behavior with your approval."*

3. LISTEN WITH YOUR EYES

A few years ago, I was talking to someone who was listening so intently that I was concerned that what I was saying was not important enough to demand that intense attention. However, I did feel special in that someone I respected and admired was listening to every word I spoke.

Children are no different than adults when it comes to being listened to. We feel special and children feel special when whomever we are speaking to listens as if he or she really is interested in what we are saying. Listening, and listening with your eyes as well as your ears, is a way of showing respect and love for the person speaking.

"Listening with your eyes is really a marvelous gift of the heart and one which you can give to your children every day. It is a gift that costs nothing, yet makes the recipient feel like a million dollars." Children want you to listen and they want to be understood. And just as we as adults tell our children *"to look at me when I am speaking to you"* they want us to look at them when they talk and they really want us to listen with our eyes. When we truly give children our undivided attention we convey a special feeling of self worth because they feel worthy of the attention we give them.

4. BE CONSISTENT

"Children need stability and consistency in their lives. One of the most difficult challenges that caring parents have to face when it comes to effective discipline and the desire to raise ethical children is the need to be consistent in how they react to the behavior of their children."

In his hierarchy of needs, Abraham Maslow stipulates that our basic needs include both physiological needs and security needs. And children need to feel the security of knowing what to expect in their environment so they develop an inner sense of security that helps them grow and succeed in life. Security and stability are to children what water and fertilizer are to plants. Stable and secure surroundings support the emotional equilibrium a child needs to develop a positive value system and solid character growth.

When parents are consistent in their relationship with their children and the discipline they apply, they implicitly convey an attitude of openness to their children that facilitates the two-way communication process so essential to raising ethical children. Long after the parents' words of wisdom stop, children hear the voice of their conscience repeating and reenforcing the message from their parents.

5. HAVE INTEGRITY, MEAN WHAT YOU SAY

The common thread that I observed with the moral heroes that I described in Chapter Three was the powerful example of integrity manifested by one or both parents. Norman Augustine speaks of the strength of character of his father and his father's admonition to be a good person now and not to wait until he grew up to be a good man. Coach Mike Krzyzewski speaks of the sacrifices his parents made to send him to parochial school and their desire for him to attend West Point. Congresswoman Sue Myrick stated that her father was the most ethical person she knew. Dr. Earl Hess revealed the tremendous admiration he had for his father and for what his father stood for. President James O. Freedman describes his parents' example as complementary and commendable. Monsignor James Treston describes the integrity of his mother and the persuasive influence she had on his life. Having integrity is much like having a friend — if you want to have a friend you have to be a friend. And if you want your child to have integrity then you as a parent must manifest integrity in all your endeavors. You must be responsible and reliable, you must mean what you say, you must not lie, cheat or steal and you must honor your commitments. Children are quite perceptive and a parents' admonishment "*to do as I say not what I do*" doesn't really serve as a model of integrity.

6. DEMONSTRATE UNCONDITIONAL LOVE

Love and appreciation by parents are essential elements for nurturing a child's self-esteem and self-respect. And self-esteem and self-respect are the underpinning for positive ethical and social behavior. Children look for approval and love from their parents.

> *"Positive loving attachment to a parent figure is the first crucial step toward building the requisite self-esteem and self-image necessary for ethical, social behavior as an adult. Holding, touching, kissing, demonstrating love for your children from their earliest infancy is the single most important gift you can give them. It is the one linch-*

pin that holds all of the other emotional, social psychological and spiritual building blocks of personality together. Without it, your children are doomed to a life of inner conflict, pain, and turmoil. With it, anything is possible and there are no limits to what they accomplish. Nothing can hold them back from becoming the kind of people that any of us would be proud to have in our lives."

When we talk about demonstrating unconditional love, there are three operative words that parents should remember — there needs to be **LOVE**, it should be *unconditional* and must be *demonstrated*.

7. WHEN THEY ASK "WHY?" TELL THEM.

Children want to be taken seriously. As suggested earlier, when we said that parents should listen with their eyes, it is also important to give appropriate attention to the questions your children ask you. If you react to a child's questions in a serious way, you create an excellent environment for meaningful conversation and open communication. When the communication between parents and children is straightforward and honest, the opportunity to influence their behavior and value system is enhanced. The important feature here is that, with open, sincere communication, parents can share with their children the values they deem important. If parental words are in harmony with parental deeds, then we have the necessary ingredients for teaching and role modeling. But, it all starts with honest communication.

8. GIVE THEM WHAT THEY NEED, NOT WHAT THEY WANT

Your children will test your limits and they will tell you time and time again their friends are getting better treatment from their parents than you are giving them. Your children will tell you that their friends get bigger allowances, get to stay out later, get to use the family car more often, etc., etc. Parenting is serious business — it is not a popularity contest. Parents should not go out of their way to be contentious, but their children are their responsibility. As teachers and mentors, parents must emphasize what is right, not what is popular. Children need limits — they need to know that their parents stand for something, that their value systems are anchored on a solid ethical and moral base that does not change. I have heard it said that the two most important things you give to your children are roots and wings. Make sure the roots you give your children are grounded in morals and ethics.

9. GIVE THEM A SENSE OF BELONGING

Being part of a family or being part of a team helps a person, especially a child, feel supported or connected. It is a way of feeling not alone or a way of having a support system. When the going gets tough, when one's moral fiber and one's integrity are challenged, a support system helps one stand tall — helps one to resist temptation. Synergy results when the parts of a whole add up to more than the whole. This phenomenon generally occurs when component parts of a system are interdependent, synchronized, and mutually supporting. The family is a perfect place for such synergy. For a child to develop with the family, he or she needs to feel loved and feel that he or she belongs. If the family has a strong value system, then each family member practices these values and everyone benefits.

10. RESPECT THEM AND DEMAND RESPECT IN RETURN

Almost without exception when anyone enumerates a list of values, the word respect appears. Respect is a fundamental, core value. Respect is the fundamental underpinning of most religions — it is the basis of the Golden Rule.

To live morally and ethically, one must understand the nature of respect. Without respect there can be no love, and to love your children is the first step in creating an environment wherein ethics and morals can be introduced and developed in an effective rational way.

If we are truly concerned about ethics in the twenty-first century, then we must pull out all the stops and do whatever we must to raise ethical children all over the world. It is a Herculean task and there should be no illusions about the degree of difficulty in achieving effective results. Nevertheless, to walk a thousand miles you have to take the first step. Let us not underestimate the power of example and the difference each of us can make if we each will stand for a more ethical world and if we teach our children how to be mature, positive, constructive, and ethical.

I extracted some interesting thoughts from an article written by Dr. Laura Schlessinger and published in **USA WEEKEND**. The article was entitled "Which are better...Smart Kids or Good Kids?" Dr. Laura observes that many parents worry more about how their children appear — smart, attractive, successful — than about the content of their children's character. Dr. Schlessinger goes on to say that parents should send their kids the right messages by:

- instilling respect for authority in your children by properly modeling that behavior.
- establishing consequences for moral lapses and following through.
- eating meals together and, during this time, exploring meaningful issues.
- attending worship services as a family regularly.
- paying attention to what your children watch, read and listen to. Take issue with immoral and unethical conduct.

Our children can't help but be negatively influenced by the examples set by some of our sports heroes and Hollywood celebrities. Dr. Laura's recommendation to counter that trend is:

"Make it clear to children that no amount of scoring, fame or fortune make up for a lack of responsibility and character. Find examples of virtuous behavior in the world and celebrate it. Create your own Hall of Fame in the family by rewarding decent behavior; and in the

world, by having your children write letter of appreciation to those who 'do good'."

With so many external influences affecting the minds and behavior of children, it is absolutely essential that parents get "their oar in the water" early and often to educate, impress and inspire their children to know and live the values that relate directly to the family and cultural heritage. The apple does not fall far from the tree, so make sure that the tree is healthy, strong, and straight.

CHAPTER TWENTY

WHERE DO WE GO
FROM HERE?

L ET'S TAKE A CLOSE LOOK at where we are now.
Although I have talked to many people and have done a
reasonable amount of research the conclusions and judgments presented herein are mine. I have reflected on what
the great moral philosophers have written; I have read many of the current books and editorials on leadership, ethics and values and morality;
I have completed a series of interviews with successful people. I have
reviewed and examined a number of codes of ethics and honor codes,
and I have worked with and learned from the Institute of Global Ethics
of Camden, Maine, and the United States Military Academy at West
Point. Much of what I have presented in this book is the result of interviews, polls, newspaper editorials, book research, seminars, codes of
ethics and surveys.

All of that having been said let me return to the following questions
on ethics: WHERE ARE WE? and WHERE DO WE GO FROM
HERE? As I strive to answer the first question, let me put my

comments in a time frame because of the highly charged ethical debate concerning the President Clinton-Monica Lewinsky scandal and the lies and alleged cover-up. The moral issues concerning this case are real and revolve around extramarital sex and deceit on one hand and loyalty on the other hand. In any event, the entire drawn-out affair is forcing a most difficult introspection and review of our national values, our morality, and our sense of ethics. Because of the conduct, sacrifices, and contributions made by many Americans, the moral authority of America in the world has been high. It is important that our leaders not dissipate that reservoir of moral authority.

When I wrote the first chapter of this book and entitled it *Moral Meltdown*, I thought that perhaps the title was too strong and a bit melodramatic. Now, I think maybe the title is not strong enough. Perhaps I should stop "soft soaping" and give you my primary conclusions: **AS A NATION WE ARE IN A MORAL FREE FALL**. For those of you who think I am an alarmist, let me ask you to consider the following:

There is an alarmingly high divorce rate in our country and, putting aside the causes and emotional trauma of the divorces, the result is that many children receive the day-to-day supervision of only one parent. More often than not, the single supervising parent has a full time job and cannot give full attention to the difficult, time consuming, and arduous task of parenting.

- There is also an alarmingly high number of children conceived out of wedlock. The situation in this latter case may even be worse because, often, the fathers in these cases will not or cannot assume responsibility for the child.

- There are relatively high numbers of families wherein both parents work, and although these families may be earning more money, they have less time and less energy for their children.

- The number of positive examples among parents, leaders, heroes, peers, and role models appears to be diminishing.

Adults are compromising their values, and their behavior is far removed from what they were taught as children. Some of this is attributed to the notion of *ethical relativism or situational ethics,* wherein ethical issues are considered relative to a specific social group or culture. The ethical relativist believes that there are no universal ethical norms or standards. It is fine for one to assert: "By my conscience I will decide if something is right or wrong." It is quite another to rationalize with: "I will decide by circumstance when something is right or wrong." The former is based on principled reasoning. The latter is narcissistic and very dangerous. The bottom line is waffling or rationalizing on important ethical issues leads to questionable behavior that in turn undermines the power of example.

• There appears to be an addiction to "mindless" TV among both parents and children. Many children spend more time in front of the television screen than they do studying, reading, writing, and exercising. There has to be a mind conditioning that occurs when one spends 15 to 20 hours or more per week watching bad examples on television. The average child has watched 8,000 televised murders and 100,000 acts of violence on TV before finishing elementary school. Are we so naïve as to assume that the cumulative effect of all of the TV violence and sex is neutral? Is there any way that the bottom-line effect of the mental conditioning that results from the majority of TV shows is not harmful?

• When you look at the statistics concerning students cheating in schools; the number of teenagers who are sexually active; the number of violent acts on and by teenagers; the number of young people who feel that it is necessary and acceptable to lie to get ahead or succeed; and the number of young people who abuse alcohol and drugs, one must conclude that from an ethical and moral standpoint, *things are not good.*

- Fifty years ago the major problems that teachers encountered in our schools concerned students talking or chewing gum in class, running in the halls or an occasional student prank. Today, the problems teachers face in schools are considerably more severe: they involve drugs, violence, guns, knives, defiance, and apathy. We can't expect schools to solve all of society's problems. The teachers need parental cooperation in disciplining students and inculcating shared ethical values.

- I feel it is imperative to exhort religious leaders, churches, and other faith organizations to do more. I have no evidence that they are seriously at fault, but, I will say that they can and should get more proactive in doing their part to turn the tide because they can have a significant impact.

- The desensitizing of America is neither a healthy process nor a pretty sight. Inch by inch, foot by foot, and yard by yard *we are gradually and incrementally lowering our standards.* At every level, we see examples of people who are rationalizing their behavior. There is more time and energy spent in rationalizing and conducting campaigns to discredit others than in trying to do what is right. There appears to be a lack of accountability, a lack of responsibility, a lack of courage and a willingness by so many of us to tolerate unethical or immoral conduct. We have seen many examples of national figures who have violated our trust and confidence. We have a president who had lied about extramarital affairs and still gets a high approval rating. Rationalizations such as: *it's only sex, everybody does it*, and *it's okay to lie as long as he's being a good president* are indications of ethical compromise as we approach the twenty-first century. As we continue to accept lies, and devastating counterattacks on the accusers, we continue to lower the bar. We no longer have a high jump standard at seven feet; it is at four feet and heading lower. If we continue on this course of moral relativism or subjective morality and if each of us insists on crafting our behavior to suit our own selfish interests, we will continue to gradually diminish our moral compass. The truth is the truth; we must seek it; we must live it. *The truth is that with all the freedoms we enjoy, in the end the only freedom that matters is the freedom to discipline ourselves.*

As the only global superpower with a democratic political system and a capitalistic free enterprise system, we are still regarded as the leader of the free world. Without moral authority and the trust that moral authority engenders, we stand to lose our position of leadership in the world. Moreover, in the worst case, despite our superpower status, we face the real possibility of destroying ourselves from within. Please do not be too quick to dismiss this possibility.

- In Chapter Two, I draw the conclusion that regardless of our religion, race or ethnic background we all share a common set of values. These are not imposed values but shared values. **Honesty, respect, responsibility, freedom, fairness, love, service, and loyalty** are values that most American profess. Time after time, when Americans are asked to define their values, the same or similar themes are expressed. So, our problems are not due to misguided values, per se. THE PROBLEM IS A DISCONNECT BETWEEN THE VALUES WE PROFESS AND THE BEHAVIOR WE DEMONSTRATE.

For whatever reason, the self-discipline, courage, and the commitment required to forge the connection between values and behavior are missing. I firmly believe that most people know what is right and that there is latent goodness in everyone. It seems, however, that many people are more concerned about appearing to be honorable as opposed to really conducting themselves honorably. It is my observation that there is more interest in style than in substance. This is a very appropriate time to repeat the quotation that appears at the beginning of Chapter One:

The shortest and surest way to live with honor in the world is to be in reality what we would appear to be. All human virtues increase and strengthen themselves by the practice and experience of them.

— *Socrates*

- The bottom line is that there is a moral meltdown and the trendline is in my view on a seriously downward slope. When you combine deteriorating ethics with the leverage that modern technology provides you have a situation wherein a few unethical people can do a considerable amount of harm to all of the rest of us. So we need to pay attention to the ethos and moral fiber that we carry into the 21st century. Now is the time to pay attention to the problem, do everything within our power to stem the tide, and convert a negative trendline into a positive one.

THE ANATOMY OF CHARACTER

The largest portion of this book is devoted to identifying and describing a number of moral exemplars — more specially a number of people who succeeded in their chosen fields because they did so with integrity. Their example was meant to show that true, enduring success must come from trust. Integrity is essential to success. These people's ethical behavior was their source of strength — they are what they appear to be. They trust and they are trusted; they pursue the truth; they lead by example; they appeal to the best that they see in their colleagues and followers; they align and they empower; they create environments where others can do their best and be their best; they truly believe that to lead is to serve. Their vision, their actions, their demeanor and their conduct allow them to develop a large positive balance in their moral bank account. In addition, to their positional authority, they have earned moral authority and it is this moral authority coupled with their professional competence that adds an additional dimension of effectiveness. In a word they are leaders of character.

There are a number of personal traits that describe or define leaders, and they all play some role in the leadership and success formula. Vision, judgment, intelligence, know-how, stamina, energy, personality, charisma and diligence are all important. I don't like to denigrate these wonderful qualities, because they are important, but as important as they are, they are secondary because by themselves, without character, they will lead to ruin. If leaders are to be trusted with the big important decisions, they must be leaders of character. It is a magic concept and it is described in one word — CHARACTER.

There is a wholeness about a person of character. He or she is not divided against himself or herself. He doesn't think one thing and say another, and it is virtually impossible for him to lie. He or she is not in conflict with his or her own principles. He doesn't believe in one thing and do another. With the absence of that inner warfare, there is extra energy and clarity of thought that makes success and achievement, if not inevitable, at least probable.

CHARACTER MEANS LIVING UP TO THE BEST IN YOURSELF.

Years ago, a writer who had lost a fortune in bad investments went into bankruptcy. His intention was to pay off every cent he owed, and three years later he was still working at it. To help him, a newspaper organized a fund. Important people contributed heavily to it, and it was a temptation to accept the contributions because accepting them would have meant the end of a big burden. But Mark Twain refused and returned the money to the contributors. Seven months later, with his new book a hit, he paid the last of his debts in full.

CHARACTER MEANS HAVING A HIGHLY DEVELOPED SENSE OF INTEGRITY.

What is the mark of true integrity in a person? It is how he or she conducts himself or herself when no one is looking. It is an individual who is true to his own standards and hence to himself. It is that person who practices total honesty in the little things as well as the big things. That person not telling the small white lie when it is inconvenient to tell the truth; not repeating that juicy bit of gossip that is quite possibly untrue; not charging the personal phone call to the office.

Such disciplines may sound small, but when you really seek integrity, it develops its own power that sweeps you along. Finally you begin to see that anything worth having has an integrity of its own that must not be violated.

CHARACTER MEANS HAVING A CONSCIENCE AND LISTENING TO IT.

Harry Emerson Fosdick told how Abraham Lincoln was warned by his friends not to give a certain speech while campaigning for the Senate in 1858. Lincoln allegedly replied: "If it is decreed that I should go down because of this speech, then let me go down linked to the truth." He did lose the senate election, but two years later he became President.

CHARACTER MEANS HAVING THE COURAGE OF YOUR CONVICTIONS.

This includes the capacity to cling to what you think is right, to go it alone if necessary, and to speak out against what you believe is wrong.

CHARACTER MEANS THE OBEDIENCE TO THE UNENFORCEABLE.

In a way, this is the heart of it. No one can force you to live up to the best in yourself. No one can compel you to get involved. No one can make you obey your conscience. A person of honor does these things anyway.

Yeah! Difficult — not easy at all. No one said it was easy, and that is why it is rare. But, oh, how it is admired. And in terms of ultimate reward, it is worth all of the effort. It pays dividends in so many other ways — in boldness —it gives you the strength to take chances, to welcome challenges, to reject the safe but unsatisfactory approach and select a bold superior approach. A person of honor can do this because he has no reason to distrust himself.

SOME OTHER ASPECTS OF CHARACTER ARE PERSISTENCE, COMMITMENT, AND COURAGE.

Honor brings with it an unshakable singleness of purpose, a tenacity that refuses to give up. "Never give in," said Winston Churchill when England was under attack and siege in WWII. "Never, never, never. In nothing great or small, large or petty, never give in except to convictions of honor and good sense," and he never did.

AND STILL ANOTHER DERIVATIVE OF CHARACTER IS SERENITY.

People of character are shock resistant. They seem to have a built-in equanimity that enables them to rebound from setbacks, or even injustices, without rancor or thoughts of revenge.

There are many other benefits that character brings to a person: friendship, trust, admiration and respect. One of the hopeful things about the human race is that people seem to recognize character almost instinctively and are irresistibly attracted to it. And that is why I say it is the fundamental cornerstone of leadership and the essential ingredient to the formula for success.

So far in this final chapter we have looked at where we are and where we would like to be. Specifically, we have observed what I consider to be a serious decline in our moral behavior. We have also looked at the benefits and wisdom of conducting all of our affairs, personal and professional, on a high moral plane as evidenced by the success and ethics of the moral exemplars presented in Section II.

WHERE DO WE GO FROM HERE?

So the big questions is HOW DO WE GET FROM WHERE WE ARE TO WHERE WE WANT TO BE? This is a huge challenge and we need to give it serious attention. Let me repeat, this is, in my view, a Herculean task that is going to take a major effort from people at all levels and people of all ages: children, parents, grandparents, teachers, preachers, leaders, followers, corporations, and universities. We are swimming upstream, and we have our work cut out for us. We as a people have admirable values and there is latent goodness in most of us but that is not enough. In this light, let me offer some serious recommendations intended to improve the overall moral condition of the nation:

- Government at all levels should publish and practice ethical principles for professional conduct and decision making.

- Parents must accept full responsibility for their behavior and for the ethical and moral development of their children. This is serious business, and it must be treated seriously.

- Our schools, including teachers, administrators, coaches and counselors, can and should play an important role in the ethical development of students. They must instruct and they must also help students connect with their values. Some may think that this approach is tantamount to imposing values, someone else's values, on children. As our research has shown, this is hardly the case. As a society, we share our fundamental values in common. *The Institute of Global Ethics, Character Counts,* and the *Josephine Institute* are organizations that can provide training and assistance to teachers who want to help their students with ethical fitness.

- Church and religious leaders have a built-in structure and value framework that make them uniquely qualified to teach and exemplify values for adults and children. I would hope that church leaders will reach out, set up community programs, and emphasize ethics in all life's aspects.

- Corporations have learned that good ethics are good business. More and more corporations are developing codes of ethics and ethics education programs. The key to success for these programs is the genuine commitment and example of the CEO and the senior leaders of the company.

- If you are an athletic star, famous politician, entertainer, journalist, military hero or industry leader, you are automatically a role model, whether you want to be one or not. At some point in your life, you are going to ask yourself how you can pay society back for your good fortune. I suggest you not wait too long to stand up for the best that is within you and utilize your personal leverage to make a positive moral contribution in your sphere of influence.

- Last, but not least, if you have concerns about the moral and ethical fiber of the community or culture in which you live, you can and should still contribute to their betterment. By living and exemplifying the shared values that we hold dear, you will make a difference. Do not underestimate the power of your example. One person can make a difference, and you can be that one person.

Before I conclude this chapter, I want to interject Charles Colson's suggestions on ways to recover and renew our character. Charles Colson has had reason to give this subject some very serious thought. As the Special Counsel to President Nixon, Chuck Colson got carried away with re-electing President Nixon because he was committed to ending the war in Vietnam and getting our prisoners back. Despite his strong value system and good intentions, he wound up in the middle of the Watergate scandal, which turned out to be one of the biggest political scandals in American history. He ultimately concluded that loyalty — if not attached to a cause that is moral and just — can be the most dangerous of all virtues. Chuck Colson makes a good point when he says that being a man or woman of character requires something more than an intellectual commitment to noble goals.

"It is the disposition to do what is right. It is not enough to know what is good; we must love the good and have the will to act in accord with it."

After much soul searching and much serious thought, Colson offers the following four suggestions as ways to recover and renew our character:

1. *"We must rediscover our belief in binding, unchanging moral truths. Our crisis of character is understandable in the absence of absolutes. We must be able to appeal to an objective rule, not a subjective feeling or a majority decision that might change tomorrow."*

2. *"We must restore a sense of shame and stigma in our society. When social disapproval is strong, it is more effective than laws, policies and the courts. So long as there is shame, it has been said there is hope for virtue."*

3. *"We need to respect and strengthen the character-forming institutions of society, particularly the family, supported by the*

church and local community. Intellectual virtue — knowing what is good is not enough."

We must connect with our values and act accordingly. The last step requires commitment and moral courage.

Colson goes on to say that a relationship with God helps breach the chasm between knowing what is right and doing what is right.

So we come to end of this journey in search of ethics. There is much to be done in this fast-paced, ever-changing, technology-driven world in which we live. There is genuine concern about *"surviving the 21st century with the ethics of the 20th century,"* but there is every reason to be hopeful. We know it is right to be ethical and to behave in a moral manner. We can live it, we can teach it, and we can make it happen one person and one day at a time. You are the one and today's the first day. Let's go! Let's all stand together for the possibility of a more ethical world.

A P P E N D I C E S

CODE OF ETHICS

SELECTED REFERENCES

APPENDIX A

LOCKHEED MARTIN

CODE OF ETHICS
AND BUSINESS CONDUCT

A T LOCKHEED MARTIN, we believe that ethical conduct requires more than compliance with the laws, rules, and regulations that govern our business. We are a company that values teamwork, sets team goals, assumes collective accountability for actions, embraces diversity, and shares leadership. We are an organization that is deeply committed to excellence and pursues superior performance in every activity. Underlying and supporting ethics at Lockheed Martin is the personal integrity of each of our employees and the highest standards in their personal and professional conduct. Our Code deals with "doing things right" and with "the right thing to do" so as to maintain our personal and institutional integrity.

NOTE: *The following has been adapted from* Setting the Standard, *as adopted by the Board of Directors of Lockheed Martin.*

While maintaining sensitivity to the diverse social and cultural settings in which we conduct our business, Lockheed Martin aims to *set the standard* for ethical conduct at all of our localities throughout the world. We will achieve this through behavior in accordance with six virtues: Honesty, Integrity, Respect, Trust, Responsibility, and Citizenship.

HONESTY: to be truthful in all our endeavors; to be honest and forthright with one another and with our customers, communities, suppliers, and shareholders.

INTEGRITY: to say what we mean, to deliver what we promise, and to stand for what is right.

RESPECT: to treat one another with dignity and fairness, appreciating the diversity of our workforce and the uniqueness of each employee.

TRUST: to build confidence through teamwork and open, candid communication.

RESPONSIBILITY: to speak up – without fear of retribution — and report concerns in the workplace, including violations of law, regulations and company policies, and seek clarification and guidance whenever there is doubt.

Thank you for doing your part to create and maintain an ethical work environment…and for *Setting the Standard.*

—Vance D. Coffman
Chief Executive Officer

TREAT IN AN ETHICAL MANNER THOSE TO WHOM LOCKHEED MARTIN HAS AN OBLIGATION

For our employees we are committed to honesty, just management, fairness, providing a safe and healthy environment free from the fear of retribution, and respecting the dignity due everyone.

For our customers we are committed to produce reliable products and services, delivered on time, at a fair price.

For the communities in which we live and work we re committed to observe sound environmental business practices and to act as concerned and responsible neighbors, reflecting all aspects of good citizenship.

For our shareholders we are committed to pursuing sound growth and earning objectives and to exercising prudence in the use of our assets and resources.

For our suppliers and partners we are committed to fair competition and the sense of responsibility required of a good customer and teammate.

We are committed to the ethical treatment of those to whom we have an obligation.

OBEY THE LAW

We will conduct our business in accordance with all applicable laws and regulations. The laws and regulations related to government contracting are far-reaching and complex, thus placing responsibilities on Lockheed Martin beyond those faced by companies without government customers. Compliance with the law does not comprise our entire ethical responsibility. Rather, it is a minimum, absolutely essential condition for performance of our duties.

We will conduct our business in accordance with all applicable laws and regulations.

PROMOTE A POSITIVE WORK ENVIRONMENT

All employees want and deserve a workplace where they feel respected, satisfied, and appreciated. As a global enterprise, we respect cultural diversity and recognize that the various countries in which we do business may have different legal provisions pertaining to the workplace. As such, we will adhere to the limitations specified by law in all of our localities, and further, we will not tolerate harassment or discrimination of any kind — especially involving race, color, religion, gender, age, national origin, disability, and veteran or marital status.

Providing an environment that supports honesty, integrity, respect, trust, responsibility, and citizenship permits us the opportunity to achieve excellence in our workplace. While everyone who works for the Company must contribute to the creation and maintenance of such an environment, our executives and management personnel assume special responsibility for fostering a work environment that is free from the fear of retribution and will bring out the best in all of us. Supervisors must be careful in words and conduct to avoid placing, or seeming to place, pressure on subordinates that could cause them to deviate from acceptable ethical behavior.

WORK SAFELY. PROTECT YOURSELF, YOUR FELLOW EMPLOYEES, AND THE WORLD WE LIVE IN

We are committed to providing a drug-free, safe, and healthy work environment, and to observe environmentally sound business practices throughout the world. We will strive, at a minimum, to do no harm and where possible, to make the communities in which we work a better place to live. Each of us is responsible for compliance with environmental, health, and safety laws and regulations. Observe posted warnings and regulations. Report immediately to the appropriate management any accident or injury sustained on the job, or any environmental or safety concern you may have.

We are committed to providing a drug-free, safe, and healthy work environment.

298

KEEP ACCURATE AND COMPLETE RECORDS

We must maintain accurate and complete Company records. Transactions between the Company and outside individuals and organizations must be promptly and accurately entered in our books in accordance with generally accepted business practices and principles. No one should rationalize or even consider misrepresenting facts or falsifying records. It will not be tolerated and will result in disciplinary action.

No one should rationalize or even consider misrepresenting facts or falsifying records.

RECORD COSTS PROPERLY

Employees and their supervisors are responsible for ensuring that labor and material costs are accurately recorded and charged on the Company's records. These costs include, but are not limited to, normal contract work, work related to independent research and development, and bid and proposal activities.

Employees and their supervisors are responsible for... the Company records.

STRICTLY ADHERE TO ALL ANTITRUST LAWS

Antitrust is a blanket term for laws that protect the free enterprise system and promote open and fair competition. Such laws exist in the United States, the European Union, and in many other countries where the Company does business. These laws deal with agreements and practices "in restraint of trade" such as price fixing and boycotting suppliers or customers, for example. They also bar pricing intended to run a competitor out of business; disparaging, misrepresenting, or harassing a competitor; stealing trade secrets; bribery; and kickbacks.

Antitrust laws are vigorously enforced. Violations may result in severe penalties such as forced sales of parts of businesses and significant fines against the Company. There may also be sanctions against individual employees including substantial fines and prison sentences.

KNOW AND FOLLOW THE LAW WHEN INVOLVED IN INTERNATIONAL BUSINESS

Corruption erodes confidence in the marketplace, undermines democracy, distorts economic and social development, and hurts everyone who depends on trust and transparency in the transaction of business. The Company is committed to conduct its activities free from the unfair influence of bribery and to foster anti-corruption awareness among its employees and business relations throughout the world. The Foreign Corrupt Practices Act (FCPA) is a United States law that prohibits corruptly giving, offering or promising anything of value to foreign officials or foreign political parties, officials or candidates, for the purpose of influencing them to misuse their official capacity to obtain, keep, or direct business or to gain any improper advantage. In addition, the FCPA prohibits knowingly falsifying a company's books and records or knowingly circumventing or failing to implement accounting controls. Employees involved in international operations must be familiar with the FCPA and with similar laws that govern our operations in other countries in which we do business.

International transfers of equipment or technology are also subject to laws and regulations — such as the International Traffic in Arms Regulations (ITAR) in the United States — that may contain prior approval, licensing, and reporting requirements.

Additionally, it is illegal to enter into an agreement to refuse to deal with potential or actual customers or suppliers, or otherwise to engage in or support restrictive international trade practices or boycotts.

It is always important that employees who conduct international business know and abide by the laws of the countries which are involved in the activities or transactions. These laws govern the conduct of Lockheed Martin employees throughout the world. If you participate in these business activities, you should know, understand, and strictly comply with these laws and regulations. If you are not familiar with these rules, consult with your supervisor and the Legal Department prior to negotiating any foreign transaction.

FOLLOW THE LAW AND USE COMMON SENSE IN POLITICAL CONTRIBUTIONS AND ACTIVITIES

Lockheed Martin encourages its employees to become involved in civic affairs and to participate in the political process. Employees must understand, however, that their involvement and participation must be on an individual basis, on their own time, and at their own expense. In the United States, federal law prohibits corporations from donating corporate funds, goods, or services, directly or indirectly , to candidates for federal offices — this includes employees' work time. Local and state laws also govern political contributions and activities as they apply to their respective jurisdictions and similar laws exist in other countries.

CAREFULLY BID, NEGOTIATE, AND PERFORM CONTRACTS

We must comply with the laws and regulations that pertain to the acquisition of goods and services by our customers. We will compete fairly and ethically for all business opportunities. In circumstances where there is reason to believe that the release or receipt of non-public information is unauthorized, we do not attempt to obtain and do not accept such information from any source.

Appropriate steps should be taken to recognize and avoid organizational conflicts in which one business unit's activities may preclude the pursuit of a related activity by another Company business unit.

If you are involved in proposals, bid preparations, or contract negotiations, you must be certain that all statements, communications, and representations to prospective customers are accurate and truthful. Once awarded, all contracts must be performed in compliance with specifications, requirements, and clauses.

AVOID ILLEGAL AND QUESTIONABLE GIFTS OR FAVORS

The sale of Lockheed Martin products and services should always be free from even the perception that favorable treatment was sought, received, or given in exchange for the furnishing or receipt of business courtesies. Employees will neither give nor accept business courtesies that constitute, or could be reasonable perceived as constituting, unfair business inducements or that would violate law, regulation or policies of the Company or customer, or customer, or could cause embarrassment to or reflect negatively on the Company's reputation. Although customs ad practices may differ among the many marketplaces in which we conduct our business, our policies in this regard are substantially similar within the United States and elsewhere throughout the world. As a matter of respect for the rich and diverse customs practiced among our business relations internationally, permissive conduct may differ somewhat in accordance with applicable policy or upon guidance from the business unit's Ethics Officer and Legal Department.

Gifts, Gratuities, and Business Courtesies to U.S., State, and Local Government Employees

Federal, state and local government departments and agencies are governed by laws and regulations concerning acceptance by their employees of entertainment, meals, gifts, gratuities, and other things of value from firms and persons with whom those government departments and agencies do business or over whom they have regulatory authority. It is the policy of Lockheed Martin to comply strictly with these laws and regulations.

Federal Executive Branch Employees

Lockheed Martin employees are prohibited from giving anything of value to federal executive Branch employees, except as follows:

* Lockheed Martin advertising or promotional items of little intrinsic value (generally $10.00 or less) such as a coffee

mug, calendar, or similar item displaying the Company logo,

- Modest refreshment such as soft drinks, coffee, and donuts on an occasional basis in connection with business activities; or

- Business-related meals and local transportation having an aggregate value of $20.00 or less per occasion, provided such items do not in aggregate exceed $50.00 in a calendar year. Although it is the responsibility of the government employee to track and monitor these thresholds, no Lockheed Martin employee shall knowingly provide meals and/or transportation exceeding the $20.00 individual or $50.00 annual limit.

Certain other exceptions regarding widely attended gatherings and business activities outside U.S. borders are detailed in company policy.

Federal Legislative and Judiciary Branches, and State and Local Government Employees

Employees of the federal Legislative and Judiciary Branches and employees of state and local government departments or agencies are subject to a wide variety of different laws and regulations. These laws and regulations and Corporate Policy Statements pertaining to them must be consulted prior to offering such employees anything of value.

Business Courtesies to Non-Government Persons

Meals, Refreshments and Entertainment

It is an acceptable practice for Lockheed Martin employees to provide meals, refreshments, entertainment, and other business courtesies of reasonable value to non-government persons in support of business activities, provided:

- The Practice does not violate any law or regulation or the standards of conduct of the recipient's organization. It is the offeror's responsibility to inquire about prohibitions or limitations of the recipient's organization before offering any business courtesy; and

- The business courtesy must be consistent with marketplace practices, infrequent in nature and may not be lavish or extravagant. While it is difficult to define "lavish or extravagant" by means of a specific dollar amount, a common sense determination should be made consistent with reasonable marketplace practices.

Gifts

Lockheed Martin employees are prohibited from offering or giving tangible gifts (including tickets to sporting, recreational, or other events) having a market value of $100.00 or more, to a person or entity with which the Company does or seeks to do business, unless specifically approved by his or her supervisor, and the business unit's Ethics Officer or the Corporate Office of Ethics and Business Conduct.

Business Courtesies to Foreign Governmental Personnel and Public officials

The Company may be restricted from giving meals, gifts,, gratuities, entertainment, or other things of value to personnel of foreign governments and foreign public officials by the Foreign Corrupt Practices Act and by laws of other countries. Employees must obtain prior Legal department approval where the hospitality (i.e., meal, gift, gratuity, entertainment or other thing of value) to be given is not clearly permissible under the Hospitality Guidelines and Matrix maintained by the Legal Department.

Employees must discuss such situations with Legal Counsel...

Business Courtesies to Lockheed Martin Employees

Meals, Refreshments and Entertainment

Although an employee may not use his or her position at Lockheed Martin to foster obtaining business courtesies, it is permissible to accept unsolicited meals, refreshments, entertainment, and other business courtesies on an occasional basis, provided:

- The acceptance will foster goodwill and successful business relations;

- The courtesies are not lavish or extravagant under the circumstances;

- The courtesies are not frequent and do not reflect a pattern or the appearance of a pattern of frequent acceptance of courtesies from the same entities or persona; and

- The employee accepting the courtesies would feel comfortable about discussing the courtesies with his or her manager or coworker, or having the courtesies known by the public.

It is the personal responsibility of each employee to ensure that his or her acceptance of such meals, refreshments, or entertainment is proper and could not reasonably be construed in any way as an attempt by the offering party to secure favorable treatment.

It is the personal responsibility of each employee...

Gifts

Lockheed Martin employees are not permitted to accept compensation, honoraria, funds or monetary instruments in any form or amount, or any tangible gift (including tickets to sporting, recreational, or other events) that has a market value of $100.00 or more, from any entity, representatives of any entity, or any person that does or seeks to do business with the Company, unless approved by his or her supervisor, and the business unit's Ethics Office or the

Corporate Office of Ethics and Business Conduct. Solicitation of gifts is always prohibited. If you have any questions about the propriety of a gift, gratuity, or item of value, contact your supervisor, Ethics Officer or the Corporate Office of Ethics and Business Conduct for guidance.

Gifts to Lockheed Martin Employees Who Procure Goods or Services

If you buy goods or services for Lockheed Martin or are involved in the procurement process, you must treat all suppliers uniformly and fairly. In deciding among competing suppliers, you must objectively and impartially weigh all facts and avoid even the appearance of favoritism. For this reason, gifts from suppliers or vendors must not be accepted, except advertising or promotional items of nominal value such as a pen, key chain, water bottle, visor, cup or glass or similar items displaying a company's logo. Established routines and procedures should be followed in the procurement of all goods and services.

STEER CLEAR OF CONFLICTS OF INTEREST AND KNOW THE RULES ABOUT EMPLOYING FORMER GOVERNMENT OFFICIALS

Playing favorites or having conflicts of interest — in practice or appearance — runs counter to the fair treatment to which we are all entitled. Avoid any relationship, influence, or activity that might impair, or even appear to impair, your ability to make objective and fair decisions when performing your job. There are extensive conflicts of interest laws and regulations regarding the employment or use of former military and civilian government personnel. These rules extend to contract or negotiations with current government employees to discuss their potential employment by the Company or their use as consultant or subcontractors. Conflict of interest laws and regulations must be fully and carefully observed. When in doubt, consult corporate and company policies and procedures and share the facts of the situation with your supervisor, Legal Department, Human Resources, or Ethics Officer.

When in doubt, share the facts of the situation with you supervisor, Legal Department, Human Resources or Ethics Officer.

Here are some ways a conflict of interest could arise:

- Employment by a competitor or potential competitor, regardless of the nature of the employment, while employed by Lockheed Martin;

- Acceptance of gifts, payment, or services from those seeking to do business with Lockheed Martin;

- Placement of business with a firm owned or controlled by an employee or his/her family;

- Ownership of, or substantial interest in, a company which is a competitor or a supplier; and

- Acting as a consultant to Lockheed Martin customer or supplier.

MAINTAIN THE INTEGRITY OF CONSULTANTS, AGENTS, AND REPRESENTATIVES

Business integrity is a key standard for the selection and retention of those who represent Lockheed Martin. Agents, representatives, or consultants must certify their willingness to comply with the Company's policies and procedures and must never be retained to circumvent our values and principles. Paying bribes or kickbacks, engaging in industrial espionage, obtaining the proprietary data of a third party without authority, or gaining inside information or influence are just a few examples of what could give us an unfair competitive advantage in a government procurement and could result in violations of law.

PROTECT PROPRIETARY INFORMATION

Proprietary Company information may not be disclosed to anyone without proper authorization. Keep proprietary documents protected and secure. In the course of normal business activities, suppliers, customers, and competitors may sometimes divulge to you information that is proprietary to their business. Respect these confidences.

Keep proprietary documents protected and secure.

OBTAIN AND USE COMPANY AND CUSTOMER ASSETS WISELY

Proper use of Company and customer property, electronic communication systems, information resources, material, facilities, and equipment is your responsibility. Use and maintain these assets with the utmost care and respect, guarding against waste and abuse, and never borrow or remove them from Company property without management's permission. Be cost-conscious and alert to opportunities for improving performance while reducing costs. While these assets are intended to be used for the conduct of Lockheed Martin's business, it is recognized that occasional personal use by employees may occur without adversely affecting the interests of the Company. Personal use of Company assets must always be in accordance with corporate and company policy — consult your supervisor for appropriate guidance and permission.

All employees are responsible for complying with the requirements of software copyright licenses related to software packages used in fulfilling job requirements.

DO NOT ENGAGE IN SPECULATIVE OR INSIDER TRADING

In our role as a multinational corporation and a publicly owned company, we must always be alert to and comply with the security laws and regulations of the United States and other countries.

...we must always be alert...

It is against the law for employees to buy or sell Company stock based on material, non-public "insider" information about or involving the Company. Play it safe: don't speculate in the securities of Lockheed Martin when you are aware of information affecting the Company's business that has not been publicly released or in situations where trading would call your judgment into question. This includes all varieties of stock trading such as options, put and calls, straddles, selling short, etc. Two simple rules can help protect you in this area: (1) Don't use non-public information for personal gain; (2) Don't pass along such information to someone else who has no need to know.

This guidance also applies to the securities of other companies (suppliers, vendors, subcontractors, etc.) for which you receive information in the course of your employment with Lockheed Martin.

FOR MORE INFORMATION

In order to support a comprehensive Ethics and Business Conduct Program, Lockheed Martin has developed education and communication programs in many subject areas.

These programs have been developed to provide employees with job-specific information to raise their level of awareness and sensitivity to key issues.

Interactive Video Training Modules are available on the following subjects:

Antitrust Compliance	International Military Sales
Domestic Consultants	Kickbacks & Gratuities
Drug-Free Workplace	Labor Charging
Environment, Health and Safety	Leveraging Differences (Diversity)
Ethics	Material Costs
Ex-Government Employees	Organizational Conflicts of Interest
Export Control	Procurement Integrity
Foreign Corrupt Practices Act	Product Substitution

Government Property   Record Retention
Harassment in the Workplace   Security
Insider Trading   Software License Compliance
International Consultants   Truth in Negotiations Act

The current list of Interactive Video Compliance Training Modules and Corporate Policy Statements relating to the above topics and others can be accessed via the Lockheed Martin Information Network at http://pageone.global.lmco.com/ or obtained from your supervisor.

WARNING SIGNS — YOU'RE ON THIN ICE WHEN YOU HEAR...

"Well, maybe just this once..."

"No one will ever know..."

"It doesn't matter how it gets done as long as it gets done..."

"It sounds too good to be to good to be true."

"Everyone does it."

"Shred that document."

"We can hide it."

"No one will get hurt."

"What's in it for me?"

"This will destroy the competition."

"We didn't have this conversation."

You can probably think of many more phrases that raise warning flags. If you find yourself using any of these expressions, take the Quick Quiz that follows and make sure you are on solid ethical ground.

QUICK QUIZ — WHEN IN DOUBT, ASK YOURSELF…

Are my actions legal?

Am I being fair and honest?

Will my action stand the test of time?

How will I feel about myself afterwards?

How will it look in the newspaper?

Will I sleep soundly tonight?

What would I tell my child to do?

How could I feel if my family, friends, and neighbors knew what I was doing?

If you are still not sure what to do, ask…and keep asking until you are certain you are doing the right thing.

OUR GOAL AN ETHICAL WORK ENVIRONMENT

We have established the Office of Vice President — Ethics and Business Conduct to underscore our commitment to ethical conduct throughout our company.

This office reports directly to the Office of the Chairman and the Audit and Ethics committee of the Board of Directors, and oversees a vigorous corporate wide effort to promote a positive, ethical work environment for all employees.

Out Ethics Officers operate confidential Ethics Help Lines at each operating company, as well as at the corporate level. You are urged to use these resources whenever you have a question or concern that cannot be readily addressed within your work group or through your supervisor.

CONTACT THE ETHICS OFFICE

In addition, if you need information on how to contact your local Ethics Officer — or wish to discuss a matter of concern with the Corporate Office of Ethics and Business Conduct — you are encouraged to use one of the following confidential means of communication:

Call: Here is listed a series of telephone numbers in English, Spanish and for the hearing or speech impaired.

Write: Here is listed the address of the Office of Ethics and Business Conduct

Fax: Here is listed the fax number of the Office of Ethics and Business Conduct

E-Mail: Here is listed the e-mail address of the Office of Ethics and Business Conduct

When you contact you Company Ethics Officer or the Corporate Office of Ethics and Business Conduct:

- You will be treated with dignity and respect.
- Your communications will be protected to the greatest extent possible.
- Your concerns will be seriously addressed and, if not resolved at the time you call, you will be informed of the outcome.
- You need not identify yourself.

Remember, there's never a penalty for using the Ethics HelpLine. People in a position of authority can't stop you; if they try, they're subject to disciplinary action up to and including dismissal.

RECEIPT AND ACKNOWLEDGEMENT

I acknowledge that I received my personal copy of Setting the Standard, the Lockheed Martin Code of Ethics and Business Conduct. I understand that each Lockheed Martin employee, agent, consultant, or representative is responsible for knowing and adhering to the principles and standards of the Code.

Signature _____

Print Name _____

Employee Number _____

Company _____

Location _____Date _____

APPENDIX B
SELECTED REFERENCES

BOOKS

Audi, Robert, *Moral Knowledge and Ethical Character.* Oxford, UK: Oxford University Press, 1997.

Bennett, William J., *The Death of Outrage: Bill Clinton and the Assault on American Ideals.* New York: Simon and Shuster, 1998.

Bennis, Warren, *On Becoming a Leader.* Reading, MA: Addison-Wesley Publishing Company, 1994.

Bennis, Warren, *Organizing Genius: The Secrets of Creative Collaboration.* Reading, MA: Addison-Wesley, 1997.

Bennis, Warren, *Why Leaders Can't Lead: The Unconscious Conspiracy Continues.* San Francisco, CA: Josey-Bass Publishers, 1989.

Blanchard, Kenneth, Zigarmi, Patricia, Zigarmi, Drea, *Leadership and the One Minute Manager.* New York: William Morrow and Company, Inc., 1985.

Callahan, David, *The Cheating Culture: Why More Americans are Doing Wrong to Get Ahead.* Orlando, FL: Harcourt, Inc., 2004.

Clancy, Tom, with General Fred Franks, Jr., Retired, *Into the Storm: A Study in Command*. New York: G.P. Putnam's Sons, 1997.

Covey, Stephen R., Merril, A. Roger, Merrill, Rebecca R., *First Things First*. New York: Simon and Shuster, 1994.

Damon, William, *Greater Expectations: Overcoming the Culture of Indulgence in America's Homes and Schools*. New York: The Free Press, 1995.

DePree, Max, *Leadership Is an Art*. New York: Bantam Doubleday Dell Publishing Group, Inc., 1989.

DePree, Max, *Leadership Jazz*. New York: Dell Publishing, 1992.

Devlin, Patrick, *The Enforcement of Morals*. London, UK: Oxford University Press, 1965.

Donnithorne, Col. Larry R., Retired, *The West Point Way of Leadership*. New York: Doubleday, 1993.

Fitton, Robert A., *Leadership: Quotations for the World's Greatest Motivators*. Boulder, CO: Westview Press, 1997.

Goodman, Joan F., Lesnick, Howard, *The Moral Stake in Education: Contested Premises and Practice*. New York: Longman, 2001.

Hayward, Steven F., *Churchill on Leadership: Executive Success in the Face of Adversity*. Rocklin, CA: Forum, 1998.

Hemstra, Bruce, *Why Good People Do Bad Things: How to Make Moral Choices in an Immoral World*. Secaucus, NJ: Birch Lane Press, 1996.

Hunter, James Davison, *The Death of Character: Moral Education in an Age Without Good or Evil*. New York: Basic Books, 2000.

Kidder, Rushworth M., *An Agenda for the 21st Century*. Boston: The Christian Science Publishing Society, 1998.

Kidder, Rushworth, M., *Heartland Ethics: Voices from the American Midwest.* St. Louis: The Principia Corporation, 1992.

Kidder, Rushworth M., *How Good People Make Tough Choices: Resolving the Dilemmas of Ethical Living.* New York: Fireside Books, 1996.

Kidder, Rushworth M., *In the Backyards of Our Lives and Other Essays.* Yankee Books, 1992.

Kidder, Rushworth M., *Shared Values for a Troubled World: Conversations with Men and Women of Conscience.* San Francisco: Josey-Bass, 1994.

Lee, Blaine, *The Power Principle: Influence with Honor.* New York: Simon and Shuster, 1997.

McDowell, Josh and Hostetler, Bob, *The New Tolerance: How a Cultural Movement Threatens to Destroy You, Your Faith, and Your Children.* Wheaton, Illinois: Tyndale House Publishers, 1998.

Naber, John, *Awaken the Olympian Within: Stories from America's Greatest Olympic Motivators.* Torrence, CA: Griffin Publishing Group, 1999.

Newberger, Eli H., *The Men They Will Become:The Nature and Nurture of Male Character.* Cambridge, MA: Perseus Books, 2000.

Phillips, Donald T., *Lincoln on Leadership.* New York: Warner Books, 1992.

Pojman, Louis P. and Westmoreland, Robert, *Equality: Selected Readings.* New York: Oxford University Press, 1997.

Puryear, Edgar F., Jr., *19 Stars: A Study in Military Character and Leadership.* Novato, CA: Presidio, 1971.

Robbins, Anthony, *Awaken the Giant Within.* New York: Summit Books, 1991.

Reuben, Steven Carr, *Children of Character: A Parent's Guide*. Santa Monica, CA: Canter and Associates, 1997.

Schlessinger, Laura, *How Could You Do That?! The Abdication of Character, Courage, and Conscience*. New York: Harper Collins Publishers, 1996.

Sommers, Christina H., Sommers, Fred, *Vice and Virtue in Everyday Life (6th ed.)*. Belmont, CA: Wadsworth Publishing Co., 2003.

Stevens, Rex P., *Kant on Moral Practice: A Study of Moral Success and Failure*. Macon, GA: Mercer University Press, 1981.

Sykes, Charles J., *A Nation of Victims*. New York: St. Martin's Press, 1981.

Telushkin, Joseph, *The Ten Commandments of Character: Essential Advice for Living and Honorable, Ethical, Honest Life*. New York: Harmony/Bell Tower, 2003.

Vessenes, Katherine, *Protecting Your Practice*. Princeton, NJ: Bloomberg Press, 1997.

* * * *

MOTION PICTURES WITH ETHICAL AND CHARACTER THEMES

All the President's Men
And the Band Played On
Any Given Sunday
Apartment, The
Baby Boom
Barbarians at the Gate
Boiler Room, The
Broadcast News

Citizen Kane

Civil Action, A

Death of a Salesman

Disclosure

Erin Brockovich

Executive Suite

Firm, The

Glengarry Glen Ross

Hoffa

How to Succeed in Business Without Really Trying

Hudsucker Proxy

Jerry Maguire

Man in the Gray Flannel Suit, The

Nine-to-Five

Norma Rae

Office Space

Quiz Show

Rainmaker, The

Roger & Me

Save the Tiger

Silkwood

Swimming with the Sharks

Take this Job and Shove It

Tin Men

Truman Show

Tucker

Wall Street

Working Girl

* * * *

**If you found this book thought provoking...
If you are interested in having this author...
or other of our consulting authors
design a workshop or seminar for your
company, organization, school, or team...**

Let the experienced and knowledgeable group of experts
at *The Diogenes Consortium* go to work for you.
With literally hundreds of years of combined experience in:

*Ethics • Human Resources • Employee Retention
Management • Pro-Active Leadership • Teams
Encouragement • Empowerment • Motivation
Attitute Modification • Energizing • Delegating Responsibility
Spirituality in the Workplace
Presentations to start-ups and Fortune 500 companies,
tax-exempt organizations and schools of all sizes
(public & private, elementary through university)*

**Call today for a list of our
authors/speakers/presenters/consultants**
Call toll free at 866-602-1476
Or visit:
www.FocusOnEthics.com

320